ACTS OF RESISTANCE

Subversive Teaching in the English Language Arts Classroom

"ELA teachers—now more than ever—are faced with awful decisions in the current context of teaching: Should they do what is best for their students or what will allow them to keep working with students? Dyches, Sams, and Boyd emphatically say, "Both" and I agree the way forward in ELA instruction is to be subversive, to be acutely aware of the dominant discourses and work constantly to help students write themselves into the discussions, texts, and narratives of their multi-faceted and complex lives. These editors and authors provide just what the profession needs at just the right time."

—*Christian Z. Goering, Ph.D.*
University of Arkansas
Professor, English Education
Chair, English Language Arts Teacher Education

"How else to abandon the status quo of generations of inequitable schooling than through sub-version? By giving voice to silenced topics, advocating for crafty, alternative assessments, and showcasing the ways these changes ignite their students into lovers of language and advocates in the world, teachers in this book dignify and insist upon the ethics of subversion in the English classroom."

—*Sophia Tatiana Sarigianides, Ph.D.*
Professor & Coordinator of English Education
Westfield State University

"*Acts of Resistance: Subversive Teaching in the English Language Arts Classroom* is timely, thoughtful, and important. Now, more than ever, we need subversive English language arts teachers—public intellectuals and professionals who deeply understand their discipline and know how to use that disciplinary knowledge to engage students in critical, transformative learning. Together, the narratives featured in this book offer a complex, compelling, and accessible picture of what it means to be subversive and to enact change"

—*Amanda Haertling Thein, Ph.D.*
University of Iowa
Associate Provost for Graduate and Professional Education
and Dean of the Graduate College, Professor

"The portraits in this collection highlight teachers, curriculum, and pedagogy that enact sub-versive teaching—a critical stance in classrooms that promotes opportunity for all students. Situated within our current era of external mandates that are increasingly aimed at standard-izing instruction, this text pushes the field to consider what possibilities exist for generative action and agency in ELA classrooms today."

—*Heidi Hallman, Ph.D.*
University of Kansas, Chair, Department of Curriculum and Teaching
Professor

ACTS OF
RESISTANCE

ACTS OF RESISTANCE

Subversive Teaching in the
English Language Arts Classroom

SECOND EDITION

EDITED BY
JEANNE DYCHES, BRANDON SAMS,
AND ASHLEY S. BOYD

Myers
Education
Press

GORHAM, MAINE

Myers Education Press

Myers Education Press is an academic publisher specializing in books, e-books, and digital content in the field of education. All of our books are subjected to a rigorous peer review process and produced in compliance with the standards of the Council on Library and Information Resources.

Library of Congress Cataloging-in-Publication Data available from Library of Congress.

13-digit ISBN 978-1-9755-0560-8 (paperback)
13-digit ISBN 978-1-9755-0561-5 (library networkable e-edition)
13-digit ISBN 978-1-9755-0562-2 (consumer e-edition)

Printed in the United States of America.

All first editions printed on acid-free paper that meets the American National Standards Institute Z39-48 standard.

Books published by Myers Education Press may be purchased at special quantity discount rates for groups, workshops, training organizations, and classroom usage. Please call our customer service department at 1-800-232-0223 for details.

Cover design by Teresa Lagrange

Visit us on the web at **www.myersedpress.com** to browse our complete list of titles.

For our professors at the University of North Carolina at Chapel Hill, including Drs. Jim Trier, Lynda Stone, Jocelyn Glazier, Dana Griffin, George Noblit, Dana Thompson Dorsey, and Madeleine Grumet, who brought us together and inspired our own thinking, teaching, and scholarship.

CONTENTS

FOREWORD

I AM HONORED TO invite you into solidarity with the educators, students, activists, visionaries, and creators who offer their experiences and insights in this powerful collection.

As part of this invitation, I want to offer you a simple embodied practice that has helped me find my stand in many different challenges. I hope that it will support you as you consider how to bring the ideas of this book into your own teaching, learning, and living.

> Put all your attention on the sensations in your right hand. Notice the experience of air touching skin, the blood moving in your tissues, the tightness or softness of muscle, whatever else you can sense.
>
> Now put all your attention on the sensations in your left hand. Again, notice the experience of your skin, and feel deep into your tissues and muscles. See what you observe.
>
> Next, see what it is like to notice both of your hands. See how it is that you really can sense them both, fully and deeply, at the same time. The reality of your right hand, the reality of your left hand, the reality of them at the same time. You can hold the truth of both at once.

In recent months and years, I have turned to this practice when I experience distress or paralysis because of conflicts between the reality of the present and my intentions, values, or hopes for the future.

For example, I believe that teachers, students, and communities can create spaces of liberation. But I also recognize that many schools have been and continue to be spaces of harm and oppression.

Try consciously holding these two realities present. Keep naming them internally.

Sometimes it feels as though one or the other must win out. Either we dance and fight for change, or we surrender to helplessness and fatigue in the face of the structures that hold change back. But the simple exercise of feeling our hands, separately and then together, reminds us that these experiences can be present at the same time. In fact, we must learn to experience them simultaneously as we ask ourselves where and how and with what resources and actions—however small—we can resist oppression and amplify possibility.

We cannot pretend that our efforts outweigh the harms that exist. We each stand at a unique intersection of challenges and possible change, but we share a broader educational situation: the compounding crisis of diminished resources as needs have increased; de facto racial and economic segregation; relentless testing and pressures toward standardization; epidemic levels of anxiety and other mental health challenges for youth. The last few years have added a global pandemic, school shutdowns, ever-more-devastating school shootings, and assaults on women's bodily autonomy.

Language arts educators have been especially impacted by widespread, coordinated attacks on books that address identities and issues that right-wing groups have tried to make controversial, from histories of enslavement and racism to the diversity of our society, to basic information about sexuality and reproductive health, to narratives that even acknowledge the existence of queer folks. As of this writing, my 2015 novel *Out of Darkness* is the third-most-banned book in the United States. The official banning of the novel in at least 41 school districts across 17 states (as of this writing), is likely the tip of the iceberg of actual removals. Although of course I want my books to be available to the young people I write for, what concerns me far more is what these assaults on literature mean for young people's right to read, learn, and mature—and what they mean for the educators doing the hard work of engaging in transformative learning alongside their students.

My transformation as an educator and a novelist for young people began with a decision to write *with* my students, initially inspired by my experiences as a National Writing Project fellow. I committed to moving my pen (or overhead marker, in most cases) at the same times that I asked students to be writing in class. I intended it as an act of solidarity and vulnerability that also modeled an authentic shared writing process. It was such a small shift at first, but it opened spaces for us to come to know each other as people, and writers, who were always *becoming*. It made writing a live experience, rather than a performance task.

I also began a practice of writing *to* my students about reading, writing, and learning. I shared memories of my own positive and negative experiences with school and books, and they wrote back in kind. These "literacy letters," inspired by Randy Bomer's *Time for Meaning*, humanized my teaching because they dissolved unhelpful stories I had about my students as readers and scholars. For example, when my kids wrote back, I learned that they had very good reasons for the fears, frustrations, and resistance they felt around reading and other aspects of language arts. These letters shattered a single story of "we don't like to read" into many manageable shards of experience that I could respond to and build from. In these ongoing exchanges, I wrote short individual letters in response to each student as well as a longer letter to the class as a whole. I was able to cultivate greater relevance in my framing of our work together because I understood what mattered to my students and showed them that I heard them. The outcome was that I got to experience my students as collaborators in resistance. Together, we stealthily remade the 12th-grade curriculum to serve them as *people*, not as test-takers or bodies in seats. For example, we reframed the class research project to focus on planning for the future. We used interviews of experts and mentors, community experiences, and resource-gathering to learn and teach each other about college, careers of interest, and strategies for being supports to family while also pursuing our own goals. I did this assignment alongside my students to research the challenges and advantages of becoming a college professor, a path I pursued after my students graduated.

Writing with my classes was also how I began writing my first novel in 5 and 10 minutes at a time, often on the overhead. I wrote with a powerful sense of my students as my most important audience. They told me stories about themselves and about what they wanted to find in books but couldn't because these books did not yet exist in 2004. My students' longings and frustrations inspired my determination to center marginalized people and experiences in my novels for young adults. They are the reason that I create characters who, in whatever ways they can, resist the systemic inequities in their lives and choose the conditions of their own thriving. I published my first novel, *What Can't Wait*, in 2010, but long before that, I gave my students the draft of the story as a graduation present. They filled the margins of the stapled copies of that manuscript with notes, stars, and objections. Their reading, not the book's publication, was what made me an author.

It is in solidarity with you and your students that I share my modest efforts to change a destructive status quo. And it is in solidarity that I challenge you to approach *Acts of Resistance* with a sense of purpose, mission, and curiosity. This collection is full of mentors and models for what resistance and subversion can look like in the ELA classroom. It is a book that can change or clarify your path forward.

Welcome these fellow educators and students as part of your broader community of resistance. Invite new strategies into your imagination and your day-to-day experiences. Stand in the truth that *you are not doing this work alone*. But please do not think that you must duplicate or enact what someone else did. Instead, pay attention to the experiments, trickster tactics, and countermeasures that resonate with you. What sparks your curiosity or excitement? How would you feel in your body having a *real* discussion with your students about a problem or issue that does not have any easy answers? In what ways might you include your students in decisions about their learning, whether on the scale of the next 10 minutes or the next 10 weeks?

As you read on and explore these possibilities, I want to invite you also to connect them to your stand for young people, your work, your positive vision. For example, even as authors, teachers, and librarians fight *against* attacks on youth access to books, we can find strength by articulating, to ourselves and to others, what we stand *for*. In fact, we must state what we are for, because we can't hold a stand that we haven't yet defined for ourselves. Once we name our values, explicitly, we can keep our actions—and acts of resistance—aligned with our mission even where there may be pressure to take another course. For example, as I face dozens of efforts to ban my novel, as I weather the accompanying hatred and vitriol, I remind myself:

My stand is for *every* student's right to read.
My stand is for books that turn kids into readers.
My stand is for telling the stories that haven't been told.

Post your stand in multiple places where you will see it. Announce it to students and colleagues. Repeat it internally when you are in hostile or unsupportive spaces. If you advocate from a grounded place, every action will be more impactful. And since the struggle and need for strategic action isn't going away, we need to conserve energy and renew our inner resources.

In these pages, you will find inspiration. You will find a community of partners in transformation. You will find a context for your own meaningful action. Above all, you will find reminders of what it means to hold your stand for and with youth.

Bring on the acts of resistance! Bring on the subversive teaching and learning!

Ashley Hope Pérez
October 28, 2022

What Is Subversive Disciplinary Literacy?

JEANNE DYCHES, BRANDON SAMS, AND ASHLEY S. BOYD

I N 1969, NEIL POSTMAN and Charles Weingartner published *Teaching as a Subversive Activity*, offering readers their ruminations on the state of education and how stakeholders might disrupt problematic traditions and ideologies. In the 50 years since its publication, the text has proved foundational to the field of education. Subversive teaching today, however, looks very different from subversive teaching in 1969. Teachers today must deliver their instruction in an era of formidable challenges related to curriculum, educational policy, and cultural and political ideology. For example, the rise in anti-CRT legislation across many states attests to the anti-intellectualism and reactionary political milieu that teachers face daily. Students learn to read and write in the context of active-shooter drills and increasingly violent public policy that assaults immigrants, persons with disabilities, people of color, women, and the LGBTQIA+ community. A robust public education is needed now more than ever, although the resources to provide it dwindle consistently.

Despite efforts to dismantle public education, to de-intellectualize and delegitimize the profession, teachers persist. Teachers are, and always have been, powerful agents of change. But who are these teachers, and why must they work in subversive ways? What experiences and identities have influenced their work? How do they navigate the demands of their instructional context? How do they teach subversively and maintain their employment? How, and in what ways, does subversive teaching work in discipline-specific ways?

These questions, among others, are taken up in the second edition of *Acts of Resistance: Subversive Teaching in the English Language Arts (ELA) Classroom*. The collection understands subversive teaching as instruction that purposefully works to satisfy traditional markers of mainstream success and academic conventions (such as addressing national standards or following a prescribed curriculum) while intentionally moving students toward effecting more socially just, anti-oppressive futures (Dyches & Boyd, 2017). This collection honors the multiplicity of subversive pedagogy by making space for narratives that show its myriad forms and how teachers variously understand, interpret, and perform subversion. Indeed, subversive teaching is just *one* form of social justice teaching—one that, somewhat surprisingly, garners little attention.

Subversive teaching is contextually bound; place, time, and teachers' bodies are just a few factors that inform subversive pedagogy. But another important (if under-recognized) element of context lies in disciplinarity. In recent years, disciplinary literacy has entered academic discourse, a shift that moves away from generic treatments of literacy instruction and instead advances the unique qualities of, and skills needed to access, the disciplines (Shanahan & Shanahan, 2008). Across disciplines and grade levels, national standards reflect this shift by requiring students to develop discipline-specific skills. From writing a literary analysis to crafting a geometric proof, disciplinary literacy asserts that students require a particular skill set to read, write, and communicate effectively while participating in various disciplinary activities (Fang & Coatoam, 2013).

But disciplines—which advance certain knowledges, traditions, perspectives, and skills—are not neutral bodies. Because disciplines are specialized cultures and communities (Moje, 2015), the ways in which teachers must work for social justice shift with the discipline at hand. Because each discipline advances its own knowledges, skills, and norms, social justice teaching looks different in math or science than it does in history classrooms (Dyches, 2018).

In keeping with a focus on disciplinarity, the second edition of *Acts of Resistance: Subversive Teaching in the ELA Classroom* explains how teachers both satisfy *and* subvert a particular ELA disciplinary convention. In these chapters, authors name an ELA disciplinary convention—close reading, writing, and canonical curriculum, to name a few—and take time exploring its history with, and relationship to, the ELA classroom. Then authors describe how their lesson subverts the same disciplinary convention it attempts to satisfy. This nuanced approach allows authors to distill the synergistic relationship between ELA disciplinary conventions and their subversive approaches and to dispel the notion that disciplinarity and social justice are isolated, mutually exclusive entities (Cochran-Smith et al, 2009).

The narratives in this second edition of *Acts of Resistance* open new possibilities for critical, social justice–oriented teaching in ELA. The collection showcases examples of subversive pedagogy to instruct and inspire other teachers and to contextualize subversive ELA pedagogy in the contemporary educational moment. The chapter authors, in-service teachers and teacher educators alike, draw from case study, narrative inquiry, or other qualitative methodologies to explain how they have variously taken up subversive pedagogy in the ELA classroom.

Teachers and other stakeholders resist oppressive structures—including disciplinary confinements—when they locate and teach from subversive viewpoints. Thus, we believe that each of the chapters describes a disciplinary "act of resistance" that illuminates possibilities for countering uncritical, "traditional" handling of ELA experiences. In each chapter, authors describe their disciplinary-specific approach to satisfying and subverting particular ELA conventions.

The second edition opens with a foreword from young adult literature novelist Ashley Hope Pérez, author of *Out of Darkness*, one of the most frequently banned books across U.S. classrooms at the time of this writing. Pérez's foreword acts as an invitation to embodied practice—a critical and generous noticing and feeling of our anchors to truth, justice, and our communities—that subversive pedagogy both needs and sustains. Four new chapters reflect sociopolitical changes since the book's publication: a widespread, coordinated uptick in the banning of books centering authors and characters from marginalized communities; the COVID-19 pandemic and with it, increased acts of violence against folks identifying as Asian, Asian American, and Pacific Islander; the murders of George Floyd, Breonna Taylor, and countless other victims of police brutality; the January 6 insurrection; and the closing of the Trump era. Chapters specifically illustrate the storied practices of subversive teachers across the 6-12 ELA context. They provide educators with instructional ideas on how to "do" anti-oppressive work while also meeting "traditional" ELA disciplinary elements.

Chapter 1, Latrise Johnson's "We Write Here: Academic Movement in the Writing and Being of Black Learners," takes up ELA and intellectual practices that maximize the development of Black writers and the academic potential of Black youth. In Chapter 2, Betina Hsieh and Jung Kim draw from research around text sets and culturally affirming instruction, as well as their own practice, to discuss the integration of humanizing, diverse Asian American texts into curriculum as an act of resistance. Stephanie Anne Shelton and Tamara Brooks contribute "Reciprocating Care and Vulnerability through a Pedagogy of Tenderness: Resistance and Transformation in ELA Classrooms," situating teaching within the current political contexts that work to control what teachers are allowed to say and do, while subverting classroom discussion and literary analysis. In Chapter 4, "Subverting the Canon through Culturally Relevant Young Adult Literature," Sandra Saco and E. Sybil Durand explore how a former ELA teacher who taught at a Title I high school serving a majority of Latinx and Black students subverted her school and district's prescribed canonical curriculum.

In Chapter 5, "Black Words Matter: Bending Literary Close Reading Toward Justice," Scott Storm examines a student's development of subversive close reading skills while enrolled in the "Black Words Matter" course. Crystal Sogar and Melanie Shoffner posit empathy as an essential component of the ELA classroom in Chapter 6, examining how the teaching of argumentation might account for students' vulnerability and sharing of personal experiences. In Chapter 7, "'Well, I Took It There': Subversive

Teaching to (Disrupt) the Test," Leah Panther and Selena Hughes describe an American literature teacher's attempts to help her students recognize and push back against the White supremacy imbued within their end-of-course state exam. In Chapter 8, "Inquiry Ignites!" Jill Stedronsky and Kristen Hawley Turner subvert traditional approaches to close reading instruction through a yearlong, inquiry-based reading program.

Anna Mae Tempus and Carey Applegate take on White savior approaches to teaching *To Kill a Mockingbird* (Lee, 1960) in Chapter 9, "'Climb Into Their Skin': Whiteness and the Subversion of Perspective." In Chapter 10, Caroline T. Clark and Jill M. Williams subvert the traditional multicultural literature course through a cultural studies approach and an Open Mic assignment, allowing students' lived experiences to serve as meaningful and authoritative text.

Heather Coffey and Steve Fulton, in Chapter 11, describe a schoolwide effort to create a justice-oriented curriculum that centered inquiry and examine the complications that arise for both teachers and students when they attempt to work outside traditional classroom boundaries. In Chapter 12, "Disability as Pedagogy," Katie Roquemore subverts traditional writing instruction using a disability-studies lens and helps readers understand the power of vulnerability for social justice teaching in ELA. Ryan Burns and Janine Boiselle, in Chapter 13, show the power of queer and gender-inclusive approaches to teaching Shakespeare. In Chapter 14, Lori Garcia and Michael Manderino present a series of lessons designed to interrupt "single stories" and traditional approaches to rhetorical analysis through the inclusion of media texts relevant to students' lives. Dorothy E. Hines, Jemimah Young, Rossina Zamora Liu, and Diana Wandix-White then take up, in Chapter 15, anti-oppressive ELA curriculum for girls of color in an after-school, social justice enrichment program. In Chapter 16, Amanda Lacy and Angela M. Kohnen challenge dominant views of literacy and reimagine curriculum for remedial reading courses built on student interest and engagement. To conclude the volume, Meghan A. Kessler and Angela L. Masters take up English teacher evaluation and show how Courtenay, a secondary ELA teacher, transformed neoliberal reform policies to advance student learning.

From the beginning, we conceptualized *Acts of Resistance: Subversive Teaching in the ELA Classroom* as a tool for pre- and in-service teachers aspiring to subvert traditional instruction and teach for social justice. Additionally, we believe the collection can help teacher educators consider the realities secondary teachers face and how to respond to these realities when designing coursework and experiences for preservice teachers.

In 1969, Postman and Weingartner asserted that students deserve "an education that develops in youth a competence in applying the best available strategies for survival in a world filled with unprecedented troubles, uncertainties, and opportunities" (p. xv). Indeed, subversive teaching should acknowledge troubles and uncertainties, and should work to show students opportunities for resistance. Postman and Weingartner (1969) go on to charge that "our task . . . is to make these strategies for survival visible and explicit in the hope that someone somewhere will act on them" (p. xv). The need for explicitly described subversive *action* compels this project. *Acts of Resistance: Subversive Teaching in the ELA Classroom* offers readers a contemporary look at subversion that acknowledges the role of ELA disciplinarity; in sharing these stories, we hope to honor—and inspire more—disciplinary-bound "acts of resistance."

References

Cochran-Smith, M., Barnatt, J., Lahann, R., Shakman, K., & Terrell, D. (2009). Teacher education for social justice: Critiquing the critiques. In W. Ayres, T. Quinn, & D. Stovell (Eds.), *The handbook for social justice in education* (pp. 625–639). Routledge.

Dyches, J. (2018). Investigating curricular injustices to uncover the injustices of curricula: Curriculum evaluation as critical disciplinary literacy practice. *High School Journal*, *101*, 236–250.

Dyches, J., & Boyd, A. (2017). Foregrounding equity in teacher education: Toward a model of Social Justice Pedagogical and Content Knowledge (SJPACK). *Journal of Teacher Education*, *68*(5), 476–490.

Fang, Z., & Coatoam, S. (2013). Disciplinary literacy: What you want to know about it. *Journal of Adolescent & Adult Literacy*, *56*, 627–632.

Lee, H. (1960). *To kill a mockingbird*. J. B. Lippincott & Co.

Moje, E. B. (2015). Doing and teaching disciplinary literacy with adolescent learners: A social and cultural enterprise. *Harvard Educational Review*, *85*(2), 254–278.

Postman, P. N., & Weingartner, C. (1969). Teaching as a subversive activity: A no-holds-barred assault on outdated teaching methods—with dramatic and practical proposals on how education can be made relevant to today's world. Dell Publishing.

Shanahan, T., & Shanahan, C. (2008). Teaching disciplinary literacy to adolescents: Rethinking content-area literacy. *Harvard Educational Review*, *78*(1), 40-59.

CHAPTER ONE

We Write Here: Academic Movement in the Writing and Being of Black Learners

LATRISE P. JOHNSON

"A language is only worth ... writing ... if you can see a future in it." — Toni Morrison, Sixo from Beloved

IN THIS CHAPTER, I reexamine and reanalyze data from my Professor-in-Residence study, Creative Writing class with high school students, and work with other Black writers. I offer a critique of how compositions (of Black bodies, of Black being, and of Black writing) can be misread and misinterpreted by writing mentors (i.e., teachers) who ground literate practice in correctness and racialized/classist views of the "academic." I name and focus on ELA and intellectual practices that maximize the development of Black writers and the academic potential of Black youth. When teachers ground their teaching in thinking/intellectual moves that humans/learners make that lean into historical legacies, they can locate how to reread and reinterpret how to teach Black learners in ways that can prepare them to build their own bridges toward academic and intellectual growth.

Writing while Black: Subverting Traditional Aspects of Academic Writing

I am a Black writer. I am and write with/in a community of Black writers—with high schoolers whose teachers relate their "inability to write" well as a reflection of the way that they "talk"; with PhD students whose professors are "not comfortable" supporting their scholarship because of writing "issues"; and with other Black scholars who suppress their voice so that their work is publishable in academic journals. Too often, Black writers receive feedback that doubts their academic or intellectual prowess, imposes normative standards of form and language, and questions their positionalities, including ontological beliefs and understandings. Across these communities, I have noted the ways that other writing mentors (e.g., teachers, professors, advisors, reviewers) have misread and discouraged Black writers. Those writing mentors perpetuate the dominant narrative that lays claims of black intellectual inferiority. The ways that Black youth have been written into literacy research suggest that they do not read, write, or think as well as other youth. Research suggests that there is a "gap" between how well Black students do versus others. There has been little to no success in closing the so-called "gap" and scholars continue to cite it as an educational issue since the Coleman Report first noted a gap in 1966. There have also been attempts to make sense of why some populations do well while others do not, including blaming irrelevant and unresponsive instruction.

According to Yagelski (2009), "school-sponsored writing is about separating self from experience by changing an experience into a stylized textual artifact" (p. 19). In addition, the type of writing practiced in high school classrooms often requires that students remove, deny, and ignore important aspects of their writing identities. For Black writers developing writing and intellectual identities, the expectations of writing and being in ELA- and writing-focused classrooms at the secondary and postsecondary levels often require Black writers to deny aspects of their being. Writing instruction and expectations feature hegemonic, heteronormative, patriarchal, and "standard" discourses aligned with normalized white, middle-class views of what it means to be intellectual (Johnson, 2017) or be considered "academic." For emerging writers who are developing their skills and voices, the ways that their writing abilities are read by teachers and other writing mentors have a long-lasting impact on how they see themselves as writers or not and shape the ways that academic communities invite or disinvite Black voices.

In Morrison's (1988) *Beloved*, Sixo (quoted in the epigraph) stops speaking English because he sees no future in it. He understands that he has a right to make sense of (t)his world in his own language—a fact that teachers of writing are slow to claim. Teachers of writing and ELA must resist normalized writing teaching and assessment that teach Black English speakers that they must change, translate, and adapt toward more standard ways of using language to make sense of their worlds. Instead, I argue for a rereading of Black writing that focuses on the intellectual moves that writers make in their writing as opposed to assessing writing based on racism and stereotypes of academic discourse.

Reexamining Ecologies of Writing Where Black Writers Be At: Theoretical Considerations

An ecology of writing encompasses more than individual writers and their immediate context. It invites one to explore how writers interact to form systems. With/in writing ecologies, "all characteristics of individual writers or a piece of writing both determine and are determined by the characteristics of all the other writers and writings in the systems (Cooper, 1986). Systems reflect "the various ways writers connect with one another through writing: through systems of ideas, of purposes, of interpersonal interactions, of cultural norms, of textual forms" (p. 369). Because of the racist and anti-Black practices and structures of academic writing discourses, Black writers face judgment "against an academic discourse that clearly privileges middle class white students" (Inoue, 2015, p. 8) that can also be anti-Black (Baker-Bell, 2019), culturally misaligned (Ladson-Billings, 2014), and dehumanizing (Goff et al., 2014; Johnson & Sullivan, 2020). Hence, even when teachers of writers claim to invite students' multimodal, relevant, and/or authentic writing, teachers judge and assess writers against white, mainstream ELA doing.

Examining Black writing ecologies can guide educators (teachers and writing mentors, specifically) toward more restorative relationships with/in textual worlds and enable teachers of writing to push back against myths of Black educational apathy and writerly (in)ability. For teachers of writing who use learners' "funds of knowledge"—that is linguistic practice, lived experiences, histories, and family and community perspectives on writing (and learning) spaces—they are able to create opportunities to improve learners' academic discourse(s) without costing them their language and being (Fisher, 2009; Gonzalez et al, 2006).

In the following section, I review literature that represents various ecologies of writing and attempt to name the ways that (Black) writers, writing, text, and readers are positioned and work together within different writing systems as well as theoretical and material ways that racist and anti-Black instructional writing practices destroy and diminish developing Black voices. Findings from my own analysis of Black students' writing follow as a way to fill in writing pedagogical gaps that can be used to center Black (and othered) voices and subvert problematic reading and teaching of Black learners/writers.

Racial and Racist Foundations of "Academic" Writing Discourse

Racist histories of writing instruction and assessment testify to the fact that past and present "English language writing assessment has dovetailed uncomfortably with those of colonialism and [white] supremacy—converging on what Inoue (2015) calls 'white language supremacy'" (Hammond, 2019, p. 42). Understanding how race functions in our assessment of Black writers/writing, specifically, requires an understanding of the ways that linguistic difference from dominant academic discourse is racialized and used to distinguish who does and does not use academic language. According to Inoue (2015), "In short, those who identify as African American, or Latino/a, or Asian Pacific American often are the multilingual students or the linguistically different in schools" (p. 26). In other words, the ways that academic discourse is constructed position white middle-class English speakers as superior and create false racial hierarchies with material and discursive consequences for Black youth in writing classrooms. Academic discourses are linguistically tailored for white learners. "In practice," according to Spence (2021), "the white speaker/listener/[reader] marks certain language characteristics of racialized people, while leaving the language of other groups unmarked" and therefore unacknowledged as part of academic discourses (Flores & Rosa, 2015).

When assessing writing, "teachers depend on their interpretations of the written product and these interpretations may be based on deficit perspectives" (Spence, 2021, p. 101). Even when invited to engage in generous readings of Black writing, teachers use raciolinguistic ideologies to make judgments about learners' academic (in)ability. As illustrated in Spence's study, during a discussion about Shamika's math writing, Amy, one of the teachers, claims that ". . . she tried, she put out words, she used her numbers, she's got pictorial representation. She did what was asked . . ." but another teacher, Jean, still dismisses her as a "good BSer" (pp. 106–107), implying that even though Shamika made the right academic moves, her effort and ability are a result of her *bullshitting*–assigning an unacademic quality based on Shamika's race and language. Such readings of Black writing use a deficit lens and relegate Black learners to the academic margins.

Poe (2015) argues to localize racial identity instead of starting with generalizations about teaching writing to racially diverse learners. While learner identity is dynamic and Black learners are not monolithic, focusing on local racial identity where Black people are can perpetuate the "exceptional Negro" (Attolino, 2022) concept in which Black people are viewed as possessing qualities that exist outside of Black cultural norms. Results of such perspectives have yielded little related to actually interrupting racist readings of Black learners' (and other Learners of Color) writing as these perspectives call for practices that dismiss their literacy practices as "alternative literacies" that decenter Black, African-centered, and/or Diasporic ways of knowing and doing with/in academic writing.

Related to the teaching of writing of culturally and linguistically diverse students, Ball and Ellis (2008) assert that "Whether an individual sees him or herself as a writer will be influenced by whether others respond to them as if they are a writer" (p. 619). As a pedagogical approach, they offer that:

Teachers can begin to introduce alternative perspectives in curricular discussion and classroom activities that allow students to bring their own culturally influenced perspectives and identities into the classroom in critical
ways. (p. 620)

While such pedagogical approaches are useful for centering the lives and experiences of all learners, *"alternative perspectives* in curricular discussion and classroom
activities"* implies that culturally and linguistically diverse perspectives (read Black)
are alternatives to academic discourses. What if we invited all languages with/in
academic writing discourse(s)? What if we focused on teaching writing in ways that
invited learners to make thinking moves in their own languages and redefine academic discourse that includes all voices?

Rereading Writing: Sankofa as Research Method

Sankofa methodology is based on the concept of the Adinkra symbol, which literally
translates as "It is not taboo to go back to the source and fetch what you forgot"
(Bangura, 2011, p. 175). I use the past writing of Black students in order to construct a future for how we might teach them to write. In addition, I go back to reexamine how writing mentors might read writers and their writing in ways that depart
from standardized approaches of assessment and evaluation. In order to address the
question: How might teachers and other writing mentors develop (and teach others
to develop) competence in critical (relevant, sustaining, diasporic, subversive) writing practices and pedagogies with/in and through ELA/Literacy being and teaching
of and writing with Black writers, I go back to the writing (text production and the
act of writing) of Black learners whom I have mentored as a writer, teacher, and
professor in their school. Their writing and experiences of being (mis)read lend to
a tapestry of Black writer experiences that beckons for revision in the ways writing
mentors consider how Black writers make sense of the(ir) worlds in writing.

  As a result of being in spaces with other Black learners writing, including ELA
classrooms, writing club, and a Creative Writing course, I have compiled essays,
poems, emails, and texts, that are data for understanding how Black writers are read
and misread by writing mentors (e.g., teachers, professors, advisors, reviewers). For
this study, I focus on a collection of Black writing from West High School where I
was Professor-in-Residence, to make a case for exposing possible cultural (in)com-
petence and racism in mentoring and reading of Black writers and to illustrate how
academic movement (i.e., critical analysis) shows up in the writing of Black learners.
In order to make a case for undoing problematic readings of Black writing, I analyze
the writing of Black youth to explicate the academic moves (see Burke & Gilmore,
2015) present in their essays, poems, and other texts[1] created and shared with me.

---

1   Data come from a larger ethnographic study where I was Professor-in-Residence and spent 6 years
at a high school that served a majority African American population.

With each unit of data, I consider the writing ecologies present, in this case, the relationship between the human writing with physical and social material as well as interrelated and dynamic systems where writers and writing mentors make sense (or not) of academic movement of Black writers. Data include 310 handwritten essays from a schoolwide writing assessment that asked 11th grade students whether colleges should use social media to make admission decisions; artifacts and course material from a Creative Writing course I taught for 9th to 12th graders at West during the Spring semester of 2017; and 40 journals from learners who participated in writing club in 2014 to 2015, 2017, and 2019.

Findings

I rely on the misreadings represented in the literature (and in some cases, in practice) on writing and assessment of Black writers to center writing pedagogical possibilities when teaching and writing with Black learners. I highlight how (Black) writing is academic and ripe for extending thinking skills to illustrate how teachers of writing may teach in ways that help all learners build their own bridges toward academic and intellectual growth.

In the following sections, I lay out ways that writing mentors and teachers of writing might reread Black writing and build on writerly assets; cultivate positive writerly identities; and encourage and support complex, abstract, and higher order thinking.

The Missing "s" Does Not Change the Argument: Focusing on Writers' Assets

Early in the Fall semester of 2015, English teachers at West administered a practice writing test to all 11th graders to assess students' essay-writing ability and to guide their teaching of writing for the semester. The essays were read and scored anonymously using an adapted rubric according to students' ability to "demonstrate effective skill in writing an argumentative essay." Of the 310 essays, 119 of them scored either 1 or 2 on the rubric, suggesting that responses demonstrate little, no, weak, or inconsistent skill in writing an argumentative essay. The assessment was supposed to inform how teachers in all grade levels might approach teaching argumentative writing for the school year.

Assessors did not address writers' (in)ability to write an argument. Instead, most of the comments for essays that scored in this range addressed grammar mistakes—mainly, subject–verb agreement—or essay length. As a result, teachers missed opportunities to identify writer assets on which to build. For example, in a paper that scored 2 on the adapted rubric, the writer made several grammar mistakes (mainly a missing "s" in possessive nouns) and included only two paragraphs, which no doubt resulted in the low score. However, a reread of this paper revealed that the writer used creative ways to support their argument that "College should not be permitted to use applicants Facebook content in their considerations because the information they find may not always be accurate" (student essay, 2015). The writer continues to offer reasons and evidence to support their claim:

> You can be one way on the internet and a whole other person in real life. My social media accounts does not determine my test score, that status didn't take the ACT for me, the status wont walk across the stage with me, but yet colleges want to use Facebook, etc to see if they would consider accepting me into their school or not.

The student has provided personal reasons that support their opposition to colleges' use of social media accounts. The writer uses a creative writing element, personification, in order to suggest their level of opposition. It is evident that the writer generates an argument and has a clear thesis. According to the rubric, what would move this paper into a higher score category is not an apostrophe "s," but an additional perspective on the given issue.

Another paper that scored a 1 on the adapted rubric revealed that while the writer had some trouble with organization and grammar, they were able to offer multiple perspectives on the given issue, use transitions between ideas, and offered support for their argument. In addition, the writer uses rhetorical questions as a data-seeking move that "recognizes . . . tensions and/or underlying values and assumptions" (language from the adapted rubric at level 4). For example, the writer provides their first position:

> Why I disagree to this is because what if you love taking pictures and uploading them and some college look into your profile and see nudes, videos of fights and much more. Do you think that you'll get into a college then? Yes or No? (student essay, 2015).

In addition to offering one side of the argument, the writer identifies tensions related to the issue (e.g., privacy and inappropriate content) that are not reflected in their score and is unnoted in the brief feedback at notations of the essay that point out the lack of punctuation and "no distinct paragraphs."

When assessors of Black writing read with only deficit lenses, they miss (and often ignore) writerly assets on which to build deeper thinking and improve other characteristics of writing (not just grammar and mechanics). It was clear that writers who scored in the 1–2 range were able to make an argument and offer support for their argument (with few exceptions). However, when writing mentors and teachers of writing focus on the ways that Black writers do not use language in ways that reflect standardized English, they are unable to identify the intellectual moves needed to build arguments.

Unexpected Places: Cultivating Positive Writer and Learner Identity

One of the essays from the 2015 practice writing test did not receive a score because the writer did not respond according to the assigned topic. Instead, the essay chronicles the writer's matriculation through school and the ways that they struggled and triumphed in Pre-K through 12th grades. The writer makes clear their departure from the assigned writing prompt in the first sentence of the essay, which read, "I am going to tell you about my school life." The writer explains with some detail for one and one-half pages about how they struggled with fighting, sleeping, and going to an alternative school. They also note that they and a friend started "a little intramural basketball league" at their elementary school.

While the writer did not write according to the assigned topic, what is evident is that the writer has a story to tell and engages in several intellectual moves, namely support, organize, and summarize. The writer uses clear transitions and includes descriptive detail. However, the only feedback the writer received was "NS–Did not write on topic." Their writing teacher failed to provide any useful feedback upon which to build and did not take any opportunity to recognize aspects of the writing to improve. In addition, the feedback does not capitalize on the writer's own positive relationship with school/ing that is developing. They write, "I am a 12th grader now and I graduate 2K16. I didn't think I would make it this far, but I did and I am proud of myself." For learners who struggle with identifying positively with school and who are tracked into alternative schooling, cultivating positive writer and learner identities is key to repairing fractured relationships.

Black learners may also be reluctant to write given their prior experiences with school-sanctioned writing. Traditional writing pedagogies invite students to use various writing processes, read and mimic textual form, and learn about elements and characteristics of "good" writing. These approaches may even use students' cultural knowledge and experiences as content and context for writing. At times, however, these approaches do not reach the most reluctant writers. So, I call for inspiration as pedagogy—one that is personally tailored for individual learners and spontaneously reactive to a moment. For example, during one of our creative writing classes, one of my learners, Jahia, struggled with the poetry warm-up activity that invited learners to compose a haiku to practice with the syllable requirement. In order to provide some modeling for Jahia, I sat next to her and composed the following haiku entitled Jahia: "Sitting next to you/I want to inspire one/If only one poem." A few moments later, Jahia shared her haiku: "Do remember me/The goofy one in class that/always made you laugh." While I used modeling and proximity in order to facilitate Jahia's engagement, I also aimed to inspire her to write. Another time I composed poetry that bore out of my frustration with the atmosphere of the classroom one day. Learners, on the whole, seemed reluctant and hesitant to engage with the day's assignments. I took the board and wrote:

> My teaching is unrequited love
> I stand with my arms out
> You fold yours
> I bring food for us to share
> You eat it all
> Perhaps there is some place in the middle
> I only need a little of you
> You can have the world
> There is potential in your standing there
> You are here
> and that is a great start. (9/28/17)

These writing pedagogical moves are important for Black writers, especially since much of what they experience within writing spaces dismisses their voices in order to perpetuate standards of writing and doing that have very little to do with thinking and intellectual growth. What I modeled for them was a way that they can use their own writing as subversion or subversive text as well as be inspired by present and real moments (Spiro & Dymoke, 2015). My poem was a way to share with the class how I felt in that moment. It was a way to share my voice without overexerting my power as the teacher. After some of the learners read the poem, I noted a shift in the atmosphere—one that moved away from lethargy towards measured enthusiasm. As writing mentors and writing teachers, it is important to model how you may compose honest and direct writing even in moments when feelings (teachers' and/or learners') are less than positive.

Feedback That Actually Feeds: Responding to Black Writers' Writing

When learners have a positive relationship with teachers, they are more likely to do well in classes. It is important that feedback is specific and points to the strengths of learners' writing. When providing feedback to my learners in the Creative Writing class, I made specific pedagogical moves that cultivated their developing voices and that changed some of their opinions about writing. When providing feedback to learners' journals, I made sure to make it personal and reflective of the ways that I engaged writing beyond looking for the holes in the writing.

Offering feedback for Black writers learning to use and love their own voices requires a delicate balance of flattery and truth. As their writing mentor, I refused to lie to them about their writing or use stipulated methods like a compliment sandwich. Instead, I listened and talked back to their writing. I used post-it notes to pose questions that asked them to go deeper or use more description. I offered ideas where I felt they may be stuck and provided references to information that they could use to enhance their writing. I suggested beautiful words for them and encouraged them to make up words when there was no word that would work. I wrote when their writing style or a subject reminded me of other brilliant Black writers like Octavia Butler and Alice Walker. I encouraged them to read passages from these writers and followed up to make sure they had. I also let them know how their writing made me feel—even when I felt very little. My feedback provided ways toward letting writers know that their writing is important and meaningful enough to improve.

For the final project in Creative Writing, learners were directed to create a portfolio of the texts they were most proud of. Learners were also required to include a reflection of the course and their writing, as well as cull their feedback received from the teacher and peers. JP's portfolio, 15 slides using an online presentation application, includes outcomes that resulted from useful and positive feedback. JP wrote:

> When I first got into this class I didn't know much about writing and I was not very good at it. Taking this class gave me a new perspective on writing and a new way of approaching it. I've learned plenty of new words and their meaning more than I have learned in any other class. My goal in this class was to get better at expanding my writing. This class helps because we explore different types of writing and different styles of writing. This course brought out a way of writing I never knew I had. I was only taught one way of writing and it was the only writing I would use when it came down to writing. I didn't know that a lot of these other writing styles even existed before. My writing has gotten better since I first started. I also learned some new stuff about myself. I learned that I'm more creative than I thought before. My creativity when writing is almost on the same level as when I'm drawing. I am very happy that I have found a new outlet for my thoughts and ideas. I'm confident that this class has helped me in other areas of school such as english. During my time at [HBCU down the street], we were required to type essays, and I could not formulate my thoughts that well. After some time in this class, I can say it has helped me drastically. Originally, I was thinking about dropping this class because I had other plans, but then I realized that it was more important and that my writing was in need of improvement. I am highly confident in my writing now, and when an essay is due, I won't be stressed out. (12/7/17)

JP reflects thoughtfully about their relationship to writing, claiming that they were not "very good," but sets a goal for themself to get better. JP also mentioned that over the course, their writing has improved, but that they also "learned some new stuff about myself." While there are still opportunities for growth in their writing (and in all of our writing, actually), JP's experiences in the Creative Writing class included feedback that improved their writing and relationship to writing, exposed them to different types of writing, and gave them the confidence to keep writing—goals that teachers and writing mentors should have for their students.

Subverting Traditional Reading of Black Writing: A Conclusion

Writing teachers and mentors have traditionally relied on stereotypes of academic writing (Biber & Gray, 2010). They have learned to hear white speech and read white writing as academic and Black voices, particularly, as nonacademic—in need of correction and standardization. Educators have an opportunity to subvert the "academic" reading of Black writing by focusing on developing a language of thinking and intellectual discourse(s) that allow them to build fortified bridges toward academic success. Kiriakos and Tienari (2018) call for making academic writing social again through a framework of love. They posit that "For love to reach full expression [in writing], it requires an academic environment that supports epistemic and social diversity and justice—the free creative play of thoughts, knowledge, and bodies" (p. 272). For Black writers specifically, this requires that teachers and writing mentors learn to read Black writing in ways that are not grounded in deficit foundations of writing, writing instruction, and assessment. Doing so means that we might truly maximize the intellectual potential of all our learners, no matter the color of their writing.

References

Attolino, P. (2022). "Yo word is yo bond": Black semantics, discourse communities, and translanguaging spaces. *Bi-and Multilingualism from Various Perspectives of Applied Linguistics*, 21.

Baker-Bell, A. (2019). Dismantling anti-Black linguistic racism in English language arts classrooms: Toward an anti-racist Black language pedagogy. *Theory Into Practice*, 59, 8–21.

Ball, A. F., & Ellis, P. (2008). Identity and the writing of culturally and linguistically diverse students. In C. Bazerman (Ed.), *Handbook of research on writing: History, society, school, individual, text* (pp. 499–513). Taylor & Francis Group/Lawrence Erlbaum Associates.

Bangura, A. K. (2011). *African-centered research methodologies: From ancient times to the present*. Cognella.

Biber, D., & Gray, B. (2010). Challenging stereotypes about academic writing: Complexity, elaboration, explicitness. *Journal of English for Academic Purposes*, 9(1), 2–20.

Burke, J. & Gilmore, B. (2015). *Academic moves for college and career readiness*. Corwin.

Cooper, M. M. (1986). The ecology of writing. *College English*, 48(4), 364-375.

Fisher, M. T. (2009). *Black literate lives: Historical and contemporary perspectives*. Routledge.

Flores, N., & Rosa, J. (2015). Undoing appropriateness: Raciolinguistic ideologies and language diversity in education. *Harvard Educational Review*, 85(2), 149–171.

Goff, P. A., Jackson, M. C., Leone, D., Lewis, B. A., Culotta, C. M., & DiTomasso, N. A. (2014). The essence of innocence: Consequences of dehumanizing Black children. *Journal of Personality and Social Psychology*, 106, 526–545.

González, N., Moll, L. C., & Amanti, C. (Eds.). (2006). *Funds of knowledge: Theorizing practices in households, communities, and classrooms*. Routledge.

Hammond, J. W. (2019). Making our invisible racial agendas visible: Race talk in assessing writing, 1994–2018. *Assessing Writing, 42.* DOI:10.1016/j.asw.2019.100425.

Inoue, A. B. (2015). *Antiracist writing assessment ecologies: Teaching and assessing writing for a socially just future.* The WAC Clearinghouse; Parlor Press. https://doi.org/10.37514/PER-B.2015.0698

Johnson, L. P. (2017). Writing the self: Black queer youth challenge heteronormative ways of being in an after-school writing club. *Research in the Teaching of English, 52,* 13–33.

Johnson, L. P., & Sullivan, H. (2020). Revealing the human and the writer: The promise of a humanizing writing pedagogy for Black students. *Research in the Teaching of English, 54*(4), 418–438.

Kiriakos, C. M., & Tienari, J. (2018). Academic writing as love. *Management Learning, 49*(3), 263–277.

Ladson-Billings, G. (2014). Culturally relevant pedagogy 2.0: a.k.a. the remix. *Harvard Educational Review, 84,* 74–84.

Morrison, T. (1988). *Beloved.* Plume.

Poe, M. (2015). Re-framing race in teaching writing across the curriculum. *Anti-Racist Activism: Teaching Rhetoric and Writing,* 1–14.

Spence, L. K. (2021). Deconstructing generous reading: Revising a writing assessment. *Critical Questions in Education, 12*(2), 100-113.

Spiro, J., & Dymoke, S. (2015). Translating writing worlds: Writing as a poet, writing as an academic. In R. Jones and J. Richards (Eds.), *Creativity in Language Teaching* (pp. 77–94). Routledge.

Yagelski, R. P. (2009). A thousand writers writing: Seeking change through the radical practice of writing as a way of being. *English Education, 42,* 6–28.

CHAPTER TWO

We Are Not the Same, We Deserve to be Seen: Diverse Asian American Text Sets as Resistance

Betina Hsieh and Jung Kim

"[Watching K-Dramas] made me appreciate a lot more that across the Asian American label, there are so many vast differences . . . . [W]hen I think of myself as an Asian American, I think a lot of the shared part, and I feel like I am not very well informed, to quote/unquote "own" that label . . . only because I feel like there are so many cultures that it can encompass that I know really nothing about." Abdul, Pakistani American ELA teacher

"[C]ommunity care has been very rare in my children's school. We live 10 miles from [the Atlanta] mass shooting. The school admin and teachers never talked about or checked in with students including Asian American students the day or the week or the month; NEVER! . . . so my daughter and her Asian American friends began [a] virtual book club to support each other and learn about Asian American histories and current stories in the making." Sohyun, Teacher Educator

Introduction

SUBVERSIVE TEACHING CENTERS PERSPECTIVES too often relegated to the margins or viewed through stereotypical lenses that reduce our collective humanity. As Asian American mothers, former secondary English teachers, and current teacher educators, the words of Abdul and Sohyun echo many of our own thoughts and experiences as

19

well as those of more than 40 Asian American educators we have interviewed about
their experiences as students and teachers in ELA classrooms and beyond (Kim &
Hsieh, 2021). While Asian Americans represent racial, ethnic, and linguistically diverse groups from 20 different nations (López et al., 2017), they are often treated
as a monolith and racialized narrowly, being perceived as "foreigners," "model mi-
norities," or "yellow perils" (An, 2020; Iftikar & Museus, 2018), despite diverse
immigration experiences and experiences as multigenerational Americans.

Asian Americans have been present on the continent of North America since the
1500s (Lee, 2015) and are the fastest-growing racial minority group in the United
States (López et al., 2017). The Pew Research center estimates there will be over 35
million Asian Americans by 2060 (Budiman & Ruiz, 2021). Yet in spite of rich and diverse histories in the United States, and growing numbers, Asian Americans are rarely
seen in school curricula or texts, a form of "curricular violence" as described by An
(2020) and a way to reinforce through curricular absence ideas of Asian Americans
as a foreign other (Goodwin, 2010). While the presence of Asian Americans in social
studies curriculum is changing with legislative mandates like the TEAACH (Teaching
Equitable Asian American Community History) Act in Illinois, which requires the
teaching of Asian American history in K-12 public schools, Asian American representation is generally still missing or limited in ELA classrooms. The diversity of the
Asian American diaspora too often is ignored and many Asian Americans are left to
feel invisible in classrooms and communities, even after painful public events like the
political rhetoric and scapegoating of Asian people as COVID-19 became a global
pandemic; the meteoric rise in anti-Asian racist and xenophobic violence captured in
viral social media attacks on elders; and the killing of eight people, including six Asian
women, in Asian-owned spas in the metro Atlanta area in 2021. Asian American inclusion is particularly necessary when one-quarter of all AAPI youth have experienced
racism since the beginning of the pandemic (Stop AAPI Hate, 2020).

As Abdul and Sohyun indicate in the epigraphs that begin this chapter, access to
more stories, histories, and media that contain nuanced Asian American characters that
challenge dominant stereotypes are critical in affirming Asian American students' identities. These narratives also provide "windows" (Bishop, 1990) for non-Asian American
students to better understand the experiences of individuals within diverse Asian American families and communities.

In this chapter, we challenge the curriculum violence, the design and use of
curriculum that compromises learners' well-being (An, 2020; Ighodaro & Wiggan,
2010; Jones, 2020), inflicted upon Asian Americans when teachers rely only upon
traditional ELA canonical texts that center Whiteness or White perspectives of Asian
cultures in ELA classrooms. We propose subverting this practice through integrating contemporary thematic Asian American text sets, written by Asian American
authors, that are taught in culturally responsive and affirming ways to all students.

Curricular Violence: Erasure and Essentialization of Asian American Experiences in the Traditional ELA Classroom

The "classic" literary canon, which overwhelmingly contains White male–centered European and American texts, has been challenged based on the increasing diversity of U.S. secondary students. Despite longstanding debates as to the canon's relevance in high school ELA, a curriculum designed around such persists through structural mechanisms—for example, the suggested texts on Advanced Placement examinations (Barshel, 2020; Miller & Slifkin, 2010). Similarly in middle schools, strong notions of the importance of maintaining literary traditionalism—that is, reading texts written by well-known authors or historically celebrated authors—abound (Thein & Beach, 2013). These middle level texts also lean heavily towards centering White authors and perspectives, erasing Asian Americans' existence in the larger American narrative. Even when Asian protagonists or stories are included in ELA classrooms, they often rely entirely upon White-authored texts with Asian foreign characters like *The Good Earth* (Buck, 1931); focus on a few selected award-winning authors and works like Lawrence Yep's *Dragonwings* (1975), Amy Tan's *The Joy Luck Club* (1989), or Maxine Hong Kingston's *Woman Warrior* (1976) (whose texts represent important but specific Chinese American diasporic voices); and/or center on particular historical events like Japanese incarceration (Rodriguez, 2020; Uchida, 1971). These texts tend to highlight experiences of cultural difference and negotiation that can reinforce trauma and othering, a form of curriculum violence (An, 2020; Jones, 2020) against Asian Americans.

The inclusion of Asian American texts and experiences in ELA classrooms must move beyond the rare appearance of a handful of dated texts from certain East Asian perspectives that reinforce ideas of cultural otherness. Our prior work (Kim & Hsieh, 2021) speaks to the direct experiences of Asian American teachers who felt missing or misrepresented in the curriculum. As ELA teachers and teacher educators, we have both a responsibility and opportunities to confront curriculum violence by introducing diverse Asian American texts to ELA curriculum, thereby addressing Asian American "narrative scarcity" (Nguyen, 2016) and move towards "narrative plenitude" (Nguyen, 2018) and a richness of representation and multiple perspectives in school-sponsored reading.

Diverse Asian American Text Sets as Subversive Practice

A fundamental act of subversion is demanding the affirmation of one's existence, particularly in the face of marginalization. This can be seen historically in landmark cases like *Tape v. Hurley*, which fought the segregation of Asian Americans in schools; *Lau v. Nichols*, which fought for supplemental English instruction for multilingual students; and *U.S. v. Wong Kim Ark*, which established U.S. citizenship as a birthright. Asians in America have, for generations, insisted on their inclusion in American society. Even the emergence of the "Asian American" label in the 1970s was an act of self-determination in opposition to "the passive Oriental" stereotype (Espiritu, 1992). Used as an umbrella term to bring together disparate groups to help solidify political power, the creation and claiming of an Asian American identity was a revolutionary act. Despite stereotypical depictions of Asian Americans as passive and subservient, Asian Americans have fought to be seen and heard for a long time.

One way to engage in the subversive practice of confronting dominant stereotypes of Asian Americans and supporting the inclusion of more authentic and affirming Asian American voices in ELA curriculum is through text sets. A text set is a group of texts centered around a central theme, topic, or essential question (Barshel, 2020). We define texts broadly to include various and multimodal forms of written, visual, and/or performance-based artifacts from which students can derive meaning. A rich body of literature on text sets as part of a rigorous ELA curriculum (Barshel, 2020; Cervetti & Hiebert, 2019; Ward & Young, 2008) demonstrates that text sets are effective tools to promote deeper understanding and knowledge around topics, greater engagement and achievement among more students, and enhanced vocabulary and conceptual development (Stevens, 2016; Ward & Young, 2008). When modern texts are used alongside more canonical works around a common theme, student motivation and connection to the relevance of reading to their own experiences increases (Barshel, 2020). Text sets can also be used to introduce and humanize characters who are different from students (Hsieh, 2012; Scullin, 2018) and to promote more diverse perspectives, extending (from) the canon to promote critical investigations of relevant justice-based topics (Babino et al., 2019, Dyches et al., 2021). Further, when various genres, including digital texts, media, and artifacts are included in text sets, students have greater opportunities to engage in rich disciplinary, digital, and critical literacies (Castek et al., 2017).

Diverse texts and text sets can be a cornerstone best practice of culturally responsive ELA teaching (Walker-Dalhouse & Risko, 2020), particularly, but not exclusively, in multiethnic and multilingual classrooms and communities (Ramirez & Jimenez-Silva, 2014). Culturally responsive teaching (Gay, 2018) includes the incorporation of cultural and societal knowledge alongside cultural caring and cross-cultural communications. By using the well-researched practice of integrating text sets to broaden and diversify traditional and canonical ELA curriculum, contemporary Asian American voices that promote inclusion can be achieved when combined with teaching that promotes connections with the characters, perspectives, and experiences brought forth in the text.

Contemporary Asian American texts, particularly those authored by Asian Americans themselves, can provide "windows, mirrors, and sliding glass doors" (Bishop, 1990) into diverse Asian American experiences. By introducing a multitude of Asian American perspectives that challenge harmful stereotypes, Asian American and non-Asian American students can begin to explore and better understand these nuanced experiences, drawing connections between their experiences and the experiences of the diverse Asian American characters and authors they encounter. Asian American students may also be able to see mirrors of their own identities and lived experiences acknowledged, affirmed, and explored in such text sets.

The use of diverse Asian American text sets considers the rich cultural and linguistic funds of knowledge and funds of identity (Esteban-Guitart & Moll, 2014; Moll et al., 1992) that Asian American students bring into the classroom and reflects some of those identities, experiences, and knowledge in ways that affirm this home knowledge as an asset in reading the word and the world (Freire & Macedo, 2005). In this way, diverse Asian American text sets can be seen as a way to enact culturally responsive pedagogy to move away from asking students to assimilate into dominant forms of knowledge (Au, 2007), and instead to center, affirm, and validate the multidimensionality of Asian American cultural experiences.

Considering Diversity & Challenging Stereotypes in Asian American Text Sets: Resources and Examples from Practice

Given the power of text sets to provide multiple stories and perspectives, we highlight two examples of incorporating Asian American voices using text sets in secondary ELA classrooms. The first example looks at an Asian American high school level standalone text set involving multiple texts (including a picture book, graphic novels, and a memoir) that could be taught sequentially as a complete unit. The second example looks at how Asian American texts might be integrated into larger thematic text sets that include additional diverse voices either at the middle school or high school levels. Both these examples go beyond a focus on East Asian (Chinese, Japanese, Korean) perspectives as representative of all Asian American experiences. They offer examples from a range of Asian diasporic experiences in the United States that can be connected with or explored in conjunction with stories focused on characters (and written by authors) from other backgrounds. This decentering of East Asian Americans (particularly the movement away from Chinese- and Japanese-only narratives) and the integration of Asian American perspectives alongside perspectives of other communities of color also are acts of subversion that challenge monolithic portrayals of a singular Asian American experience. By highlighting the diversity of the Asian diaspora in the Americas and the similarities across Asian Americans and other immigrant groups in the United States, it pushes back against "wedge" minority narratives that are part of the model minority myth (Poon et al., 2016).

Using Text Sets to Highlight Refugee Narratives

In the last several years, there has been a robust conversation about the plight of refugees globally. However, refugees are not new to the United States, and in some cases—like those coming from Vietnam—are partially a result of America's empire abroad. Thus, the view of Asian immigration as "East comes West" is better contextualized to understand that some Asian immigration was more of a response to "West goes East," as American involvement in Vietnam and Korea brought waves of immigration from those areas (Lowe, 1996). While the popular conception of Asian Americans is that of voluntary immigrants who came for their chance at the American Dream, the truth is that large swathes of Asians came to America fleeing war and conflict.

The model minority myth (Poon et al., 2016) obscures the "truth" of Asian American success—that the first large waves of Asian American immigrants after 1965 came with better education, financial resources, and connections than both previous Asian immigrants and than those who did not immigrate from their home countries (a phenomenon called *hyperselection* by Zhou & Lee, 2017). This made educational and financial success for their children and themselves much more attainable. This is in stark contrast to the second wave of Asian immigrants in the later 20th century, which was mostly refugees from Southeast Asia.

This text set, which was also partly introduced in *Graphic Novels in the English Language Arts Classroom* (Boerman-Cornell & Kim, 2020), includes texts that describe a variety of Vietnamese American refugee experiences. They both push back on the model minority myth, unveiling the hardships many Asian Americans encounter, and counter the deficit-laden views of refugees by highlighting their inner strength and rich backgrounds. While this text set centers on stories of Vietnamese Americans, the diversity of narrative perspectives and experiences in the set challenges monolithic views of them. Because of the different levels of complexity and contextual background needed for understanding the stories, the texts in this set (Figure 2.1) can work well together to build upon and complement one another or can be pulled out as standalone texts in a different unit.

Bao Phi's (2018) picture book *A Different Pond*, illustrated by Thi Bui, is told from the perspective of a little boy who is woken up in the pre-dawn to go fishing with his father. While this seems like a simple enough tale, there are deeper layers that speak to both the poverty in which they live—the fish they catch will supplement the groceries they purchase—and the intimacy that develops between the father and son in the story. While Asian American parents are often cast as unfeeling "tiger" parents who prioritize their children's academic achievement over their social-emotional well-being, this book reveals the love and joy that can exist between Asian American parent and child. And while the poverty the family struggles with is not the focus of the book, there are enough details for the reader to understand that this is not the classic upper-middle class Asian American success story that is often portrayed in mainstream media.

As the text set continues, the level of complexity and difficulty evolves as well. Trung Le Nguyen's (2020) graphic novel *The Magic Fish* may be seen as more fitting for middle school by some readers. However, Nguyen's multilayered storytelling and use of metaphor offers nuanced opportunities for meaning-making for older read-

Figure 2.1.

Refugee Narratives

Author	Title	Asian American Ethnic Identity Group	Additional Notes
Bao Phi (author) Thi Bui (illustrator)	*A Different Pond*	Vietnamese American	Father–son relationship, poverty, refugee, memoir
Trung Le Nguyen	*The Magic Fish*	Vietnamese American	Second generation son, LGBTQIA+ coming out story, multiple storylines, allegory
Nam Le (author) Matt Huynh (graphic adaptation)	*The Boat matthuynh.com/ theboat*	Vietnamese American	Migration, transnational contexts, death
Thi Bui	*The Best We Could Do*	Vietnamese American	Migration story, transnational contexts, flashback, memory, symbolism
Kao Kalia Yang	*The Song Poet: A Memoir of My Father*	Hmong American	Transnational contexts, migrant refugee experiences, American Dream, storytelling

ers as well. Nguyen uses three different color schemes to tell three stories, at times overlapping/intersecting, from the perspective of a young boy grappling with his sexuality, his mother's story of being a refugee, and a fairy tale. Drawing upon multi-modal resources, readers must unpack how these stories inform and build upon one another. Scholars have critiqued the tendency in literature to emphasize coming out stories as ones filled with pain and trauma (Bittner, 2016), and Asian Americans are not often portrayed as being particularly sympathetic towards LGBTQIA+ issues. *The Magic Fish* subverts both of these depictions by telling a story of self-love, support, and acceptance. The many layers of the story create opportunities for readers to connect on historic, emotional/aesthetic, and political levels. *The Magic Fish* also highlights the many intersectional identities that make up Asian American identity, such as socioeconomic status, religion, linguistic proficiency, immigration status, and sexuality, to name a few.

Part of *The Magic Fish* includes the mother's escape from Vietnam by boat. While some readers may have seen images of capsized boats or boats detained by local authorities, many will not be very familiar with the details of such experiences. "The Boat" is an acclaimed short story by Nam Le (2009) that has been adapted into an interactive graphic novel by Matt Huynh (found on Huynh's personal website). It is a brutal and unflinching look at one young girl's escape by boat from Vietnam. Teachers should use their discretion as the multimodal aspect of it—the illustrations and accompanying background sounds—can make the reading a particularly difficult one for sensitive readers. The fact of the matter is, though, that too often in American society we say things like "never again," yet we have seen over and over American indifference to the plight of people feeling violence and persecution. "The Boat" offers opportunities to not only make the historical more personal but still speaks to contemporary issues. The death of a child at the end of "The Boat" has a striking resonance to the viral 2016 image of the young Syrian boy who drowned. History *does* repeat itself.

The culmination of this text set is the most difficult—in structure, complexity, and subject matter—Thi Bui's (2018) *The Best We Could Do: An Illustrated Memoir*. Bui, who also illustrated *A Different Pond*, tells the story of her family's journey to the United States from Vietnam. However, to better understand her own childhood, she investigates her parents' childhoods. Through unpacking who her parents were as children and young adults, she is better able to understand the various traumas and life experiences that shaped her own childhood and her relationships to her parents. Jumping back and forth between perspectives and timelines, Bui's book includes several historical references, which may require some additional teaching as well. Addressing themes of intergenerational trauma, healing, and hope, Bui's book not only reveals the difficulties and trauma refugee adults and children must contend with, it also sheds light on the constant "becoming" Asian American children and adults are grappling with.

Some of these ideas are also reflected in Kao Kalia Yang's (2016) *The Song Poet*, which we discuss in greater detail below. There are many parallels between Yang's book about being a Hmong refugee and the others in the previously described set, just as there are many other books about non-Asian refugees that could be incorporated into this text set as well (See Boerman-Cornell & Kim, 2020 for other ideas). Many of these texts challenge traditional views of "the American Dream" and trouble overly easy narratives of success and plentitude. Even the texts' multiple-voiced narratives and nonlinear storytelling challenge traditional understandings of plot structure and narrative. Just as they trouble set ideas of what being Asian or American means, these stories can also trouble canonical understandings of ELA curriculum.

Adding Asian American Perspectives to Coming-of-Age Text Sets

Another way that text sets can be used to include and highlight Asian Americans in curriculum is by integrating contemporary Asian American texts alongside more traditional texts within preexisting text sets. In many secondary settings, texts like *The Diary of Anne Frank* (Goodrich & Hackett, 1955) and *The House on Mango Street* (Cisneros, 1984) have become a part of a coming-of-age canon. While short stories like Amy Tan's "Fish Cheeks" (1987) are sometimes included in anthologies, additional texts that include a greater diversity of Asian American experiences can help students to understand more diverse and complex Asian American coming-of-age stories. The texts in this section thus highlight additional Asian American texts that can be integrated into larger units of texts with additional texts from nondominant groups around the common theme of coming of age.

Graphic novels (see Figure 2.2) including the aforementioned *The Magic Fish* (Nguyen, 2020) and *The Best We Could Do* (Bui, 2018) powerfully illustrate coming-of-age stories for transnational and refugee children, exploring generational trauma as well as the power of self-acceptance. *I Was Their American Dream*, a graphic memoir by Malaka Gharib (2019), offers a different perspective, as she describes her experiences as a second-generation daughter of Egyptian and Filipina parents who grew up in a predominantly Asian American city. Gharib's humorous, honest stories of struggling to fit in, even among other Asian Americans, highlights diversity within the Asian diaspora in America and themes that came up in our research among Southeast, South Asian, and multiracial Asian American participants of not feeling like they were "the right kind" of Asian American. Booki Vivat's *Frazzled* series (2016) offers a light-hearted exploration of the transition to middle school for younger readers, which also deals with issues of fitting in, within, and outside of one's family, offering a universal theme through an Asian American middle school main character.

Figure 2.2.
Coming-of-Age Graphic Novels

Author	Title	Asian American Ethnic Identity Group	Additional Notes
Trung Le Nguyen	*The Magic Fish*	Vietnamese American	Second generation son, LGBTQIA+ coming out story
Thi Bui	*The Best We Could Do*	Vietnamese American	Migration story, transnational contexts
Malaka Gharib	*I Was Their American Dream*	Egyptian/ Filipina American	Multiethnic Asian Americans, growing up in a predominantly Asian American Community
Booki Vivat	*Frazzled* (series)	Chinese American	Middle school transition/ fitting in (appropriate for MS, late elementary)

Middle grade novels (see Figure 2.3) like Mike Jung's (2020) *The Boys in the Back Row* and Debbi Michiko Florence's (2020) *Keep it Together, Keiko Carter* or *Just Be Cool, Jenna Sakai* (2021), like Vivat's *Frazzled* (2016), provide contemporary coming-of-age friendship stories that feature Asian American protagonists (including a multiracial Asian American main character in *Keiko Carter*) navigating the challenges of adjusting to middle school and adolescence. Andrea Wang's *The Many Meanings of Meilan* (2021) explores similar themes, but also brings forth how changing contexts and regions (i.e., moving away from family, interfamily conflict, moving away from an Asian American community on the East Coast to a town in the Midwest with no other Asian American families) lead the protagonist to explore her identity, resist identities placed upon her, and build deeper connections within her family and across communities.

Figure 2.3.

Middle Grade (Grades 6–8) Asian American Coming-of-Age Novels

Author	Title	Asian American Ethnic Identity Group	Additional Notes
Mike Jung	*The Boys in the Back Row*	Korean American	Friendship between boys
Debbi Michiko Florence	*Keep it Together, Keiko Carter; Just Be Cool, Jenna Sakai*	Multiracial Japanese American; Japanese American	Middle school transition, friendships, divorce
Andrea Wang	*The Many Meanings of Meilan*	Chinese American	Moving/ changing regions, leaving family

At the high school level (see Figure 2.4), a short story like Ken Liu's *The Paper Menagerie* (2016) powerfully explores intersections of race, class, intergenerational communication, and belonging. In order to fit in with his White American peers, the protagonist wrestles with the rejection of his Chinese heritage and language and his mother's expressions of love. Eventually, after his mother passes away, into his adulthood, he discovers the origami she made him, and on the back of his "old friend," a magic paper tiger, he finds a letter written to him in Chinese about the pain of his rejection and how much he meant to her.

Young Adult novels like Randy Ribay's *Patron Saints of Nothing* (2019) and Emily X. R. Pan's *The Astonishing Color of After* (2018) both deal with painful reckoning after the traumatic loss of family members close to the protagonists. In *Patron Saints of Nothing*, the protagonist, Filipino American Jay Reguero, is forced to reckon with the complex truth of his cousin Jun's death in the Philippines. Ribay's

Figure 2.4.

High School Appropriate/YA Asian American Coming-of-Age Texts[1]

Author	Title	Genre	Asian American Ethnic Identity Group	Additional Notes
Ken Liu	*The Paper Menagerie*	Short Story	Chinese American	Intergenerational relationships, rejected connection to heritage
Randy Ribay	*Patron Saints of Nothing*	YA Novel	Filipino American	Transnational contexts, trauma, drug references
Emily X. R. Pan	*The Astonishing Color of After*	YA Novel	Taiwanese American	Multiracial Asian American, suicidality, transnational contexts
Kelly Yang	*Parachutes*	YA Novel	Chinese American, Filipino American	Sexual assault, racism, classism, familial expectations, parachute children

1   The three YA novels listed (and several of the texts that deal with refugee experiences) deal with trauma and potentially triggering content. They should be carefully previewed before being taught and students and families should receive specific content warnings prior to reading these texts.

storytelling brings us from Michigan to the Philippines and back again to explore the devastation of Duterte's drug war and the complexities of family, humanity, and identities. In *The Astonishing Color of After*, the multiracial Taiwanese American protagonist, Leigh Chen Sanders, must reconcile her identity and how to continue with her life, following her mother's death by suicide. As she struggles with grief, she also discovers more about who she is, who her mother was, and forms a new relationship with her maternal grandparents in Taiwan.

A final young adult novel that explores challenging coming-of-age experiences is *Parachutes* (2019) by Kelly Yang. The title refers to the idea of parachute children, who come to the United States without their parents to stay with friends or family members to complete part of their schooling, and the text, with complex explorations of sexual assault, racism, classism, and familial expectations, could be paired with another powerful text about sexual assault like *Speak* (1999) by Laurie Halse Anderson.

Finally, memoirs (see Figure 2.5) like *The Song Poet* by Kao Kalia Yang (2016), *All You Can Ever Know* by Nicole Chung (2019), and *Year of the Tiger* (2022) by Alice Wong also bring to light powerful perspectives from across the Asian American diaspora. Yang's *The Song Poet* is a memoir of the author's father, in two parts, the first told from her father's perspective in his voice about how he became a song poet, a revered tradition in the Hmong culture of recounting history, joy, and loss, and how he loses his songs as he moves from his homelands in Laos through refugee camps in Thailand and eventually to Minnesota with his family. The second part of the memoir is told from the author's perspective as daughter of the Song Poet, born in refugee camps, coming of age in the United States in poverty. The memoir moves both away from and towards her father as she comes of age and he ages in the cold of Minnesota, so far from their Hmong ancestors. *All You Can Ever Know* is told from Chung's perspective as a Korean adoptee raised in a White family. It is a story about a struggle for belonging, dealing with loss, and the complexities of reckoning with hard truths about one's family and past. *Year of the Tiger,* while extending beyond a coming-of-age memoir, explores intersectional issues of race, gender, and disability, in a variety of genres (visually, in science fiction-like reflections, and in more traditional narrative), as Wong reflects on the evolution of her relationship with herself, her family, and how she navigates coming of age, as her disability progresses.

Figure 2.5.

Coming-of-Age Memoirs

Author	Title	Asian American Ethnic Identity Group	Additional Notes
Kao Kalia Yang	*The Song Poet*	Hmong American	Transnational contexts; migrant refugee experiences
Nicole Chung	*All You Can Ever Know*	Korean American	Transnational, transracial adoption
Alice Wong	*Year of the Tiger*	Chinese American	Intersectional issues of race, gender, and disability

These texts could be part of a larger unit that looks at family relationships (particularly parent–child relationships) and establishing one's identity, which could also include texts from other communities of color like: *I Am Not Your Perfect Mexican Daughter* (Sánchez, 2017); *How the Garcia Girls Lost Their Accents* (Alvarez, 1992); *Accents* (Frohman, 2016); *Everyday Use* (Walker, 1994); and *Beloved* (Morrison, 2007), as well as others named earlier. Integrating Asian American voices and perspectives like these into larger text sets with diverse voices can help to challenge some of the harmful stereotypes and homogenization of Asian American stories, showing both universal and diverse experiences that Asian Americans may face.

Subverting Asian American Erasure: Visibility & Voice as Resistance

In integrating rich and diverse voices across the Asian diaspora in America, we provide "mirrors" (Bishop, 1990) for some Asian American students who are rarely able to see their perspectives reflected in classrooms and "windows" and "sliding glass doors" into the experiences of diverse Asian Americans for other students, both Asian American and non-Asian American. Integrating diverse Asian American stories refuses to play into monolithic portrayals of Asian Americans and evokes a sense of Asian American belonging within the larger fabric of American society. Through visibility and voice, ELA teachers can engage in active resistance to curricular violence that erases or misrepresents Asian American experiences and challenge notions of Asian Americans as "all the same." While we recognize that representation is not the only or highest level of resistance, it is an opening that allows ELA teachers and students to move past reductionist ideas about what it means to be Asian American and explore the diverse experiences that Asian diasporic people have in the Americas.

The inclusion of diverse Asian American perspectives in text sets in ELA classrooms begins to push back on the notion that Asian Americans are always "foreign" and disconnected from the experiences of other communities in America. One heartbreaking statistic from the Stop AAPI Hate report (2020) revealed that when Asian American youth experienced racist incidents, it was often in the presence of an adult who did not intervene. It is beyond time for ELA educators to intervene in symbolic, curricular violence and in actual violence against Asian American youth. Engaging with text sets like those described can help both teachers and students develop greater empathy and understanding towards Asian Americans which might, in turn, prevent hateful incidents in the future. Teachers must actively resist the entrenched belief that Asian Americans are doing "just fine" and don't need representation in school curricula. It's become clear that this is not the case, and there is much work to be done.

References

Alvarez, J. *(1992). How the García girls lost their accents.* Plume.

An, S. (2020). Disrupting curriculum of violence on Asian Americans. *Review of Education, Pedagogy, and Cultural Studies, 42(3),* 141–156.

Anderson, L. H. (1999). *Speak.* Farrar, Straus and Giroux.

Au, K. H. (2007). Culturally responsive instruction: Application to multiethnic classrooms. *Pedagogies: An International Journal, 2(1),* 1–18.

Babino, A., Araujo, J. J., & Maxwell, M. L. (2019). Critical, compelling, and linguistically scaffolded literature: Implementing text sets multilingually for social justice. *Texas Journal of Literacy Education, 7(1),* 44–64.

Barshel, A. (2020). Using text sets to engage students while reading canonical literature in a language arts classroom. *Learning to Teach, 9(1),* 14–19.

Bishop, R. S. (1990). Mirrors, windows, and sliding glass doors. *Perspectives, 6(3),* ix–xi.

Bittner, R. (2016). (Im) Possibility and (in) visibility: Arguing against 'just happens to be' in Young Adult literature. *Queer Studies in Media & Popular Culture, 1(2),* 199–214.

Boerman-Cornell, B. & Kim, J. (2020). *Using graphic novels in the English Language Arts classroom.* Bloomsbury Academic.

Buck, P. S. (1931). *The good earth.* Simon & Schuster.

Budiman, A. & Ruiz, N. G. (2021). Asian Americans are the fastest growing racial or ethnic group in the U.S. https://www.pewresearch.org/fact-tank/2021/04/09/asian-americans-are-the-fastest-growing-racial-or-ethnic-group-in-the-u-s/

Bui, T. (2018). *The best we could do.* Abrams ComicArts.

Castek, J., Manderino, M., Rainey, E. C., & Storm, S. (2017). Teaching digital literary literacies in secondary English language arts. *Journal of Adolescent & Adult Literacy, 61*(2), 203–207.

Cervetti, G. N., & Hiebert, E. H. (2019). Knowledge at the center of English language arts instruction. *The Reading Teacher, 72*(4), 499–507.

Chung, N. (2019) *All you can ever know: A memoir.* Catapult.

Cisneros, S. (1984). *The house on Mango Street.* Arté Publico Press.

Dyches, J., Boyd, A. S., & Schulz, J. M. (2021). Critical content knowledges in the English language arts classroom: examining practicing teachers' nuanced perspectives. *Journal of Curriculum Studies, 53*(3), 368–384.

Espiritu, Y. L. (1993). *Asian American panethnicity: Bridging institutions and identities.* Temple University Press.

Esteban-Guitart, M., & Moll, L. C. (2014). Funds of Identity: A new concept based on the Funds of Knowledge approach. *Culture & Psychology, 20*(1), 31–48.

Florence, D. M. (2020). *Keep it together, Keiko Carter.* Scholastic.

Florence, D. M. (2021). *Just be cool, Jenna Sakai.* Scholastic.

Freire, P., & Macedo, D. (2005). *Literacy: Reading the word and the world.* Routledge.

Frohman, D. (2016). Accents. https://folukeafrica.com/accents-by-denice-frohman/

Gay, G. (2018). *Culturally responsive teaching: Theory, research, and practice* (3rd ed.). Teachers College Press.

Gharib, M. (2019). *I was their American dream: A graphic memoir.* Clarkson Potter.

Goodrich, F., & Hackett, A. (1955). *The diary of Anne Frank.* Random House.

Goodwin, A. L. (2010). Curriculum as colonizer: (Asian) American education in current U.S. contexts. *Teachers College Record, 112*(12), 3102–3138.

Hsieh, B. (2012). Challenging characters: Learning to reach inward and outward from characters who face oppression. *English Journal, 102* (1), 48–51.

Iftikar, J. S., & Museus, S. D. (2018). On the utility of Asian critical (AsianCrit) theory in the field of education. *International Journal of Qualitative Studies in Education, 31*(10), 935–949.

Ighodaro, E., & Wiggan, G. (2010) *Curriculum violence: America's new civil rights issue.* Nova Science.

Jones, S. P. (2020). Ending curriculum violence. *Teaching Tolerance, 64,* 47–50.

Jung, M. (2020). *The boys in the back row.* Levine Querido.

Kim, J., & Hsieh, B. (2021). *The racialized experiences of Asian American teachers in the US: Applications of Asian Critical Race Theory to resist marginalization.* Routledge.

Kingston, M. H. (1976). *The woman warrior: Memoir of a girlhood among ghosts.* Alfred A. Knopf.

Le, N. (2009). *The boat: Stories.* Vintage.

Lee, E. (2015). *The making of Asian America.* Simon & Schuster.

Liu, K. (2016). *The paper menagerie.* Head of Zeus.

López, G., Ruiz, N. G., & Patten, E. (2017). Key facts about Asian Americans, a diverse and growing population. http://www.pewresearch.org/fact-tank/2017/09/08/key-facts-about-asian-americans/

Lowe, L. (1996). *Immigrant acts: on Asian American cultural politics*. Duke University Press.

Miller, S. J., & Slifkin, J. (2010). "Similar literary quality": Demystifying the AP English literature and composition open question. *The ALAN Review, 37*(2), 6–16.

Moll, L. C., Amanti, C., Neff, D., & Gonzalez, N. (1992). Funds of knowledge for teaching: Using a qualitative approach to connect homes and classrooms. *Theory Into Practice, 31*(2), 133–141.

Morrison, T. (2007). *Beloved*. Vintage Classics.

Nguyen, T. L. (2020). *The magic fish*. Random House Graphic.

Nguyen, V. T. (2016). Viet Thanh Nguyen on narrative scarcity. Library Foundation of Los Angeles. https://lfla.org/media-archive/viet-thanh-nguyen-on-narrative-scarcity/

Nguyen, V. T. (2018). Narrative plentitude: Viet Thanh Nguyen and Vu Tran: Talks at Google. https://www.youtube.com/watch?v=gqiPoZOy3VE

Pan, E. X. R. (2018). *The astonishing color of after*. Little, Brown and Company.

Phi, B. (2018). *A different pond*. Capstone.

Poon, O., Squire, D., Kodama, C., Byrd, A., Chan, J., Manzano, L., Furr, S., & Bishundat, D. (2016). A critical review of the model minority myth in selected literature on Asian Americans and Pacific Islanders in higher education. *Review of Educational Research, 86*(2), 469–502.

Ramirez, P. C., & Jimenez-Silva, M. (2014). Secondary English learners: Strengthening their literacy skills through culturally responsive teaching. *Kappa Delta Pi Record, 50*(2), 65–69.

Ribay, R. (2019). *Patron saints of nothing*. Kokila.

Rodríguez, N.N. (2020). "Invisibility is not a natural state for anyone": (Re)constructing narratives of Japanese American incarceration in elementary classrooms. *Curriculum Inquiry, 50*(4), 309–329.

Sánchez, E. L. (2017). *I am not your perfect Mexican daughter*. Alfred A. Knopf.

Scullin, B. L. (2018). Understanding those who are different: A text set for middle school language arts curriculum. In J.K. Dowdy & R. Fleischaker (Eds.) *Text sets: Multimodal learning for multicultural students*. (pp. 13–23). Brill Sense.

Stevens, N. L. (2016). Choice and rigor: Achieving a balance in middle school reading/language arts classrooms in the era of the common core. *Reading Horizons: A Journal of Literacy and Language Arts, 55*(2), 64–76.

Stop AAPI Hate. (2020). *They blamed me because I am Asian: Findings from youth-reported incidents of AntiAAPI hate*. https://stopaapihate.org/wp-content/uploads/2021/04/Stop-AAPI-Hate-Report-Youth-Campaign-200917.pdf

Tan, A. (1987). Fish cheeks. *Seventeen Magazine*.

Tan, A. (1989). *The joy luck club*. Putnam.

Thein, A. H., & Beach, R. (2013). Critiquing and constructing canons in middle grades English language arts classrooms. *Voices from the Middle, 21*(1), 10–14.

Uchida, Y. (1971). *Journey to Topaz: A story of the Japanese American evacuation*. Scribner's.

Vivat, B. (2016). *Frazzled: Everyday disasters and impending doom*. Harper.

Walker, A. (1994) Everyday use. In A. Walker & B. Christian (Eds.) *Everyday use*. Rutgers University Press.

Walker-Dalhouse, D., & Risko, V. J. (2020). Culturally responsive literacy instruction. In A.S. Dagen & R.M. Bean (Eds.) *Best practices of literacy leaders: Keys to school improvement*, (2nd ed., pp. 304–322). The Guilford Press.

Wang, A. (2021). *The many meanings of Meilan*. Penguin Random House.

Ward, B. A., & Young, T. A. (2008). Text sets: Making connections between and across books. *Reading Horizons: A Journal of Literacy and Language Arts, 48*(3), 215–226.

Wong, A. (2022). *Year of the tiger*. Penguin Random House.

Yang, K. K. (2016). *The song poet: A memoir of my father*. Metropolitan Books, Henry Holt and Company.

Yang, K. (2019) *Parachutes*. Katherine Tegen Books.

Yep, L. (1975). *Dragonwings*. Harper & Row.

Zhou, M., & Lee, J. (2017). Hyper-selectivity and the remaking of culture: Understanding the Asian American achievement paradox. *Asian American Journal of Psychology, 8*(1), 7–15.

CHAPTER THREE

Reciprocating Care and Vulnerability through a Pedagogy of Tenderness: Resistance and Transformation in ELA Classrooms

Stephanie Anne Shelton and Tamara Brooks

We two have been friends, colleagues, educators, and co-authors for over 15 years, and collectively we have over 40 years of experience in ELA classrooms. Stephanie is currently a university professor who supports ELA teachers in the United States, and Tamara teaches middle and high school ELA at an international school in Brazil. Over our years of experience, including over a decade of working together, we have subverted many forces shaping our and students' experiences, including resisting censorship, curriculum standardization, and oppression of marginalized students and colleagues. Despite—or perhaps because of—our years of experience, we find ourselves rewriting what subversive teaching means and looks like *now*. Students and we continue to reel from overlapping multiple pandemics, including COVID-19, anti-Black and anti-Asian racism, gun violence, and anti-immigration and anti-LGBTQIA+ legislation, all coupled with political efforts across the United States and the world to dictate how educators may teach, what texts we may provide, and even what language that we and students might use in our classrooms (Council of Europe, 2022; FL HB 1557, 2022; GA SB 377, 2022; HRW, 2022; PA HB 972, 2022).

Shifts in Subverting ELA

Early in our careers, we committed to upending a range of traditional ELA practices. These efforts included disrupting the literary canon by incorporating more diverse and less conventional texts and decentering teachers' perspectives by emphasizing students' voices in writing and discussions. For years, we delighted in rejecting the status quo and reenvisioning ELA, even as administrators and curricular standardization challenged this work. However, oppressive K12-focused legislation and major societal upheavals shifted teaching and learning, and we realized that these forces had also reshaped what subversive practices might be and look like. So many effective practices that we and other ELA teachers and teacher educators had adopted, including incorporating culturally sustaining pedagogies (Hines et al., 2020; Strom, 2020), disrupting canonized literature (Burns & Boiselle, 2020; Shelton, 2017), and resisting standardized testing and curricula (Panther & Hughes, 2020; Shelton & Brooks, 2019), were no longer just contested but, in some cases and spaces, *illegal*. Numerous legislative efforts across the United States and world have worked to criminalize addressing "divisive concepts" in our classrooms, including explicit attempts to prevent critical engagements with racism, classism, and cisheteronormativity. One insidious effect of these mandates is their ability to dehumanize teaching, teachers, and students with demands that educators focus exclusively on standards and "facts" (e.g., Dalton, 2022; HRW, 2022), as if classrooms are not inherently political spaces (Shelton et al., 2019), and as if students and teachers are not people rather than data points.

A New Pedagogy for Subverting ELA Traditions

This chapter shares a pedagogical approach that, within these political shifts, centers the vulnerability, kindness, and joy that these mandates have worked to erase and prohibit. Even before these shifts, traditional approaches to ELA had centered teacher perspectives in discussions, assumed teacher objectivity within students' interactions and grading, and focused on canonized literature, often as means of avoiding controversy. Within these new legislative efforts to presumably depoliticize, and thereby dehumanize, teaching and learning, we countered these influences and expectations by instead centering reciprocal care and vulnerability between students and teachers through a Pedagogy of Tenderness. This pedagogical framework emphasizes educators' and students' humanity, as it also works to reshape class content and interactions by disrupting teacher authority and engagements with literature.

We arrived at this approach while both living and working in sociopolitically conservative geographies. This meant that where we taught had proposed and newly established laws and policies explicitly prohibiting the teaching of social justice concepts, such as LGBTQIA+-affirming and racial justice-oriented topics. The political shifts outlined earlier were now in our classroom, mandating curricular standardization and teacher objectivity, while lending new authority to longstanding threats to our subversive efforts to reimagine ELA teaching. This context mattered very much relative to our social justice-focused teaching (Dyches et al., 2020; Shelton, 2022), and inevitably shaped other teachers' efforts, too. It is our hope that these efforts resonate with and empower other ELA educators who find themselves threatened and confined by similar settings and traditional approaches to ELA, as we share new possibilities that we have found through a Pedagogy of Tenderness.

Pedagogy of Tenderness

bell hooks (1994/2020) has long shaped our teacher identities and work, due to her insistence that social justice and humanity are essential to effective teaching practices. Ranges of educational mandates now demand that teachers and students somehow excise themselves and discussions of difficult and controversial topics from learning. hooks, however, emphasized that "education [. . . is] fundamentally political because," when it is framed within care and reciprocity, it has the potential to "resist every strategy of white racist [cisgenderist] colonization" (p. 2). In discussing transformative teaching specifically, hooks writes that an essential but often omitted element of working toward "education as the practice of freedom" (p. 20) is educators "being vulnerable in the classroom, being wholly present in mind, body, and spirit" (p. 21). This vulnerability is a key aspect of the framework that shapes our discussion.

Informed by hooks' work, a "pedagogy of tenderness" (Schulz et al., 2011) proved integral to our efforts to transform classrooms and to resist oppressive forces through reciprocal vulnerability, as students and teachers learned to humanize themselves, others, and the challenging topics that they explored. A pedagogy of tenderness fostered "an environment open to dialogue and active participation" that established "positive personal relationships with and among students, extending caring relationships" alongside the everyday "high expectations for quality academic performance" (Schulz et al., 2011, p. 56). In short, this pedagogical framework centers vulnerability and personal connections as integral to meaningful and transformative learning, as it disrupts traditional teacher- and canon-centered ELA approaches, as well as educational policies that seek to dehumanize teaching and learning.

ELA Classrooms' Context

This chapter explores Tamara's application of a Pedagogy of Tenderness across her work, with a focus on two ELA classrooms. The focal courses were part of an International Baccalaureate (IB) Middle Years Programme (MYP), which emphasized interdisciplinary and global interconnectedness. The first classroom was a 7th grade class in which students explored the differences between "conversation" and "discussion" during a social justice unit, and the second was a 12th grade classroom in which students read the novel *Feed* (Anderson, 2002) within a unit on social responsibility. As previously noted, Tamara taught within a sociopolitically conservative context, with a range of educational policies working to control teachers' curricula and limit engagements with equity and social justice. This setting sometimes made Tamara's efforts to push students to resist oppressive structures a delicate balancing act. Prior to starting these units, rumors swirled of schoolwide book censorship after parents' complaints about diversity-centered texts and contentious school board meetings. Knowing the texts that she had ordered included positive representations of LGBTQIA+ communities in order to center diverse student identities and to move beyond the traditional literary canon, Tamara wondered if these books would even make it out of their boxes—if her curriculum was derailed before it even started. It is within this context, so much like those other educators face, that we offer an honest discussion of Tamara's efforts, our collaborative reflections, and hope in the face of oppression. Our goal is to emphasize the potential of ELA classrooms as sites of resistance, subversion, and transformation, while acknowledging that such work is not easy but is always important and necessary.

Conversation versus Discussion in a 7th Grade ELA Class

Middle schoolers don't generally hold back from sharing their thoughts, so getting them to talk was not the concern—it was *how* they talked about issues, and particularly ones that made them uncomfortable or uncertain. Helping students with the how was especially important given the overhanging clouds of mandates and censorship stifling Tamara's efforts to extend both reading and discussion beyond traditional texts and topics. Offering "the space for change, intervention," as students considered complex topics in supportive and productive ways (hooks, 1994/2020, p. 1), demanded "reciprocity of vulnerability and humanity" between students and Tamara.

Approaching these efforts within a pedagogy of tenderness meant that Tamara, *not* the students, was expected to initiate care and openness (Jones & Shelton, 2022, p. 3). So often, hooks noted (1994/2020), instructors leave students to take risks while educators themselves refuse to be reciprocally vulnerable (hooks, 1994/2020, p. 21). We could both easily recall years of ELA teaching when we had evaluated students' verbal and written efforts to share fragile pieces of themselves, without reciprocating ourselves. We had patted ourselves on the back for creating opportunities for these vulnerabilities to subvert more traditional and impersonal student writing, while unfortunately also upholding conventional teacher authority and impersonal objectivity, by leaving them entirely unilateral.

Subverting ELA through Teacher Vulnerability

As we talked about how renewed efforts might look within a Pedagogy of Tenderness, Tamara hesitated. She noted before she had even started the unit that this teacher-initiated openness went against everything that she had been taught as a teacher. She emphasized, "My advising teacher told me numerous times, 'Don't let them see you vulnerable.' I'm not sure how this process would look? I'm sitting here thinking about how much I'm having to unlearn about what *I* had been taught about 'good' teaching. And doing all that while trying to think through how to push them to question what *they* have been taught." As we talked, we recalled that "when education is a practice of freedom, students are not the only ones who are asked to share, to confess" (hooks, 1994/2020, p. 21), and we considered how the lesson might start.

Tamara's primary goal for her 7th graders was to first understand and then engage in "conversation" as different from "discussion." Given the ELA classroom context, the etymology of the words was useful in parsing apart what she hoped that she and students might do. Both Latinate words, *discutere* emphasizes investigation, while *conversari* implies interactions that are based in comfort and familiarity (Oxford Languages, 2022). Tamara had observed that "discussion" was common in ELA instruction, as she and students readily investigated texts, though often in a decontextualized and detached way. Stephanie noted, "How often have we both facilitated discussions that leaned heavily on textual analysis? Objective, safe, ultimately teacher-centered in many cases? Useful, certainly, but not necessarily human or subversive." Tamara agreed, and we noted that "conversation" could certainly include evidence-based considerations; however, this approach would necessarily resist conventional, straightforward, presumably "fact-based" examinations that are common in ELA, in favor of instead centering connections and relationships as integral to students' understandings.

Beginning "Conversations" and Care

Tamara was already flirting with subversion when she crafted the unit. She felt a growing tension and fear of political forces that opposed thoughtful and balanced discussions of diversity and social justice. "Don't Say Gay" and anti-CRT sentiments that reverberated across the United States and the globe (FL HB 1557, 2022; GA SB 377, 2022; HRW, 2022) echoed in her school and classroom. Given her school's emphasis on interdisciplinary and global-minded curricula, alongside her refusal to avoid contested topics, she selected "social justice" as the overarching theme. Adopting a Pedagogy of Tenderness meant that this effort would work and look differently than previous similar efforts. Tamara reflected at the beginning,

> Begin with love. Begin with vulnerability. They need someone "real" to trust, not some "objective" authority figure just there to talk about learning standards. In this time of anti-CRT, anti-LGBTQIA+, anti-Black, anti–social

justice policies and laws, it's risky for a teacher to not only introduce these topics, but to share our own perspectives, emotions, and uncertainties. But, a Pedagogy of Tenderness doesn't work without an in-the-flesh-honest-to-goodness-human who—in front of them and *with* them—has emotions, makes mistakes, says "I don't know" with confidence. What is more subversive to traditional ELA than forcing the teacher to do and be different? If I want to go from "discussion" to "conversation," this is going to have to be a reciprocal effort couched in vulnerability, care, and honesty.

Subverting Traditional Teacher Roles

Tamara opened class by introducing the word "bias." Before she asked students to consider or define the word, she shared with them,

> When I hear the word "bias," I think about what I'll call our "bias baggage" (Shelton & Brooks, 2021). This is an implicit, unconscious bias that we all bring to every interaction, conversation, reading, to almost every thought we have. We have to recognize that and consider blindspots that those biases bring to our thinking. I need to do this self-reflection, and you need to do this, before we can have any type of conversation that goes beyond the superficial. Understanding our "bias baggage" allows us to ask *why* we believe what we do, and what it would take to change our minds. Each of us examining ourselves like this opens up the possibility for you to ask me, for you to ask one another, *why* without prejudice—just a genuine desire to understand others' perspectives.

She turned and drew a giant stick figure on the board, and next to it wrote various personal identities that she knew shaped her thinking, including "I am a woman. I am white." She then began to write down self-attributes about which she had no choice, including "race," "sexuality," "birthplace," etc. She emphasized to Stephanie afterward, "I laid it *all* out there, because I couldn't expect them to, if I didn't. And I made sure that they understood that I was doing this because I *cared* about them and wanted them to know me. Not just because this was some confessional." After opening the unit by sharing her uncertainties and limitations as a *human*, not just teacher, she continued this disruption of power dynamics by inviting students to help her think through other issues about which *she* might be biased. They readily pointed out her age, her single and childless status, and her being a U.S. citizen, and wondered aloud how those aspects might affect her attitude toward them.

Tamara then shifted to the *how* of conversations in the coming unit. hooks (1994/2020) remarked that a critical aspect of having a pedagogy of tenderness is "seeing the classroom always as a communal place" (p. 8) in which there is shared trust and accountability between students and teacher. In order to emphasize conversation as a collective process, Tamara shared,

> We're going to have many conversations over the next few weeks about ideas and behaviors that you may have experienced yourself or heard about from others. Before we do this, we're going to work to create a "safe space" in our classroom.

She acknowledged to Stephanie, "I know there's no such thing as a totally 'safe' space. I need for them to understand this as something that we create and share, that we're in together, and that is *ours*. They need to share ownership." She went on with the students,

> What happens or is said here *stays here* until you get a green light from everyone else. We all have a stake in what happens with what we say here, and we need to trust one another. A green light from everyone else will indicate that we've grappled with those ideas ourselves, individually and as a class, as much as we can, and now we're ready to truly listen to others' thoughts on our thoughts, beyond this classroom. So, we're going to work to not share parts of our conversations with others outside this class for a time, while knowing that we'll all be able to eventually. No one's prohibiting you from sharing. It's just that we're fully engaging with that concept as a community before we incorporate others, too.

This community ownership, Tamara noted, was critical to a Pedagogy of Tenderness, and mitigated the potential threats of censorship or legislated prohibitions. This approach to "pedagogy must insist that everyone's presence [and perspective] is acknowledged" (p. 8). It subverted how school normally worked for both the students and Tamara, by situating students to have some community responsibility and ownership over what topics they explored.

Tamara went another step to continue to disrupt the notion that she was in charge or had a hidden agenda. She told them,

> I want to clarify: the point of these conversations is not to convince you that any particular concept is true; it's not to later test you or assign an essay on a topic that we consider. The point is for you to *think about* and to have *conversations with one another* on these ideas. Forget tests or grades. What you have to say is *the point* here. We all want to be *heard*, maybe even understood eventually, but mostly we want to be *heard*.

Then she turned around and wrote on the board, "I need to think about it, but that doesn't mean that I need to believe it." Tamara explained to Stephanie later, "I was interested in the way that they did their thinking. I wasn't necessarily interested in *what* they were thinking as much as I wanted to, with tenderness and reciprocity, shake them to consider *how* they and I do our thinking." After all, "transgressing boundaries [is] frightening," for students and teachers (hooks, 1994/2020, p. 9), and "responsibility to self, respect for others" is essential in pushing education to support social justice efforts and enact a pedagogy of tenderness (Schulz et al., 2011, p. 57). Resisting oppressive contexts and policies cannot be an individualized effort and be sustainable or successful. And so they began. Together.

Table 3.1.

Pedagogy of Tenderness as Concept and Action

Pedagogy of Tenderness as a Concept	Pedagogy of Tenderness in Action
1. Modeling and offering vulnerability	• Tamara drew and verbally reflected on her personal identities for and with the students.
2. Disrupting power dynamics through vulnerability	• Tamara invited students to consider her biases and how those assumptions shaped her teaching.
3. Subverting typical discussion dynamics	• Tamara and the students establishing and agreeing to class norms about how they would engage in controversial and difficult topics, inside and outside of the classroom.
4. Engaging with microaggressions and disruptions in caring and thoughtful ways	• Tamara and the students used a series of questions to consider a classmate's reaction to LGBTQIA+ topics, to ensure a culture of care as students held one another accountable.
5. Providing ways to disagree and express uncertainty based on reciprocal vulnerability and a classroom culture of care.	• Tamara and the students moved from the questions to considerations of how they might push against the student's response without undermining reciprocal support and concern.

Focusing on "How," Not "What"

Early on, exploring the limits of their communal conversations, students chose to explore the meaning of the letters in the acronym LGBTQIA+. As Tamara and some students explained terms unfamiliar to others, one student responded to the conversation, "That's strange." With a community focus on *how* they were thinking, the class paused. Tamara took a breath and reminded herself about the importance of tenderness, and of ELA's curricular potential to examine words' power. This needed to be community-based conversation, not teacher directives or chastisement. Students, drawing on the previous emphasis on *how* and *why*—and not *what*—they were thinking, started by considering the *how* of his reaction. Tamara and the students used the following questions to thoughtfully engage with this moment of dissent, with the intent being to analyze while maintaining a classroom culture of reciprocal care and support. They took each question individually as a scaffolding process to self-reflect, examine classroom dynamics, and consider potential implications of his reaction, and of their reactions to him. They explored:

How did his response land for them?
How did they react to his response, both immediately and with some thought?

Then they shifted to the *why* of his reaction:

Why was the acronym strange, not only to him but to others?
Why was "strange" the right word?

Tamara's adoption of a pedagogy of tenderness created a community of shared exploration, accountability, and care. As the students considered these questions, they worked to actively listen—not just talk—and, with an emphasis on conversation, they shifted from defensiveness and accusations to readily sharing their uncertainties about and experiences with LGBTQIA+ identities.

Within a sociopolitical context in which such topics were technically disallowed, the community of care that they fostered enabled students to broach topics of concern to them, and to explore questions with openness and compassion. While the listening and speaking skills were aligned with traditional and mandated ELA curriculum, the focus on conversation rather than discussion crafted a space where students and teacher resisted both teacher-centered engagement with social justice and external mandates forbidding such topics. As hooks (1994/2020) notes, there is little more meaningfully subversive in educational contexts than disrupting a "classroom's politics of domination" and having "space to interrogate," without the teacher as "traditional authoritarian, and the students conform[ing]" (p. 148).

Questioning Personal Responsibility in a 12th Grade ELA Class

Shifting from conversation to reading, Tamara considered how she might incorporate a pedagogy of tenderness in exploring literature, too. Twelfth-grade students read the book *Feed* (Anderson, 2002) in a unit emphasizing social responsibility. *Feed* is a dystopian novel in which brain implants controls people's thoughts and emotions through a digital "feed." At this grade-level, unlike with the 7th graders, there were no standardized tests that might be weaponized to justify curricular control. Instead, students' impending graduations left some teachers fearful over parental and school board complaints about how students were "indoctrinated" by teachers ahead of graduation and leaving home. Tamara noted, "I sometimes just kind of waited for the ax to fall. Waited for parents who I'd heard had complained about colleagues to complain about me." But there was no executioner. The reason, Tamara insisted, was "relationships. This pedagogy of tenderness builds relationships where kids are in control, and I can trust them to be." This approach subverted traditional teacher-led discussions and analyses in ELA to position the students to not only shape discussion, but to construct the classroom culture itself, as a way to explore literature.

hooks (1994/2020) pointed out that "creating a space of emotional trust" in classrooms allows those from different perspectives to engage in politicized and difficult topics in ways that are "nourish[ing]" (p. 132). Importantly, this approach is one that would likely be challenging for ELA instructors from marginalized communities, as the risk of pushback and repercussions from various school community members is already significant, and then heightened by these additional layers of vulnerability and open transgression. hooks acknowledged that her own efforts changed shape based on both professional and personal risk, and that educators who already exist in the margins sometimes have to use those spaces as ways to reimagine teaching in ways that are both sustainable and realistic.

A Dialogic Framework of Care and Trust

In working to rework her own educational practices, Tamara's transgression was based in hooks' call "to challenge and change the way everyone thinks about pedagogical process" (p. 134), both teacher and students. Tamara approached this in two main ways. First, she structured the literary discussions so that there was, by design, never a "right" answer. The goal was to push students to "question and interrogate" *everything* (p. 134), including identity, learning, and taken-for-granted norms, with the book serving as catalyst and not basis of evidence. Second, she wanted to "try to change the classroom so that there is a sense of mutual responsibility for learning," to create a "shift in the locus [of control]" (p. 134). When recalling successes in the unit, Tamara shrugged and smiled, "Honestly? I just needed to get out of the way. Let them *actually* be in control, rather than they and I pretending that they were." This often looked like Tamara initially facilitating open-ended questions related to social responsibility and the novel, such as themes of consumerism, and then literally getting out of the way. "I would physically go over to the side. Sit out of the circle and just listen. Not interrupt or supervise."

The effect was unexpected and powerful, as students continuously noted how respected they felt in class, how much they felt that Tamara cared about them and their thoughts, because *they* were the heart of the classroom. In one instance, students considered the question "Do I have a social responsibility to anyone other than myself?" Before they even began to try to answer the question, they discussed as a group what their groundwork would be for listening to one another. Tamara was prepared to intervene or push, but she primarily moved to the side and let them decide how their community would work. They agreed that they would "Seek out the voices that oppose our voices," and when confronted with those perspectives, consider individually and collectively why others might hold those positions. Informed by multiple TED-Talk videos (TED, 2022) that Tamara assigned across various units, students decided to adopt a similar format as the initial basis of interactions. Specifically, they offered their personal stories to one another in an effort to further humanize their community and their individual positions. When invited to participate, Tamara likewise shared personal stories, both modeling and reciprocating vulnerability for and with students.

Students' stories formed a foundation of trust in their interactions with one another, as they applied their own pedagogy of tenderness that emphasized "responsibility to self, respect for others, and commitment to a just society" (Schulz et al., 2011, p. 57). With Tamara literally de-centered, the students engaged in a range of topics that might have drawn ire in a different context. At one point, students considered, "How do we listen to someone who just makes you so mad that it's hard to stay in the same room with them?" What did care and community look like in those moments? Students shared examples from personal interactions, as Tamara likewise told stories of being hung up on by family in the middle of a tough conversation over the phone. Over and over again, students emphasized that this approach both helped them to listen—because the focus was on people not sterile concepts—and to be heard.

Students applied this community-based framework as they read and discussed the novel. *Feed* opens with Auden's (1942) poem to St. Cecelia, which reads, "Oh, dear white children casual as birds" (l. 1). Using the novel's explorations of physical and class-based differences and this epilogue, students began to wonder, "Why don't we expect Black characters as a default?" and "Why don't we question that characters are white?" With substantial racial, ethnic, and language diversities in the classroom, students were stunned to consider together why they had *all*, much like the novel's main character, been influenced by "feeds" of societal beliefs and values since childhood. As anti-Black and anti–Critical Race Theory legislation raged across nations and U.S. states, these students considered the default of Whiteness, the erasure of racial diversities, and in some cases, their own invisibility in innumerable ELA texts.

Building on this discussion, students began to explore personal choice. Rather than simply critiquing the novel's characters for not assuming autonomy, they wondered, "What don't we choose?" They thought through the racialized identities that they had explored and then, to Tamara's surprise, a student told peers, "I don't think that someone chooses to be gay." In a dialectical exchange built on respect and care, students had accepted that between them there were inevitably "diverse political stances [. . . that necessarily include] the politics of race, class, and gender" (hooks, 1994/2020, p. 144), and now sexuality. Another topic sociopolitically discouraged but examined thoughtfully in this moment. This sort of exchange, hooks emphasizes, is true *revolution, reflecting* students taking ownership of their learning, and doing so in ways that do not shy away from complex and controversial topics is transgressive and remakes learning into a process that is humanizing and empowering, within and beyond the classroom.

Subverting Oppressive Forces through a Pedagogy of Tenderness

We want to emphasize that these described moments had built from months of work and community-building in Tamara's classroom. The focus here, in this chapter, is to emphasize that, even as sociopolitical forces work to prevent teachers and students from engaging in social justice work, students and teachers are both ready and able to resist. In reflecting back on these units, Tamara remarked to Stephanie, "Sometimes I'm just like, 'How did I get away with it?' I waited for the fear, the external complaints, and consequences that colleagues described. But it never happened." Concern over restrictive contexts, including ranges of anti-diversity legislation efforts in Brazil, United States, and elsewhere, left her temporarily stunned that "I didn't get into trouble. Like, how?"

The answer, we agreed, was steeped in Tamara's adoption of a pedagogy of tenderness. In the midst of concerns over censorship, censure, and legal consequences, her relationships with students had repelled those repressive regimes. Legal efforts, such as "Don't Say Gay" and anti-CRT bills, were ultimately subverted because students were empowered to choose to explore these topics. To be clear, throughout these units, there were what hooks (1994/2020) referred to as "limits of fear" (p. 201), as both students and Tamara experienced moments of trepidation again and again, as they attempted to remake their classroom and their modes of learning. It was hard, Tamara acknowledged, "to build trust and care with and between them, so that they could think and work together, with and without me." Tamara's role was not to be a conveyer of knowledge or facilitator of interactions; her purpose within this pedagogical approach was to "nurture and guide" students (p. 201). That shift was sometimes hard for all of them, as she and students were long acculturated to more traditional teacher-centered approaches in ELA, even those presumably working toward social justice. The point was that they never stopped trying and did not revert back to more familiar and traditional interactions.

We do not anticipate the onslaughts against teachers and social justice–centered education to stop, either. If anything, the time following Tamara teaching these units suggests that they are accelerating. And these suppressive and oppressive efforts leave teachers and students "bone weary" and wary (hooks, 1994, p. 201). However, pedagogical strategies that emphasize "joy in learning, [. . .] the classroom a space of critical thinking, [. . . and caring] exchange of information and ideas" are powerfully subversive and transformative (hooks, 1994, p. 202). hooks noted that classrooms are "not paradise. But learning is a place where paradise is created" (p. 207). A key part of that paradise, of that necessary resistance to forces that work to strip teachers and students of autonomy and humanity, is *community*. It was through mutual care, vulnerability, and trust that Tamara and students subverted powerful and omnipresent forces. This work, as teachers and students are smothered under prejudices and oppressions, offers life-giving breath, joy, and promises of new classrooms and new tomorrows.

References

Anderson, M. T. (2002). *Feed*. Candlewick Press.

Burns, R. & Boiselle, J. (2020). Gender bending the curriculum: Queer approaches to teaching Shakespeare in high school. In J. Dyches, B. Sams, & A. S. Boyd (Eds.), *Acts of resistance: Subversive teaching in the English language arts classroom* (1st ed., pp. 132–143). Myers Education Press.

Council of Europe. (2022). *European higher education area*. https://www.coe.int/en/web/higher-education-and-research/european-higher-education-area

Dalton, M. (2022). "I'll still teach the same way:" Atlanta teacher says despite new "divisive concepts" law. *WABE*. https://www.wabe.org/ill-still-teach-the-same-way-atlanta-teacher-says-despite-new-divisive-concepts-law/

Dyches, J., Sams, B., & Boyd, A. S. (Eds.). (2020). *Acts of resistance: Subversive teaching in the English language arts classroom* (1st ed.). Myers Education Press.

FL HB 1557. (Florida 2022). https://www.flsenate.gov/Session/Bill/2022/1557

GA SB 377. (Georgia 2022). https://www.legis.ga.gov/api/legislation/document/ 20212022/203938

Hines, D. E., Young, J. Y., Liu, R. Z., & Wandix-White, D. (2020). Can we talk?: Promoting anti-oppressive futures for girls of color through a social justice enrichment program. In J. Dyches, B. Sams, & A. S. Boyd (Eds.), *Acts of resistance: Subversive teaching in the English language arts classroom* (1st ed., pp. 158–170). Myers Education Press.

hooks, b. (1994/2020). *Teaching to transgress: Education as the practice of freedom*. Routledge.

Human Rights Watch. (2022). *Efforts to ban gender and sexuality education in Brazil*. Human Rights Watch. https://www.hrw.org/report/2022/05/12/i-became-scared-was-their-goal/efforts-ban-gender-and-sexuality-education-brazil

Jones, A. M., & Shelton, S. A. (2022). A transgressive pedagogy of tenderness in hybrid education. *Feminist Pedagogy, 2*(1), 1–6.

Oxford Languages. (2022). Conversation. *Oxford English Dictionary*. https://languages.oup.com/research/oxford-english-dictionary/

Oxford Languages. (2022). Discussion. *Oxford English Dictionary*. https://languages.oup.com/research/oxford-english-dictionary/

PA HB 972. (Pennsylvania 2022). https://www.legis.state.pa.us/cfdocs/billinfo/billinfo.cfm?sYear=2021&sInd=0&body=H&type=B&bn=972

Panther, L. & Hughes, S. (2020). "Well I took it there": Subversive teaching to (disrupt) the test. In J. Dyches, B. Sams, & A. S. Boyd (Eds.), *Acts of resistance: Subversive teaching in the English language arts classroom* (1st ed., pp. 36–50). Myers Education Press.

Schulz, L. L., Sewell, K. T., & Hirata, L. (2011). Towards pedagogy of tenderness. *International Journal of Humanities and Social Science, 1*(10), 55–58.

Shelton, S. A. (2017). A narrative reflection on examining text and world for social justice: Combatting bullying and harassment with Shakespeare. *Journal of Language and Literacy Education, 13*(1), 1–14.

Shelton, S. A. (2022). Communities of discomfort: Empowering lgbtq+ ally work in a south-eastern rural community. *English Education, 54*(3), 177–195.

Shelton, S. A., Barnes, M. E., & Flint, M. A. (2019). "You stick up for all kids": (De)politicizing the enactment of lgbtq+ teacher ally work. *Teaching and Teacher Education, 82*, 14–23.

Shelton, S. A., & Brooks, T. (2019). "We need to get these scores up": A narrative examination of the challenges of teaching literature in the age of standardized testing. *Journal of Language and Literacy Education, 15*(2), 1–17.

Shelton, S. A., & Brooks, T. (2021). Everyday reflection and addressing racism and lgbtq+ issues. *English Journal, 110*(6), 90–94.

Storm, S. (2020). Black words matter: Bending literary close reading toward justice. In J. Dyches, B. Sams, & A. S. Boyd (Eds.), *Acts of resistance: Subversive teaching in the English language arts classroom* (1st ed., pp. 7–21). Myers Education Press.

TED. (2022). *TED videos*. https://www.ted.com/recommends?utm_term=ted%20talks&utm_campaign=TED+Talks&utm_source=adwords&utm_medium=ppc&hsa_acc=7777130675&hsa_cam=218945593&hsa_grp=17379703273&hsa_ad=295614277847&hsa_src=g&hsa_tgt=kwd-257 5934383&hsa_kw=ted%20talks&hsa_mt=b&hsa_net=adwords&hsa_ver=3&g-clid=Cj0KCQiAvqGcBhCJARIsAFQ5ke4ebFOrITs6E5dkrUNvRa VUHqUxBoqfkfJZJi2f_IgrfbB8FxSM7NIaAjE8EALw_wcB

CHAPTER FOUR

Subverting the Canon through Culturally Relevant Young Adult Literature Circles

SANDRA M. SACO, E. SYBIL DURAND

THIS CHAPTER EXPLORES HOW a former English Language Arts teacher who taught at a Title I high school serving a majority of Latinx and Black students subverted her school and district's prescribed canonical curriculum. Sandra shares her pedagogical strategies and activities for meeting her students' need for reading literature that reflects their cultures and experiences while also abiding by the demands of a culturally limited school curriculum. She discusses how she implemented literature circles in her 11th grade Advanced Placement course using young adult literature that featured characters from culturally diverse backgrounds, including Latinx, Black, Indigenous, Asian, LGBTQIA+, immigrant, globally displaced, and activist youth. Sandra's unit emphasized student choice both in terms of the book students selected from a list she provided and the literature circles they formed. This unit subverted the canonical boundaries of Sandra's traditional Advanced Placement curriculum that favored European American male authors by offering students culturally relevant youth literature as an object of rigorous study. Importantly, as the students in Sandra's class were predominantly Latinx, studying literary representations of youth of color written by a majority of authors of color signaled to students that stories that mirror their experiences have a place in advanced reading and writing curriculum.

Historically, our educational system has positioned Western, Eurocentric literature as what is classic, mainstream, and normal. As Sinclair (2018) notes, "the texts we study, the ways of knowing we value, the behaviors we expect—all privilege white, middle-class ways of knowing and being" (p. 89). In contrast, students of color now account for more than 50% of students enrolled in public schools (National Center for Educational Statistics, 2022). Schools have struggled to address the needs of students from culturally diverse communities and have continued to promote "a traditional 'one-size-fits-all' model of English education and literacy teaching" (Boyd et al., 2006, p. 329). Unfortunately, when teachers are mandated to teach Western canonical texts and when these are taught uncritically, "we silence and marginalize the experiences and existence of the students who do not identify with a white, middle-class worldview" (Sinclair, 2018, p. 94).

Culturally relevant literature—texts that function as mirrors (Bishop, 1990) for youth from culturally diverse communities by reflecting "their lived experiences in ways that balance aesthetic and literary quality with relevant social, cultural, and political contexts" (Durand & Jimenez-Garcia, 2018, p. 19)—is essential to an equitable English Language Arts curriculum. Those texts also function as windows (Bishop, 1990) for students who are not from these communities but are nonetheless members of a culturally diverse society. All students benefit from engaging nuanced and diverse literary representations of communities that have been historically excluded from the English curriculum (Loh, 2006). Conversely, a lack of literary diversity creates an "imagination gap" (Thomas, 2016) for readers: "it limits them to single stories about the world around them (Adichie, 2009) and ultimately affects the development of their imaginations" (p. 112).

The curriculum in Advanced Placement (AP) English language arts (ELA) courses often reflects this imagination gap. When it comes to diversity in AP programs, concerns have primarily focused on increasing the low enrollment of students of color in advanced courses (Kolluri, 2018). Changes to the AP curriculum to reflect student diversity have been slower. AP programs have traditionally emphasized text-focused approaches, such as "close reading and critical analysis of imaginative literature to deepen [students'] understanding of the ways writers use language" (College Board, 2020, p. 7), in contrast to affective and reader-centered processes of interpreting literature (Rosenblatt, 1978). Approaches to disrupting the canon in ELA include having students enact a "critical canon pedagogy" to examine the curriculum in critical ways (Dyches, 2018), exploring how students respond to insertions of texts written by authors of color (Bender, 2017), and developing units within the AP curriculum focused on African American language (Baker-Bell, 2013).

In this chapter, we (Sandra, a Latina doctoral student and former high school English teacher and Sybil, a Black Haitian university professor of youth literature) argue that using culturally relevant young adult (YA) literature in an AP English course disrupts the canon by subverting traditional expectations for advanced curriculum study. We draw inspiration from #disrupttexts (Ebarvia et al, 2020), a movement created by teachers of color to disrupt inequitable ELA curriculum and pedagogy. These educators explain that the canon is socially constructed and thus reflects society's biases; they argue, "To disrupt texts effectively, we must *center the voices of BIPoC in literature*" (p. 100, emphasis in original). In addition to using diverse YA texts, this chapter also makes an argument for using student-centered pedagogies to further subvert traditional AP practices. Literature circles (Daniels, 2002)—small, peer-led discussion groups focused on student-selected texts—and reader response journals (Berger, 1996), for example, shift the focus from texts to readers by encouraging students to draw on their skills and lived experiences to interpret literature.

In the following sections, Sandra details how she implemented literature circles in four sections of 11th grade AP English, which included a majority of Latinx students at a Title I school in the U.S. Southwest. In this chapter, she shares examples from two AP sections, totaling 52 students. First, Sandra provides a research-based rationale for using YA literature circles in the ELA classroom and describes how she structured them. Next, she describes the process of selecting diverse YA texts, followed by activities students completed during literature circles. Last, Sandra outlines a multigenre project students completed as their culminating assignment instead of the traditional research paper. Sandra's unit highlights curricular and pedagogical strategies that subvert traditional approaches to AP English by focusing on youth voices in two ways: 1) through texts that reflect students' cultures or interests, and 2) through reader-centered literary interpretations. These subversive methods fulfill the goals of AP programs by having students engage in higher order thinking like analyzing and evaluating literature and creating new texts that demonstrate their understanding while also validating their lived experiences.

YA Literature Circle Unit

In AP classrooms, teachers typically select a single text for all students and focus on close reading and analysis to examine how authors use language (College Board, 2020). In contrast, literature circles encourage student choice and emphasize readers' interpretations of stories in ways that more closely resemble everyday reading practices while also fostering critical reading skills. Nearly 40 years ago, when Daniels (2002) and his colleagues conceived of literature circles, their goal was to foster lifelong readers. The rules were simple: small groups of students select a text they want to read, create a reading and meeting schedule, take notes to contribute to the discussion and, once they finish reading, share their insights with the larger class. This approach departed from old-fashioned ELA practices like round robin reading or answering fact-based questions towards critical thinking and reading skills and, more importantly, enjoyable collaborative discussions of stories (Daniels, 2002). In the intervening years, literature circles became a staple of ELA teaching and have been shown to improve reading levels, increase comprehension, advance gender equity, and support emergent bilingual students (Daniels, 2006). Unfortunately, as Daniels (2006) observed, many current iterations of literature circles veer away from the original intent. Most notably, the role sheets Daniels designed, such as Word Wizard or Literary Luminary, were designed to show students strategies experienced readers use during discussions. Daniels warned role sheets were meant to be temporary to avoid fostering "mechanical discussions that can stem from over-dependence on these roles" (p. 11).

I (Sandra) had previously implemented literature circles (Daniels, 2002) with leftover books from my school's book room, such as *Jane Eyre*, *My Antonia*, *Kaffir Boy*, and *Catcher in the Rye*. I noticed students enjoying the autonomy of being in book groups and managing their own learning. I assigned overall deadlines, but they decided how many pages to read and how to rotate their reading roles (e.g., discussion leader, bridge builder, diction detective, etc.). The discussions were structured; students completed reading roles prior to their discussions and shared with their groups. Although I saw potential in the structure and pedagogy behind literature circles, I wondered whether using YA literature would make it a more enjoyable experience for students by reading culturally relevant books.

I told my students I would be completing a research study on literature circles for my graduate degree. We had spent the first three-quarters of the year focused on canonical texts, which I also tried to approach in critical and relevant ways by connecting them to current events. For example, I taught *The Great Gatsby* using literary theory—Feminist, Marxist, and Archetypal critical lenses (Domingo, 2019). Students chose a theoretical lens and created graphic essays based on the theory. As we entered the fourth quarter, I told students I now wanted to know what they noticed in their reading without my prompting. I reassured students that I trusted them to make sense of the reading.

I designed a 6-week peer-led literature circle unit where students read a culturally relevant YA text in self-selected groups (Tables 4.1 & 4.2). They reviewed and engaged with the text through discussion and reader response journals. My rationale for using literature circles in my AP English class was based on research claims that "reader-centered (as opposed to text-centered)" experiences with texts can lead to deeper interpretations, positive attitudes, and appreciation towards reading (Smiles, 2008, pp. 32–33). I also wanted to encourage students to lead their book discussions rather than limit student talk to teacher-selected questions or topics. Smiles (2008) explains that "engaging students in discussions of their initial responses to a text—however incomplete or inaccurate those understandings may be—will lead to refinement and enhancement of their interpretations" (p. 33).

Culturally Relevant YA Literature and Student Choice

To find belonging in their English classrooms, students need to be able to relate to what they are reading from a linguistic, cultural, racial, and ethnic perspective among many other identities. Lopez (2011) states, "by reading alternative texts . . . students can begin to examine how their cultures and identities are represented or misrepresented. These kinds of activities increase engagement and participation, and ultimately improve grades" (p. 78). Several scholars argue that culturally diverse YA literature can introduce students to current local and global sociocultural issues relevant to students' lives, including issues related to gender, sexuality, race, ethnicity, immigrant status, as well as climate, environmental, and mental health issues (Eppert et al, 2007; Malo-Juvera, 2017; Wolk, 2009). In addition, when students read about characters from diverse backgrounds, they can engage in "critical conversations about power, equity, and analyses of how identity is both constructed and perceived" (Ginsberg et al, 2017, p. 26). When my students read culturally relevant YA literature that mirrored their lives, I found that they not only read avidly, but also created meaningful connections to their cultures and society. Most importantly, many expressed excitement and joy when they saw parts of themselves reflected in the characters they discovered and found validation that their stories matter (Saco, 2022).

Students picked their books from a list I provided (see Table 4.1). The book list featured characters from culturally diverse backgrounds, including Latinx, Black, Indigenous, Asian, LGBTQIA+, immigrant, globally displaced, and activist youth written by a majority of authors of color, and covered a variety of genres and formats—realistic fiction, memoirs, poetry, and graphic novels. I instructed students that if no book on the list captured their interest, they could choose another. Along with culturally relevant literature, this approach emphasized choice and student-led curriculum. Wilson and Kelley (2006) explain that, "When students are allowed to read texts they are interested in, they make time to read. Therefore, offering students choice is also an important variable . . . offering relevant compelling texts students would want to read" (p. 73). Providing students with choice made the reading and assignments more enjoyable because they played a part in the decision on how to spend their academic time and how to approach their reading.

Students' enthusiasm was drastically different from earlier units before I even started the culturally relevant YA literature unit. Prior to selecting their books, I created teaser flyers to increase their anticipation and to ensure attendance the day they would choose their books. Students first chose who they wanted to read and collaborate with and formed groups of two to five members. I reasoned that students would be able to have disagreements in a safer and more productive manner if they read with people they felt comfortable with. Then, each group decided which book to read from the list. I didn't limit how many groups could select a specific title. Some groups chose the same book (see Table 4.1).

Only two students across four AP classes chose a book that was not on the list—*Never Let Me Go* by Kazuo Ishiguro. Although it was not classified as a YA novel, the story still focused on the lives of youth. Both students occasionally joined a group

Table 4.1.

Literature Circle Texts Selected

Books (in Alphabetical Order by Author)	Format/Genre	# of Groups
The Poet X by Elizabeth Acevedo	Poetry	1
A Long Way Gone: Memoirs of a Boy Soldier by Ishmael Beah	Memoir	2
The Best We Could Do by Thi Bui	Graphic Memoir	2
The Perks of Being a Wallflower by Stephen Chbosky	Epistolary Novel	3
If I Ever Get Out of Here by Eric Gansworth	Realistic Fiction	0
The Distance Between Us by Reyna Grande	Memoir	1
Never Let Me Go by Kazuo Ishiguro	Science Fiction	1
Hearts Unbroken by Cynthia Leitich Smith	Fiction	2
Long Way Down by Jason Reynolds	Poetry	5
Always Running by Luis J. Rodriguez	Memoir	2
Aristotle and Dante Discover the Secrets of the Universe by Benjamin Alire Sáenz	Realistic Fiction	1
I Am Not Your Perfect Mexican Daughter by Erika L. Sánchez	Realistic Fiction	1
The Hate U Give by Angie Thomas	Realistic Fiction	2
I Am Malala: The Story of the Girl Who Stood Up for Education and Was Shot by the Taliban by Malala Yousafzai and Christina Lamb	Memoir	1

reading a different book and they would make connections between their books. Despite the variety of books, I noticed that students developed a sense of pride and ownership in their work, and those who critiqued the traditional curriculum revealed they enjoyed the process.

One group of three students chose *I'm Not Your Perfect Mexican Daughter* by Erika Sánchez. They were excited to begin reading the novel and, in preparation, one student who was skilled at drawing made bookmarks for each group member including me. Their bookmarks were Mexican American themed since all three culturally identified as such, but she drew me an alpaca bookmark because she knew that I identified as Peruvian. They approached the literature circle like their own book club, and I noticed a greater sense of unity between them. This group mirrored the level of ownership and excitement that many students felt in reading these chosen texts. Overall, students looked forward to reading. Some students started reading as soon as they got the books and many read ahead of their schedules. I overheard comments from students saying they had read ahead and their peers responded, "Don't spoil it for me!"

I recall one student who wanted to read *Aristotle and Dante Discover the Secrets of the Universe* by Benjamin Alire Sáenz, but no one in their class did, so I offered to partner with them. I wanted to ensure that all students had their choice in reading. During our meetings, that student led our discussions. One day I didn't have time to do the reading since I was working on my graduate studies at the time, and the student guided our discussion, ensuring not to spoil anything for me, and even scolding me, "Make sure to get caught up Ms. Saco!" They really loved the book and their ownership of it made it evident they benefited from the experience. I'm glad that I didn't convince them to join another group.

This approach to literature circles made significant changes in my AP classes. Compared to canonical texts, these texts were culturally relevant and focused on youth experiences, which centered youth knowledge and interpretation instead of teacher knowledge and resulted in my students taking the lead in their learning. Subverting traditional approaches may be especially necessary in culturally diverse classrooms and can be accomplished by giving students choice and leaning into the enthusiasm and agency they have when reading a text that they enjoy and chose for themselves (Wilson & Kelly, 2006).

Literature Circles

During the literature circle unit, students engaged in scheduled reading group discussions. I was nervous about not assigning reading roles for students like I had with previous literature circles, so I provided students with notebooks to serve as their reader response journals. After reading two to four chapters, students wrote written reflections using the same set of open-ended questions developed by Linda Berger (1996):

What did you notice?
What do you question?
What do you feel?
What do you relate to?

These prompts gave students more freedom in how they processed reading and provided appealing guiding questions designed to "challeng[e] adolescent readers to be more aware as they read" (Berger, 1996, p. 382). Students ultimately used these responses to frame their literature circle discussions.

In between circle discussions, I led mini-lessons and writing activities drawn from Linda Christensen's (2009) *Teaching for Joy and Justice* (see Table 4.2), which emphasized model texts and students writing about their own identities, stories and experiences using different genres and formats.

Table 4.2.

Unit Lessons & Activities

Lessons	Activities
Week 1: Unit introduction–reader response journals and planning reading schedules.	Students planned their reading schedules and began reading their chosen texts.
Week 2: Writing Poetry (Christensen, 2009, pp. 17–22) Mentor Text: "Raised by Women" by Kelly Norman Ellis	Students wrote poems using mentor text. Reader response journals & literature circles.
Week 3: Intersectionality 101 Video (Learning for Justice, 2016)	Students identified the intersectionality of the characters in their books. Reader response journals & literature circles.
Week 4: Narrative Writing (Christensen, 2009, pp. 60–75) Mentor Texts: "Thank you Ma'am" by Langston Hughes & "The Jacket" by Gary Soto	Students wrote a narrative using mentor text. Reader response journals & literature circles.
Week 5: Multigenre Book Projects	Students chose project options and began planning. Reader response journals & literature circles
Week 6: Multigenre Book Projects/Presentations	Students worked on projects and presented them to literature circle groups.

In traditional approaches to teaching literature in the ELA and AP classroom, the idea that the self is unreliable and biased can be limiting to readers. With reader response questions, I trusted students' responses and interpretations. I wanted students to have the agency to respond the way they wanted and to reflect on how they connected to the book. Instead of approaching the readings with what *I'm* going to teach them, this freedom allowed students to point out things I would never have noticed. In designing this culturally relevant YA literature circle unit, I intentionally centered my students' knowledge and knew I was going to learn just as much from them as they would from me. I allowed their observations and analysis to guide their learning.

Culminating Multigenre Book Projects

When considering options for a culminating assessment, I opted not to include the standard research paper, which reflects and reinforces white, middle class academic standards of communication and can be an exclusionary form of expression (Sinclair, 2018). This is especially true when considering students from families who do not have the means of pursuing higher education or whose home language is not English. Research papers do not take into consideration the multiple forms of expressions and languages in culturally diverse communities. I wanted to continue to emphasize choice for the culminating project and was inspired by Tom Romano's (2007) writings on multigenre projects. I wanted students to express their learning in genres they chose and that complemented their strengths, rather than assign teacher-selected projects that might not support their unique learning approaches.

I provided a list of 12 different genres students could choose to demonstrate their understanding of their literature circle book. Students selected and completed three pieces from the list and had the option to propose a new genre that was not on the list:

News Article
Digital Travel Brochure
YouTube Video Book Review
Current Event Connection
Soundtrack List and Album Cover
Free Verse Poem
Amazon Book Review
Letter to the Publisher or Author
Book Time Capsule
Infographic
Book Cover Redesign
One Pager

Students worked independently and took similar ownership of their culminating projects in the same way they had their literature circles. I believe they appreciated the opportunity of completing the project in a manner that made sense to them as individual learners. They were able to tap into their personal strengths after working collaboratively during the circles. Upon completing their culminating projects, students presented one of their genres to their literature circle group.

For example, one student, Alex (a pseudonym) chose to read *A Long Way Gone: Memoirs of a Boy Soldier* by Ishmael Beah. For their culminating book project, Alex chose to write a free verse poem, create a one pager, and write a current event connection. Alex wrote a poem about the author titled, "I Was," which described all the things Ishmael Beah once was that were taken from him when he was stolen from his family and forced to fight as a child soldier. Alex also created a one pager to visually demonstrate their understanding and interpretation of the text with thematic images that resonated with them. Lastly, Alex wrote a current event connection that discussed current events they felt connected with their chosen text, such as the ongoing civil war in Yemen involving child soldiers, episodes of posttraumatic stress disorder in child soldiers, and the benefits of talking to trained professionals. Alex concluded that, while Ishmael Beah was able to share his experiences, other child soldiers have not had this opportunity. Alex demonstrated their comprehension of the text through multiple genres and revealed the complexity of their analysis by thinking about the text from various perspectives.

These book projects subvert academic norms for writing and composition by not focusing on MLA or APA structured research papers. Multigenre projects invite students to utilize skill levels described at the top of Bloom's taxonomy—analyzing, evaluating, and creating. Structured and standardized curriculum in ELA often ignores the value, challenge, and skill of creating. Students were tasked with taking an idea from the literature and creating new knowledge or insights from their analysis, evaluation, and personal connections to the literature. Students' creations not only conveyed what they understood from the stories, but also revealed their ability to create products that helped others understand their analysis of their selected literature circle book.

Conclusion

One implied goal of teaching AP English courses is for students to succeed on the AP exam. Such an approach to the course has tacitly reinforced Eurocentric literature and writing as the exemplar and norm for advanced study. Sandra's unit demonstrates that subverting the AP curriculum can mean creating opportunities for students to move beyond conforming to a Eurocentric curriculum, and designing instruction that allows students to become advanced readers and writers on their own culturally rich and diverse terms.

It is especially important to challenge the traditional canon in AP courses with students of color so they don't assume only "dead white authors" are featured in advanced courses or that these authors represent the epitome of advanced academics. Including YA literature written by authors of color, which centers the voices of youth of color, signals to students, *especially* students of color, that these diverse texts have merit and value in terms of rigorous study. Exposing students to diverse characters, cultures, and stories that reflect their own experiences and identities is a key element of subverting traditional ELA curricula.

The pedagogical practices we discuss in this chapter are accessible to teachers and often well-established practices in the English classroom (e.g., literature circles, reader response journals, etc.). Subversive teaching does not necessarily equate dramatic or drastic action. It is not out of reach. Instead, Sandra shows that subversive teaching means deliberately choosing the texts and pedagogical strategies that best meet students' needs. For Sandra's students, subverting traditional AP English curricular and pedagogical practices meant adopting culturally relevant texts and reader-centered pedagogies. In the context of an AP English course that traditionally emphasizes a white, middle class worldview, subversive teaching means giving students of color permission to place their lived experiences at the center of learning. Reading, evaluating, and analyzing culturally diverse YA literature subverts traditional expectations for the advanced study of literature. Drawing on students' lived experiences and cultural knowledge to make sense of literature and to write, compose, and create new insights subverts traditional expectations for advanced reading and writing.

References

Adichie, C. (2009). *The danger of a single story* [video]. TED Global. https://www.ted.com/talks/chimamanda_ngozi_adichie_the_danger_of_a_single_story/c

Baker-Bell, A. (2013). "I never really knew the history behind African American Language": Critical language pedagogy in an advanced placement English language arts class. *Equity & Excellence in Education, 46*(3), 355-370.

Bender, G. (2017). Things (don't quite) fall apart: Exploring the diversity insertion in the secondary ELA canon. *Changing English, 29*(4), 368-381.

Berger, L. (1996). Reader response journals: You make the meaning . . . and how. *Journal of Adolescent & Adult Literacy, 39*(5), 380–385.

Bishop, R. S. (1990). Mirrors, windows, and sliding glass doors. *Perspectives, 5*(3), ix–xi.

Boyd, F. B., Ariail, M., Williams, R., Jocson, K., Sachs, G.T., McNeal, K., Morrell, E. (2006). Real teaching for real diversity: preparing English language arts teachers for 21st century classrooms. *English Education, 38*(4), 329–350.

Christensen, L. (2009). T*eaching for joy and justice: Reimagining the language arts classroom.* Rethinking Schools.

College Board. (2020). *AP English literature and composition: Course and exam description.* AP College Board.

Daniels, H. (2006) What's the next big thing with literature circles? *Voices in the Middle, 13*(4), 10-15.

Daniels, H. (2002). *Literature circles: Voice and choice in book clubs and reading groups* (2nd ed.). Stenhouse.

Domingo, A. (2019). *How to introduce literary theory to your students*. Prestwick House. Retrieved from https://www.prestwickhouse.com/blog/post/2019/09/how-to-introduce-literary-theory-to-your-students

Durand, S., Jimenez-Garcia, M. (2018). Unsettling representations of identities: a critical review of diverse youth literature. *Research on Diversity in Youth Literature: 1*(1), 1–24.

Dyches, J. (2018). Critical canon pedagogy: Applying disciplinary inquiry to cultivate canonical critical consciousness. *Harvard Educational Review, 88*(4), 538–564.

Ebarvia, T., Germán, L., Parker, K. N, & Torres, J. (2020). #Disrupttexts. *English Journal, 110*(1), 100–102.

Eppert, C., Ethridge, K., & Bach, J. (2007). Bridging the gap: Using young adult literature to teach a just and sustainable world. *Talking Points, 19*(1), 10–20.

Ginsberg, R., Glenn, W. J., Moye, K., (2017). Opportunities for advocacy: interrogating multi-voiced YAL's treatment of denied identities. *English Journal, 107*(1), 26–32.

Kolluri, S. (2018). Advanced placement: The dual challenge of equal access and effectiveness. *Review of Educational Research, 88*(5), 671–711.

Learning for Justice. (Summer, 2016). *Online exclusive: Intersectionality 101* [Video]. https://www.learningforjustice.org/magazine/summer-2016/online-exclusive-intersectionality-101

Loh, V. (2006). Quantity and quality: The need for culturally authentic trade books in Asian-American young adult literature. *The ALAN Review, 34*(1), 44–61.

Lopez, A. E. (2011). Culturally relevant pedagogy and critical literacy in diverse English classrooms: a case study of a secondary English teacher's activism and agency. *English Teaching: Practice and Critique, 10*(4), 75–93.

Malo-Juvera, V. (2017). A postcolonial primer with multicultural YA literature. *English Journal, 107*(1), 41–47.

National Center of Educational Statistics. (2022). Enrollment and percentage distribution of enrollment in public elementary and secondary schools, by race/ethnicity and level of education: Fall 1999 through fall 2030 [Statistics database]. https://nces.ed.gov/programs/digest/d22/tables/dt22_203.60.asp

Romano, T. (2007). The many ways of multigenre. In T. Newkirk & R. Kent (Eds.) *Teaching the neglected 'R': Rethinking writing instruction in secondary classrooms* (pp. 87–102). Heinemann.

Rosenblatt, L. M. (1978). *The reader, the text, the poem: The transactional theory of the literary work*. Southern Illinois University Press.

Saco, S. (2022). "We're like not alone": Finding validation in Latinx YAL. *The ALAN Review, 50*(1), 45–55.

Sinclair, M. N. (2018). Decolonizing ELA: Confronting privilege and oppression in textual spaces. *English Journal, 107*(6), 89–94.

Smiles, T. (2008). Connecting literacy and learning through collaborative action research. *Voices from the Middle, 15*(4), 32–39.

Thomas, E. E. (2016). Stories "still" matter: Rethinking the role of diverse children's literature today. *Language Arts, 94*(2), 112–119.

Wilson, N. S., & Kelley J. S. (2016). Avid Readers in high school: Are they reading for pleasure? In J. A. Hayn J. S. Kaplan, & K. R. Clemmons (Eds.), *Teaching young adult literature today: insights, considerations, and perspectives for the classroom teacher* (2nd ed., pp. 65–83). Rowman & Littlefield.

Wolk, S. (2009). Reading for a better world: Teaching for social responsibility with young adult literature. *Journal of Adolescent & Adult Literacy, 52*(8), 664–673.

CHAPTER FIVE

Black Words Matter: Bending Literary Close Reading Toward Justice

Scott Storm

THE STUDENTS IN MY untracked 11th- and 12th-grade English class sit in a circle and passionately discuss James Baldwin's prose. The discussion sounds like the traditional discourse of literary scholars—a focus on literary terms such as *symbolism* and *imagery* to conduct close readings of texts. A closer inspection reveals that students go beyond traditional disciplinary expectations. Students not only analyze comma placement and syntactical choices, but also examine how literary structures reify or disrupt narratives around race, gender, class, and sexuality. Students harness the traditional tools of the discipline of English literature and orient them toward justice—meeting and disrupting what it means to traditionally *do* English in high school classrooms. To meet traditional conceptions, students apply close-reading skills fundamental to disciplinary traditions and state standards. Students subvert traditional understandings by using close-reading tools to critically analyze power, privilege, and oppression.

In this chapter, I draw on data from a larger teacher-research project of classroom practice that included audio recordings of 20 hours of classroom discussions and more than 200 student essays. I illustrate how students fulfilled traditional notions of literary close reading and subverted expectations by fusing critical analysis with literary analysis. I highlight one English course titled Black Words Matter, which focused on students interpreting texts by Black authors. In particular, I focus on one student writer, Mateo, to illustrate subversive close reading. More broadly, this analysis illuminates one way that teachers might bring together disciplinary literacies and social justice teaching. I conceptualize social justice teaching as necessarily centering on students' own experiences and funds of knowledge (Gonzalez et al, 2005), providing access to dominant skills (Delpit, 1995), and creating opportunities to critique and transform our society and the construction of knowledge (Moje, 2007).

Traditional Conceptions of Close Reading in English

English disciplinary literacies include the ways of thinking, writing, and talking like a literary scholar (Rainey, 2017). This means approaching a text as an aesthetic object: identifying literary form and structure, considering multiple interpretations, and constructing interpretive claims (Rainey & Moje, 2012). In English classrooms, disciplinary literacies can serve as a potential method of teaching for social justice as these literacies can provide both access and transformation (Moje, 2007, 2015). Although the school subject of English language arts can also include disciplinary literacies around creative writing, linguistics, composition, or rhetoric, for this chapter, I focus on literature because of the prominence of literary texts in English classrooms as well as the emphasis on literary close reading in the discipline (Eagleton, 2014).

Although scholarship on English disciplinary literacies as social justice teaching is a growing area of study (Dyches, 2018; Storm & Rainey, 2018), this line of inquiry has not thoroughly investigated the relationships between close reading and social justice in classroom practice. Both Smagorinsky's (2015) and Fisher's (2018) recent conceptual articles rely heavily on imagined classrooms and do not appear to present empirical data. Studies of the literacy practices of literary scholars either exclude students (Rainey, 2017), focus only on college undergraduates (Reynolds & Rush, 2017; Warren, 2011), or include only a few high school seniors in advanced placement courses (Peskin, 1998). This chapter adds to the disciplinary literacies scholarship by offering a picture of teaching and learning one literary disciplinary skill—close reading—in an untracked, inclusive, urban high school English classroom.

Close reading describes the careful examination of textual language, literary elements, and literary devices as a way to systematically analyze texts and construct arguments about relationships between form and meaning (Wolfe & Wilder, 2016). Emerging as the dominant analytic paradigm for literary study by the mid-20th century, close reading is often associated with the rise of a group of literary scholars known today as the New Critics (Scholes, 1998). New Critics considered the text itself the object of study and believed that contextual issues, such as historical period, an author's biography, and a reader's affective response, were of little consequence to rigorous close reading (Eagleton, 2008). Although today literary scholarship recognizes the importance of contexts (Tyson, 2015), close reading is still a disciplinary foundation. Literary scholars from diverse theoretical perspectives, ranging from queer theory to psychoanalysis, employ close reading as a core practice (Eckert, 2006).

Close reading is sometimes defined as a kind of careful reading that considers explicit and implicit meanings in a text (Lehman & Roberts, 2014). Within the tradition of literary scholarship, close reading must also incorporate an analysis of literary elements, including those that extend across a literary work, such as narrative structure, motifs, genre, and theme, and sentence-level devices, such as figurative language, syntax, diction, and imagery (Wolfe & Wilder, 2016).

High school English departments traditionally value literary close reading. Discussing literary terms and writing analyses have long been the purview of English classrooms (Eckert, 2006). Furthermore, close reading is an essential skill tested in standardized assessments. Both the AP English Literature and Composition Exam and high-stakes graduation tests, such as the New York State English Language Arts Regents Exam, demand student-constructed responses centered on close reading. Close reading also holds a prominent place in local and state standards—particularly in standards focusing on looking at an author's language and literary form—cementing the centrality of close reading in American public schools.

Subverting Close Reading Disciplinary Practices

As Moje (2010) attests, the goals of disciplinary study in literature are not to make everyone into literary scholars but to engage all youth in complex thinking and to transform schools toward justice. A subversive approach to close reading fulfills these goals. Although traditional notions of close reading focus on literary reading at the expense of contexts, subversive close reading combines a focus on literary language with tools from critical theory (Appleman, 2015). Critical theory here refers to analytic lenses used to analyze systems of power, including such approaches as feminism, Marxism, queer theory, postcolonial theory, critical race theory, and (dis)ability studies. This fusion of the close analysis of literary language with critical theory allows for the deconstruction of narratives that reify stereotypical representations or perpetuate injustice.

Many critical scholars from Audre Lorde (1984/2007) to Gloria Anzaldúa (1987/2012) have long engaged in this kind of close narrative analysis. For example, in her literary criticism, Toni Morrison (1992) employs traditional close-reading practices by tracing flashback, imagery, and "narrative gearshifts—metaphors; summonings; rhetorical gestures of triumph" (p. x). However, Morrison also draws on critical tools to highlight how language can "enforce hidden signs of racial superiority, cultural hegemony, and dismissive 'othering'" (p. x). Morrison explores literary language, reveals the assumptions underlying that language, and, ultimately, interrogates language's effect on the material world. Standing on the shoulders of these literary giants, this chapter explores the ways in which subversive close reading can be operationalized in public school English classrooms.

Subversive close reading also challenges the notion that a close reading of a text is an end in itself. A traditional model of close reading with its central focus on the text often stops short of exploring the implications of literary analyses on the world. For instance, students conducting traditional close readings might analyze oppressive diction, symbols of Blackness in a novel, and their effect on narrative structure. A subversive close reading can extend this work by having students discuss how they have seen problematic diction and symbols used in everyday conversation; then, students may brainstorm ways to revise, rephrase, and reimagine this language in anti-racist ways. Over time, literary close reading may help students shift away from even subtly oppressive language. Helping students make these connections between close reading and everyday life is essential for all English teachers. Subversive close reading works toward social transformation.

Subversive close reading centers not only canonical literature but also all semiotic forms. Daily, readers are inundated with advertisements, news broadcasts, narrative television, e-mails, music, fashion, and countless other semiotic resources. Although underexamined, close readings of form, imagery, mood, and tone can help people critically construct meaning from these resources. Analyzing not only what something says but also how it is written or constructed allows for one to critically engage with words and potentially reframe oppressive narratives. This ability to contest problematic narratives potentially builds a stronger, more inclusive democratic citizenship.

A subversive approach to close reading maintains a close analysis of language. However, a subversive approach also extends the purview of traditional close reading to include (a) an analysis of power/oppression, (b) implications for the rich contexts beyond the text under study, and (c) the application of close reading skills beyond canonical literature to all semiotic forms.

Teacher Positionality

My focus on social justice issues formed when I was a teenager navigating my gay identity in my hometown's homophobic rural high school, where, on one occasion, my peers broadcast a video on the closed-circuit television in which they tie a character— possessing my name and likeness—to a stake and shout, "Burn the faggot," as he ignites in flames. Experiences such as these have driven me toward transforming oppressive school structures for all youth.

Across my 12 years of teaching high school English, interrogating my own positionality in this work has been essential. A step toward bending literacies toward justice is confronting one's own privilege. As a White man, I enter the classroom with immense, unearned privilege. Routinely, I explicitly talk about the injustice around White privilege with students. When pedagogically relevant, I also discuss my queer identity and my identity as someone who grew up working class. In this way, I work at making talk of both power structures and intersectional identities a valued part of the class community.

These identities inform my approach to subversive English teaching in that they have allowed me to see that what we do with words is inextricably linked to who we envision ourselves to be. The words we use have not only literary effects but also material consequences—words help construct reality. Literary close reading helps people gain agency over words' semiotic and material effects—literary analysis helps us learn to become metalinguistically aware of how words reify stereotypes, to police problematic societal norms, and to enforce both ideological and material oppression. This awareness allows people to actively work to quash narratives used to marginalize, subjugate, and belittle.

School Context

More scholarship on close reading and social justice in urban public schools is needed. The school where I teach students English is an in-district public high school in New York City. The school's mission centers on learning through inquiry and experience as heralded by the Coalition of Essential Schools and prepares students for collegiate study. The school focuses on equity by engaging students with both culturally sustaining curricula and rigorous performance-based assessments. Approximately 45% of students identify as Latinx, 25% as Black, 20% as White, and 10% as Asian. Approximately 75% of students receive free or reduced-price lunch, and 30% of students receive special education services. Students represent a diversity of neighborhoods and all five boroughs of New York City. The school community sees this diversity as a strength and prioritizes students' funds of knowledge in the curriculum. Structurally, this stance helps make subversive teaching possible across the school, not only in a single classroom.

The English Department

Classes are untracked and inclusive of all students. Most courses are team-taught by a special education and a general education teacher. The English department does not follow the traditional high school sequence but, instead, has designed a menu of multi-age English courses from which students select each semester. Ninth and 10th graders select from one set of courses, and 11th and 12th graders select from more advanced options. A student might choose to take Literary Que(e)ries, in which students read lesbian, gay, bisexual, transgender, and queer (LGBTQ) literature and research their own literary queries. Alternatively, students may choose Writing the Great American Novel, in which every student reads a diversity of American novels as mentor texts and writes a novel of at least 100 pages. In the course Versus Verses, students read canonical and contemporary poetry and host their own poetry slam/coffeehouse event every week.

Across these courses, students engage in close reading by analyzing syntax, diction, poetic form, and other traditional literary tools. However, students do not perform this analysis as an end in itself. Instead, students grapple with the material consequences of rhetorical choices. In Literary Que(e)ries, students question how authorial word choice in canonical literature may reify gender norms, and then students continue this kind of close reading with texts from their daily lives to investigate how popular culture also reproduces problematic assumptions. Students write papers in which they not only meticulously consider literary features, but also explore the implications of literary devices for critical frameworks and lived experiences.

The Black Words Matter Class

In another English course, Black Words Matter, students read Black authors and conduct subversive close readings that highlight literary language and social justice. I developed this course with my longtime co-teacher, a veteran special education teacher who identifies as Haitian American. We drew inspiration from the Black Lives Matter movement—a social movement cofounded by Khan-Cullors, Garza, and Tometi (Black Lives Matter Global Network, n.d.), which examines systematic violence and racism while working against anti-Blackness. The Black Words Matter class highlights Black authors' contributions while centering on issues of oppression and humanity. Course texts span multiple genres and time periods and celebrate a diversity of Black voices, including Afro-Caribbean, African, and African American writers. Table 5.1 details some of the key course texts.

As a class, we develop structures for engaging with these texts. Often, we sit in a large circle and read a short excerpt (or watch/listen for nonprint media). A student reads aloud while everyone follows along with his or her individual copy. Next, we silently annotate as we consider literary form and critical theory. My co-teacher and I crouch beside students and hold whispered conferences as students annotate. We ask questions that point students to the language features, such as "What do you notice about how this text is written?" "What words jump out at you?" "What literary devices might be causing the feelings you have as you read?" "What specific words help shape how the text treats race, class, and gender?" and "What do these words imply or assume about particular identity groups?" Because readers need time to puzzle through questions, try multiple analytic tools, and construct interpretations, we annotate for at least 10 minutes.

After annotating, students share their thinking with a partner—rehearsing and co-constructing ideas. Then, as a whole group, we discuss the text for at least another half hour. Students drive this discussion by sharing what they noticed and articulating interpretive puzzles. We highlight emerging interpretive claims and interrogate the strength of the textual evidence for these ideas. Teachers act as facilitators—avoiding lecture and creating space for students to own the conversation.

Some days the text we analyze is student-created. We analyze students' short stories, poetry, song lyrics, visual art, text messages, and fashion designs. This prac-

Table 5.1.

Select course texts used in the Black Words Matter curriculum, listed in order of course sequence

Author	Text(s)
Chimamanda Adichie	TED Talk: "The Danger of a Single Story"
Black Lives Matter Global Network	Webpage: Black Lives Matter: What We Believe
Booker T. Washington	Essay: "The Atlantic Exposition Address"
W. E. B. DuBois	*The Souls of Black Folk* (excerpt)
Langston Hughes	Poetry: "Harlem," "Ballad of the Landlord," "Theme for English B," and others
James Baldwin	Short story: "Sonny's Blues"
Frank Ocean	Song: "Bad Religion"
Zora Neale Hurston	Novel: *Their Eyes Were Watching God* (excerpt)
Audre Lorde	Essay: "The Master's Tools"
	Poetry: "Power" and others
	Television show: *RuPaul's Drag Race* (excerpt)
Assata Shakur	Autobiography: *Assata* (excerpt)
Toni Morrison	Novel: *Sula* (excerpt)
Beyoncé Knowles-Carter	Film/album: *Lemonade*
bell hooks	Essay: "Postmodern Blackness"
	Book of essays: *Talking Back* (excerpt)
Edwidge Danticat	Novel: *Breath, Eyes, Memory* (excerpt)
Barry Jenkins	Film: *Moonlight* (excerpt)
Michelle Alexander	Non-fiction: *The New Jim Crow* (excerpt)
Ta-Nehisi Coates	Essay: "The Case for Reparations" (excerpt)

tice highlights the complex literacies of youth, showing that close reading is not just for disciplinarians but can also be a tool for all.

Skill instruction is interlaced throughout these routines. We model how to annotate a text as a literary scholar would. Students explain what literary devices they employ in their analyses and walk the class through their thinking. We discuss how to self-monitor to stay on task and how to try different analytic tools when one feels stuck. Close reading also supports comprehension—even when literal meaning seems to be an obstacle, close reading can help students attend to the words on the page and grapple with comprehension on their way to crafting cognitively complex interpretations. Throughout, we discuss how to build our identities as literary scholars in an intellectual community.

Portrait of Mateo's Literacy Learning

To better describe students' close reading in this classroom, I ground this description with examples of one student's work—Mateo (a pseudonym). This student is not unusual but, rather, performs literary disciplinary literacies in ways similar to many of his peers. However, I choose Mateo for the focus of this chapter because his work exemplifies subversive close reading.

As a final project for the course, each student writes a 10-page close reading of one or more course texts. After completing several drafts, students present their papers in an hour-long oral defense to a panel of external examiners consisting of literature professors, teachers, and writers. Although the assignment asks students to engage with traditional close reading skills, students also subvert traditional notions by analyzing societal power systems. For example, one student's paper explores Zora Neale Hurston's (2006) *Their Eyes Were Watching God*. She analyzes the connotations and imagery in Hurston's descriptions of female characters to show how White conceptions of beauty serve to police Black bodies. This student engages with traditional notions of close reading by meticulously tracing connotations and imagery in every description of a female character in Hurston's text. She subverts these notions by analyzing power structures around body image and White supremacy in the text and describing the implications for today's society.

Mateo, who identifies as Latino, wrote his final paper by conducting a close reading of Black authors throughout American literary history, including Dubois, Baldwin, Shakur, and hooks. In this paper, he highlights how authors across time use similar literary techniques to show that racial injustice is a systemic issue as opposed to an individualistic one in American culture. Ultimately, Mateo demonstrates how authors use literary tools to work toward systemic social change. Throughout his paper and oral defense, Mateo demonstrates his prowess at traditional notions of literary close reading, as well as his ability to subvert these expectations to bend close reading toward justice.

Subverting Close Reading Norms: Mateo's Paper

Mateo closely reads the language in Baldwin's (2009) "Sonny's Blues," a short story in which the narrator's brother is arrested for selling drugs and the narrator, who is a teacher, goes through his day contemplating the seemingly hopeless future for the boys in his math class. Starting his close reading, Mateo explains that "the way Baldwin forms the sentence, the syntax, when he says 'boys' it's not a singular thing; it's a plural thing." Mateo focuses on the traditional grammatical tool of plural form. Although a traditional close reading might stop at this observation, Mateo goes on to connect

Baldwin's use of the plural form *boys* to an analysis of structural power. Mateo describes that "it's something that stems across many people, and it's not just a singular problem." Throughout the paper, Mateo explains that it is not merely one boy getting in trouble but, rather, that there is a systemic issue. Thus, his analysis shifts the perceived blame for misbehavior from individual boys to the school system, which is not adequately serving the men of color in Baldwin's text. Mateo builds off the traditional close-reading skills and subverts them by connecting close language study with a systemic analysis of racism. Ultimately, this analysis leads Mateo to claim that the text describes not a problem regarding an individual student but, rather, a pattern indicating a structural problem for the school system. Mateo even uses metaphorical literary language to make this point by saying, "There's too much smoke for there not to be a fire." For Mateo, Baldwin's grammatical structure highlights issues of systemic racism, and he captures this idea by crafting his own literary language—choosing the metaphor of smoke and fire wherein the smoke represents the markers of this structural problem and the fire is the underlying societal racism.

In another example of subversive close reading, when analyzing an excerpt from bell hooks's (1989) *Talking Back*, Mateo says that what he "would like to talk about is how [hooks] displaces herself—how she says 'some people.'" Here, Mateo illuminates how hooks, who is telling a personal narrative, distances herself by telling her story using the diction of "some people" instead of directly using her name or personal pronouns. Throughout his analysis, Mateo highlights hooks's pronoun choices and diction—analytic moves associated with traditional close reading. Mateo remarks that hooks "explains how she feels inadequate . . . and juxtapose[s] the word *momma*, which is in the next line." Here, Mateo uses another move traditionally associated with close reading—noticing strangeness (Rainey, 2017)—and he uses the disciplinary term *juxtaposition* to make this point. Mateo points out that this juxtaposition is strange because he questions, "Who should feel inadequate to their mom?" Mateo then says that the effect of this juxtaposition is that it "helps to show the disconnect among parent and child . . . which is what the rest of the book kind of talks about." Throughout his essay, Mateo focuses on closely reading word choice and juxtaposition. This focus enables him to frame his paper around generational trauma and healing as they relate to structural racism. By moving between a close analysis of language and critical theory, Mateo subverts traditional notions of close reading and bends his argument toward justice.

Going beyond a strict New Critical reading that does not account for historical context, Mateo couches his close reading in today's complex cultural contexts by explaining,

> I wanted to write about identity and not only how people are treated and how that affects your identity but how history affects your identity now . . .

you're not just affected by what's happening now; you're affected by your own history as well.

Mateo makes a case for why analyzing literary devices across semiotic forms can help readers understand how historically bound oppression facilitates further injustice today. This analysis goes beyond the work of many literary scholars in that, for Mateo, his close reading ultimately is used as a tool toward helping people reframe their discourse in human interaction. Thus, Mateo does not merely conduct his close reading as an end in itself but, rather, explores the implications of his close reading for everyday interactions as well.

Mateo's work is illustrative of the kinds of literacy practices with which his classmates engage. Whether we are analyzing bell hooks or Beyoncé, the students in this untracked, fully inclusive classroom in a public school demonstrate how they productively interweave their strong critical consciousness with disciplinary skills in transformative, even liberatory ways.

Conclusion

Although some see close reading as entrenched in dominant disciplinary discourses, subversive close reading helps students use the tools valued by a dominant culture of power and simultaneously transform these tools to reorient them toward justice. Importantly, this work is possible within large public school systems. Still, this work is not easy—it requires teachers to think like engineers and puzzle through how to optimally structure learning environments. Teachers must strive toward this work because racism and other oppressions are systemic issues. As Mateo reminds readers, "There's too much smoke for there not to be a fire." Teachers must address structural oppression through every aspect of English classrooms—and close reading is well suited for this kind of transformation.

References

Adichie, C. (2009). *The danger of a single story* [Video file]. Retrieved from https://www.ted.com/talks/chimamanda_adichie_the_danger_of_a_single_story?language=en

Alexander, M. (2012) *The new Jim Crow: Mass incarceration in the age of color-blindness.* The New Press.

Anzaldúa, G. (1987). *Borderlands/La frontera: The new Mestiza.* Aunt Lute Books. (Original work published 2012).

Appleman, D. (2015). *Critical encounters in high school English: Teaching literary theory to adolescents* (2nd ed.). Teachers College Press.

Baldwin, J. (2009) "Sonny's blues." pp. 17–48. In *The jazz fiction anthology* (S. Feinstein & D. Rife Eds). Indiana UP, 2009. (Original work published 1957).

Black Lives Matter Global Network. (n.d.). Black lives matter: Herstory. Retrieved from https://blacklivesmatter.com/about/herstory/

Black Lives Matter Global Network. (n.d.) Black lives matter: What we believe. Retrieved from https://blacklivesmatter.com/what-we-believe/

Coates, T. (2014) The case for reparations. *The Atlantic.com.* Retrieved from https://www.theatlantic.com/magazine/archive/2014/06/the-case-for-reparations/361631/

Danticat, E. (2015) *Breath, eyes, memory.* (Anniversary ed.) Soho Press. (Original work published 1994).

Delpit, L. (1995). *Other people's children.* The New Press.

DuBois, W. E. B. (1994) *The souls of Black folk.* Dover Publications. (Original work published 1903).

Dyches, J. (2018). Investigating curricular injustices to uncover the injustices of curricula: Curriculum evaluation as critical disciplinary literacy practice. *The High School Journal,* 101, 236–250. doi:10.1353/hsj.2018.0013

Eagleton, T. (2008). *Literary theory: An introduction* (Anniversary ed.) Minneapolis: University of Minnesota Press. (Original work published 1983).

Eagleton, T. (2014). *How to read literature.* Yale University Press.

Eckert, L. S. (2006). *How does it mean?: Engaging reluctant readers through literary theory.* Heinemann.

Fisher, R. (2018). Reconciling disciplinary literacy perspectives with genre-oriented activity theory: Toward a fuller synthesis of traditions. *Reading Research Quarterly,* 54, 237–251. doi:10.1002/rr1.233

Gonzalez, N., Moll, L. C., & Amanti, C. (Eds.). (2005). *Funds of knowledge: Theorizing practices in households, communities, and classrooms.* Erlbaum.

hooks, b. (1989). *Talking back: Thinking feminist, thinking Black.* South End Press.

hooks, b. (2018) "Postmodern Blackness" In V. B. Leitch, W. E. Cain, L. A. Finke, J. McGowan, T. D. Sharpley-Whiting, and J. J. Williams (Eds.), *Norton Anthology of Theory and Criticism* (3rd ed.) (pp. 2318–2324). W. W. Norton & Company.

Hughes, L. (1995) *The collected poems of Langston Hughes* (A. Ramersand & D. Roessel, Eds.) Vintage Classics.

Hurston, Z. N. (2006) *Their eyes were watching God.* Harper Perennial Modern Classics. (Original work published 1937).

Knowles, B. (2016) *Lemonade* [video album]. Parkwood Entertainment.

Lehman, C., & Roberts, K. (2014). *Falling in love with close reading: Lessons for analyzing texts—and life.* Heinemann.

Lorde, A. (2000) *"Power." The collected poems of Audre Lorde.* pp. 215–216. W. W. Norton & Company.

Lorde, A. (2007) The master's tools will never dismantle the master's house. *Sister outsider: Essays and speeches.* pp. 110–113. Crossing Press.

Moje, E. B. (2007). Developing socially just subject-matter instruction: A review of the literature on disciplinary literacy teaching. *Review of Research in Education,* 31, 1–44.

Moje, E. B. (2010). "Response: Heller's 'in praise of amateurism: A friendly critique of Moje's 'call for change' in secondary literacy.'" *Journal of Adolescent and Adult Literacy,* 54, 275–278.

Moje, E. B. (2015). Doing and teaching disciplinary literacy with adolescent learners: A social and cultural enterprise. *Harvard Educational Review,* 85, 254–278.

Morrison, T. (1973) *Sula.* Penguin Books.

Morrison, T. (1992). *Playing in the dark: Whiteness and the literary imagination.* Vintage Books.

Ocean, F., & Neuble, M. (2012). Bard religion [Recorded by Frank Ocean]. *On Channel orange* [CD]. Def Jam.

Peskin, J. (1998). Constructing meaning when reading poetry: An expert-novice study. *Cognition and Instruction*, 16, 235–263.

Rainey, E. C. (2017). Disciplinary literacy in English language arts: Exploring the social and problem-based nature of literary reading and reasoning. *Reading Research Quarterly*, 52, 53–71.

Rainey, E. C., & Moje, E. B. (2012). Extending the conversation: Building insider knowledge: Teaching students to read, write, and think within ELA and across the disciplines. *English Education*, 45, 71–90.

Reynolds, T., & Rush, L. S. (2017). Experts and novices reading literature: An analysis of disciplinary literacy in English language arts. *Literacy Research and Instruction*, 56, 199–216.

Romanski, A., Gardner, D., Kleiner, J. (Producers) & Jenkins, B. (Director). (2016). *Moonlight* [Motion picture]. United States of America: A24.

Shakur, A. (1987). *Assata: An autobiography*. Lawrence Hill Books.

Scholes, R. (1998). *The rise and fall of English: Reconstructing English as a discipline*. Yale University Press.

Smagorinsky, P. (2015). Disciplinary literacy in English/language arts. *Journal of Adolescent & Adult Literacy*, 59, 141–146.

Storm, S., & Rainey, E. C. (2018). Striving toward woke English teaching and learning. *English Journal*, 107(6), 95–101.

Tyson, L. (2015). *Critical theory today: A user-friendly guide* (3rd ed.). Routledge.

Warren, J. E. (2011). "Generic" and "specific" expertise: An expert/expert study in poetry interpretation and academic argument. *Cognition & Instruction*, 29, 349–374.

Washington, B. T. (1995) "The Atlantic exposition address." *Up from slavery*. (105–115). Dover Publications. (Original work published 1895).

Wolfe, J. & Wilder, L. (2016). *Digging into literature: Strategies for reading, analysis, and writing*. Bedford/St. Martin's.

CHAPTER SIX

Arguing for Empathy: Subverting the Teaching of Argumentation

CRYSTAL SOGAR AND MELANIE SHOFFNER

I (CRYSTAL) NEVER FELT more overwhelmed than when I began teaching. I had relocated from the Midwest to San Francisco, I was teaching 11th-grade English language arts (ELA) at a school using a project-based learning curriculum aligned to the California State Standards, and I was working with a new-to-me student population. My students, predominantly Latinx, were adolescents often navigating issues of immigration, poverty, homelessness, depression, sexual assault, and violence before they even entered the school doors. Despite my years studying education, months of student teaching, and hours of planning lessons, I came home and cried more days than I can count, worried that I was not doing enough to build relationships with my students, much less creating engaging, standards-based assignments. I had thrived during my student teaching, so I struggled to understand why I was failing now. Wanting to prove myself to administrators and colleagues, I was too embarrassed to admit that I needed help, so I had very little support navigating my first year.

As if all that was not enough to keep me up at night, I was terrified of a mass shooter terrorizing my own school. Despite crying whenever I saw clips of school shootings on the news, I had not felt it as a real threat until the day we practiced a safety drill. Watching my students push desks against the door and hide in a corner of the room, it hit me that if a shooter came into my classroom, I would be helpless to protect them or myself. So, when the shooting occurred at Marjory Stoneman Douglas High School (February 14, 2018), I knew I wanted to address it in my classroom. Although my students often struggled to express their emotions, whether it be through writing or in-class discussions, I knew the shooting had affected them. Students at the school had already led a walkout in response to school shootings; they seemed to be searching for ways to make their voices heard. I was not sure how to move forward, however, so I contacted my former professor, Dr. Melanie Shoffner. The lesson discussed here evolved from that conversation.

In this chapter, I focus on the teaching of argumentation, a traditional (and often required) topic in the ELA classroom. We subvert this traditional topic of study, however, by sharing a lesson that uses analysis of argumentation to support the consideration of current events and the development of students' empathy.

Argumentation in ELA

The study of argumentation is a standard convention in ELA, with students learning, practicing, and honing skills in reasoning, critical thinking, and problem solving to develop and deliver persuasive writing and speaking (Turner & Hicks, 2016). As students work with argumentation in the classroom, they need help "thinking through the complexity and complications of an issue, making inferences based on evidence, and hierarchically grouping and logically sequencing ideas" (Rex et al, 2010, p. 61). Moreover, with the amount of digital content constantly influencing our thoughts, feelings, opinions, and decisions, students learning about argumentation in digital spaces is more important than ever. As Turner and Hicks (2016) explain, if we want students to write and analyze real-world arguments, "we must teach them to understand both the logic of the argument as well as how those arguments work when they are streaming in" through digital media (p. 7); with students "now communicating to a global audience, the need for crafting successful arguments is more important than ever" (p. 9).

As part of my school curriculum, students study the Toulmin method (Rex at al., 2010), a "process of setting out a logical series of ideas that appear persuasive to readers or hearers" (p. 57). For students to analyze an argument, they break down the components that make up the argument (e.g., stance, evidence, and warrant), assess the purpose, and evaluate the effectiveness of each component. Students are then provided with a framework of questions to evaluate the effectiveness of the evidence provided in the argument (e.g., Is this evidence credible? Is this evidence sufficient? Is this evidence accurate? Which order of evidence is best?). In doing so, students learn to assess and evaluate persuasive language to explore positions, weigh evidence, and determine support for the claim.

At this point in my unit, the students had worked with the Toulmin method to define, identify, and write the different components of an argument; they were now working on critiquing others' argumentative skills. To integrate this lesson into the unit, I created the following objectives:

- Identify each component of the Toulmin method in a given text.
- Evaluate the effectiveness of each component in the text.
- Identify and explain the impact of rhetorical devices and logical fallacies in the text.
- Use understandings of argumentation to strengthen an existing argument.

The lesson aligned with the unit's standards in reading and writing, requiring students to analyze and evaluate the effectiveness of authors' arguments, determine authors' purpose and effectiveness of style, and support the resulting analysis through textual evidence.

Subverting the Teaching of Argumentation

Through their study of argumentation, my students were learning rhetorical analysis and word choice. I also wanted them to learn the power of words and the importance of empathetic response, so instead of focusing solely on the assessment and evaluation of the argument, I included the writing of a personal response. Whatever the subject under study, I want to encourage empathy in my students so that they think about their positions, consider their words, and appreciate others' perspectives.

In addition to the objectives addressing argumentation (noted earlier), students would also push themselves—potentially out of their comfort zones—to respond to an argument in a reflective, empathic manner. Although one of the school administration's goals is building students' emotional response skills, I also want to develop students' empathy by creating a safe space in my classroom for students to engage with important issues—such as the death of teenagers through gun violence—that have connections to their life experiences. My students are resilient young people who (continue to) navigate a range of difficult experiences, from leaving home to escape violence to being accosted by police officers while walking home to having friends injured through gang violence. These experiences have contributed to my students' struggles to express themselves, so I aim to create a space where students can bring their whole selves to class without worry or fear of judgment.

What I did not realize in teaching this lesson was how it would shift my own point of view; like Wender (2014), I learned that "instead of focusing on our experiences of teaching, we must focus instead on students' experiences of learning" (p. 34). I needed to work on building my understanding of their world because my students' thoughts, feelings, and exposure to violence differed so much from my own. In practicing empathy, I needed to actively and continually think, feel, and appreciate students' perspectives (Wender, 2016) while working against negative evaluations of my students by society, other teachers, and, sometimes, themselves. As Wender (2016) notes, teachers must ask themselves:

How [can] I better recognize my students' experiences, especially in difficult moments? How [can] I better understand what it is like for my students to go through school, and how [can] I let them know I [am] trying to understand their experiences? (p. 36).

In asking students to write a personal response, I was also creating a space for students to share their experiences, offering me the opportunity to gain a better understanding of their lives in and out of school.

Developing the Assignment

Immediately following the Marjory Stoneman Douglas shooting, I wrote Melanie a quick e-mail one morning:

I'm struggling with how to discuss the recent school shooting with my low income Latinx students who characteristically push back on sharing feelings. I want to discuss it at school because I don't think it will be talked about at home and I think it's important to acknowledge it with the students. I'm trying to figure out how to frame it or even where to start and would love some feedback! I was thinking about how I've framed my classroom, how our words are powerful and what we can do with our words. I wanted to start a conversation around the shooting and relate it back to using their words, then have them do a writing activity (such as an open letter) and then maybe ask students to share if they are comfortable with what they wrote. I'm just not sure how to frame the conversation or the writing prompt really. Any ideas?

Melanie pushed me to think of an activity on my own, but she also gave me additional points to consider:

Asking students directly about any difficult topic is likely to shut them down; they feel like you're looking for a specific answer and emotions don't work that way . . . you want this to be a teachable moment . . . which is why you're considering having them write an open letter. But an open letter to whom? For what? Pushing them to take a stance on something this volatile may backfire. Plus, your population is different than suburban white kids. You want to honor their differences of experience, ethnicity, socioeconomic status, location through something that only happens in suburban white schools. Your kids have likely experienced violence and loss and death but in different ways, so how do you create a commonality that will engage

them without reducing what they can bring to the table? The idea behind
using a text [like Emma Gonzalez's "We Call BS" speech] is that it allows
students to "other" the emotions that might arise. . . . "You" aren't angry,
"the character" is angry—and then you can talk about emotions in a different way. Using the text as a text offers an instructional activity—you can
find standards to suit whatever you do with it—that engages and challenges
students in a meaningful way. . . . Give them something to dig into and
allow them to share their emotions if they wish; don't force them or require
them.

The conversation that followed led to the creation of the analysis of argumentation
lesson aligned with my current unit's standards and objectives. More important, this
lesson challenged the required study of argumentative structure: moving beyond the
study of rhetoric to engage students' empathetic responses to current events. Melanie's e-mail also challenged me to think differently about my curriculum and how I
could use a text to help my students work with their emotions.

　　This lesson changed how I think about working with my students. I did not realize how much my students wanted to share their thoughts but were too scared or too
convinced that their voices did not matter. I did not realize that their discomfort with
emotion often came from not knowing what to say rather than not having something to say. After this lesson, I felt more comfortable bringing supplemental texts
into the classroom and using them as a way for students to work with characters'
emotions as well as their own. This work has encouraged me to address so many
more of the difficult issues my students face on a daily basis.

Analyzing and Subverting Argumentation

No class during my university preparation covered how to respond to school shootings with my students. Many classes, however, stressed my role in engaging students
with challenging material, developing their abilities as critical thinkers, and supporting their individual agency (Shoffner et al., 2017). If I wanted students to develop
as critical thinkers, I needed to actively engage them with the world around them as
well as texts that required them to question and respond (Pescatore, 2007).

　　I asked them to be uncomfortable and vulnerable as we engaged in a dialogue not typically found in schools. I knew that each of my students shared
different political views and had varying degrees of interaction with violence, so each student would have different thoughts and feelings. So I needed them to trust that I cared for them, as my students and as individuals,
in order to engage with the lesson. As Chiang (2019) notes, teachers must be self-aware
and respect students as thinkers and actors while creating a curriculum that "reaches
outside the classroom and gives students opportunities to exercise their moral and

political sensibilities" (para. 17). I hoped a lesson that engaged my students with a difficult, emotional topic would support the creation of the classroom I envisioned: one that works within the confines of a traditional curriculum to develop students as critical, empathetic thinkers.

As a Teacher

I grew up in a predominantly White community in the suburbs of Chicago. The lack of diversity in my town was reflected in the curriculum taught at my school: canonical classics featuring White characters. I had little exposure to texts that offered me a chance to explore other experiences and identities in any significant way, although I did not realize that until my undergraduate education. There, I learned about issues of institutionalized inequality, a lack of opportunity, and social injustice that contrasted sharply with my own experiences as a young White woman educated in an upper middle-class suburb. I engaged in difficult discussions in my education classes that addressed the intersections of race, gender, socioeconomic status, privilege, and student and instructional practice. I read books, articles, and chapters that challenged me to think differently about taken-for-granted concepts of inclusion, educational purpose, student diversity, and teacher responsibility (e.g., Dodge & Crutcher, 2015; Groenke et al., 2015; Wilson, 2014). By the time I graduated, I knew my classroom would allow students to draw on their own experiences and that my texts would provide an opportunity to critically reflect on society.

When I moved to San Francisco, I was drawn to a public charter high school with a commitment to preparing diverse learners for higher education while supporting their development as members of society. As of the 2017–2018 school year, the school enrolled 428 students, while 275 students identified as Latinx, 228 identified as male, and 59 identified as English learners (Ed Data, 2018). The school's stated mission was that all students graduated college-ready, defined as students taking several Advanced Placement (AP) classes, sitting for the SAT multiple times, and scoring at least 70% on the Smarter Balanced Assessment Consortium test, a standardized test taken by all juniors in California. As of 2018, 98% of the graduating senior class was accepted to a four year university.

Students face a number of difficulties in their lives beyond school, but inside the building, every student is considered equally capable of achievement. Students are encouraged to take AP classes, offered additional test preparation if needed, and provided access to internships. Although teachers are provided a base curriculum with specific projects, they have a significant amount of leeway to modify curriculum based on students' needs and use projects and self-directed learning in the classroom. Through mentor groups, students are assigned to a teacher who serves as their main support, ideally throughout high school. Through weekly circle activities, mentors provide a safe space for students to share thoughts and feelings and provide support to fellow mentees. These relationship-building activities also develop students' empathy by asking them to reflect on their feelings and to make connections with peers over similar fears, stresses, and wins.

Social Justice in the Classroom

As Melanie Shoffner (2018) has written, teachers are responsible for developing students' abilities to "affirm and respond to the world's diversity in ways that support and promote empathy, acceptance and understanding" (para. 8). For me, that means working to prove to students that their voices are powerful and their lives are meaningful. Too many teachers seem willing to write off my students because of their "minority status" or lower income backgrounds. I reject the inherent message that certain students are not capable of higher level thinking, so I challenge my students to consider different perspectives and question what they are told. In my classroom, we focus on building critical thinking skills. We start the year by defining what it means to be a critical thinker and why it is important to be one. Although students recognize that critical thinking is an important skill, they are not sure how they can develop it or when they would know if they have.

When students are seemingly accustomed to failure, they see it as their status quo. In helping them to develop a different perspective, I focus on changing students' responses of "I'm bad at this, so I'll never get it" to "I have this strength . . . so I can work on this." In addition, I want to recognize my students' cultural knowledge and personal experiences as strengths; many of them have faced a range of challenges, from moving to the United States from small towns in foreign countries to living with parents suffering post-traumatic stress disorder from crossing the U.S.-Mexico border to managing the fear and anguish that they will be deported. I ask my students to bring their culture and life to the table and draw on their experiences when completing assignments.

Ultimately, to me, being a teacher invested in social justice means that I fight for and with my students. I fight what society tells them: that they will never succeed. I fight what the media tells them: that they are a burden on the country. I fight the little voice in their heads that tells them they cannot do it. I am only able to be successful in my fight because of the relationships I build with my students. I have worked hard to convince them that I not only want to teach them but that I also want to learn from their experiences, which is something I want to model for their own lives. Being able to identify with others creates connections, builds relationships, promotes social responsibility, and motivates altruistic behavior (Goodman, 2000). Building empathy in my classroom, then, aligns with my efforts to teach with/for social justice by creating opportunities "to connect with others who are different, see their common humanity, and begin to care about the situation" (Goodman, 2000, p. 1067).

The Lesson

To begin the argumentation lesson, students first independently read a speech given by Emma Gonzalez, a survivor of the Marjory Stoneman Douglas High School school shooting, before I read it aloud to the class. We then watched a video of Gonzalez delivering her speech at a rally in Fort Lauderdale, Florida, three days after the shooting (CNN Staff, 2018). With each reading, students were asked to underline and note phrases or words that stood out to them. Offering multiple readings of the same text was important to students' understanding because of differing reading abilities. It also provided multiple opportunities to check their understanding and reflect on their responses to the speech before I asked them to complete their final reflection.

After reading and viewing the speech, students worked in pairs to analyze Gonzalez's speech. Each pair applied their previous work with the Toulmin method to identify different elements of her speech: main claims, subclaims, warrants, backing, counterclaims, and rebuttal. Following this activity, I stopped students for a pair/share discussion before moving them into new pairings. In these pairs, students analyzed the effectiveness of Gonzalez's arguments by identifying areas she could have included or improved, working together to determine whether each element of the speech made her arguments clear, logical, and convincing.

Once the pairs had completed their analysis, we discussed how Gonzalez's writing style connected to her content and, ultimately, the power this style gave to her speech. Discussion questions addressed issues such as the following:

- How does Gonzalez's use of language impact the quality of her speech?
- How does her word choice impact the message she is trying to send to her audience?
- What specific words or phrases do you find powerful? Why?

As we discussed, students had to identify specific evidence that supported their analysis. As a student explained, "Gonzalez's speech is good because she uses her emotions and makes the audience feel bad. People are interested because they want to help. She is using the logical fallacy pathos." In considering areas for improvement, a student explained that Gonzalez should "[make] sure to cite her facts and [include] a counterclaim." They moved past the emotional subject matter, however, to critique her words and her arguments. In these activities, students were able to meet the traditional ELA goals of argument analysis and evaluation, but they did so through analysis of a speech on gun violence given by a fellow adolescent.

Although our discussion focused on analyzing argumentation, I still wanted to provide my students with an individual opportunity to reflect on the speech and address the emotional aspect. So the last activity was a writing assignment that took one of three forms: a letter to the victims and their families expressing condolences, a letter to a state representative asking for specific action, or a personal journal response to the teacher. My goal was for students to engage in authentic writing that allowed them to use emotion in a positive way. So, although students were meeting the goals of traditional writing instruction, they were also pushed to write to an authentic audience, respond to a current event, interact with difficult subject matter, and consider theirs and others' emotions. Those goals continued with the last piece of the assignment: expressing their own thoughts and feelings through a brief reflection on their understanding of the text.

As students continued with the lesson, I could see that not all were engaged with the assignment. Although this had certainly happened before, I was surprised they did not seem to feel the weight of this event. I briefly wondered what kind of people I was sending into the world—How could they be immune to the severity of a school shooting?—as I attributed their reluctance to adolescent immaturity and discomfort with emotion. When I checked in with these students to ask why they were avoiding the work, however, I found I was very much mistaken: They were engaged in the lesson, but they were struggling with what to write. So, instead of a letter, we agreed they would write a journal entry to me.

Some were scared of writing to a state representative because of their legal status. Some were angry because they had watched the U.S. government break apart their families and knew their voice had not mattered then; as one student wrote, "I know the families don't want apologies for what happen [sic], they want action, they want something to be done about the issue." Some felt they could not write a letter to the victims because it would be insincere to write to someone they did not know:

> I wish I could say "sorry" and send my condolences, but there aren't any words to change what occurred [sic] behind those school doors, February 12 that will change the 14 students' parents [who] are grieving over their lost child.

One student's response in particular stuck out to me:

> I am unable to right [write] a sorrowful letter to the family victims because of my low level of sympathy for others . . . People die everyday [sic] in gruesome ways whether it is by government or random people, and that doesn't have any attention. Laws cannot stop a person from taking action to do what they want to do.

I wonder if this student captured what many of my students feel: helplessness. They have experienced crime and corruption, at home and in the United States, and seen how laws do not stop violence. Where, at first, I saw lack of empathy, now I see courage in naming a personal response; I also see emotion in the student's implied helplessness and anger for a situation that does not change.

The Impact of Subversive Efforts

This lesson was an eye-opening experience for me. Despite believing I had some understanding of their daily lives, I did not know my students felt so restricted and marginalized; for me to believe that they felt comfortable in their lives was easy. They seemed to have adapted to the United States, wearing the right clothes, speaking English, and acting like every other American teenager. I realized I had never offered them a chance to tell me otherwise, to tell me that they did not feel like they belonged. My own assumptions about my students blinded me to their experiences, and I was ashamed to realize that I had not seen my students for who they really were.

For my students, they were able to reflect on their emotions surrounding school shootings, but, more important, they were able to express how they felt. I have always thought that young people struggle to find their voice, perhaps because they think no one will listen. Why share your thoughts and feelings if you do not think anyone cares? I have worked hard to include activities that give my students an audience and a platform to speak their mind because they have been given few chances to do so.

My lesson was not perfect, of course. I had tasked my students with a tall order: Analyze a speech about a violent event, participate in a discussion about the speech, and write an authentic response stemming from the analysis. I was subverting the regular classroom by asking them to be uncomfortable, vulnerable, and honest with themselves in an academic space. Although I may not have gotten the perfect level of engagement, my students did engage with the lesson. Some students who had struggled throughout the school year to express emotion were clearly trying to let their guards down and complete the writing. Rather than focusing on how my students may or may not have emotionally engaged with the lesson, I choose to consider this experience a stepping-stone for the next time they are asked to do something different.

This academic year, I had the proud opportunity to watch my first students—the students who completed this lesson—the boundary-pushing, resilient kids who challenged my thinking about empathy—walk across the graduation stage. In a world of standardized tests, exclusive curriculum, limiting data, and overwhelming social media, teaching things that are not on the test is more important than ever. Teaching my students how to be thinking, feeling people is one of them.

References

Chiang, M. (2018). Nurturing student activists in the time of Trump. *Rethinking Schools*, 33(1). Retrieved from https://www.rethinkingschools.org/articles/nurturing-student-activists-in-the-time-of-trump

CNN Staff. (2018, February 17). Florida student Emma Gonzalez to lawmakers and gun advocates: "We call BS." CNN. Retrieved from https://www.cnn.com/2018/02/17/us/florida-student-emma-gonzalez-speech/index.html

Dodge, A. M., & Crutcher, P. A. (2015). Inclusive classrooms for LBGTQ students: Using linked text sets to challenge the hegemonic "single story." *Journal of Adolescent & Adult Literacy*, *59*, 95–105.

Ed Data. (2018). Summit Preparatory Charter High. Retrieved from http://www.ed-data.org/school/San-Mateo/Sequoia-Union-High/Summit-Preparatory-Charter-High

Goodman, D. J. (2000). Motivating people from privileged groups to support social justice. *Teachers College Record*, *102*, 1061–1085.

Groenke, S., Haddix, M., Glenn, W. J., Kirkland, D. E., Price-Dennis, D., & Coleman-King, C. (2015). Disrupting and dismantling the dominant vision of youth of color. *English Journal*, *104*(3), 35–40.

Pescatore, C. (2007). Current events as empowering literacy: For English and social studies teachers. *Journal of Adolescent & Adult Literacy*, *51*, 326–339.

Rex, L. A., Thomas, E. E., & Engle, S. (2010). Applying Toulmin: Teaching logical reasoning and argumentative writing. *English Journal*, *99*(6), 56–62.

Shoffner, M. (2018, January). Disrupting the world as we know it: Addressing racism in ELA education. *Journal of Language and Literacy Education*. Retrieved from http://jolle.coe.uga.edu/wp-content/uploads/2018/01/SSO-Jan-2018_Shoffner_Final.pdf

Shoffner, M., Alsup, J., Garcia, A., Haddix, M., Moore, M., Morrell, E., Shaafsma, D., . . . Zuidema, L. A. (2017). *What is English language arts teacher education?* Retrieved from http://www2.ncte.org/statement/whatiselateachereducation/

Turner, K. H., & Hicks, T. (2016). *Argument in the real world: Teaching adolescents to read and write digital texts.* Heinemann.

Wender, E. (2014). The practice of empathy. *English Journal*, *103*(6), 33–37.

Wilson, B. (2014). Teach the how: Critical lenses and critical literacy. *English Journal*, *103*(4), 68–75.

CHAPTER SEVEN

"Well, I Took It There": Subversive Teaching to (Disrupt) the Test

LEAH PANTHER AND SELENA HUGHES

Students examine three images: an oil painting of Little Red Riding Hood, a pop-art illustration of Eve and a snake in the Garden of Eden, and a photograph of Harvey Weinstein. Rapidly, they call out patterns, and then their teacher, Miss Hughes, responds, "You've said the victims are usually young females, but how about White?" Amber replies, "I wasn't going to take it there, Miss Hughes!" Looking at her student with a wry smile, she replies, "Well, I took it there."

IN MISS HUGHES'S 11TH-GRADE American Literature course, her predominantly Black and Latinx students are encouraged to use literary theories to "take it there," to name and discuss systems of oppression, difference, and examples of erasure in the texts they read. Like many English educators in an increasingly standardized educational system, Miss Hughes's instruction prepares students for a high-stakes end-of-course (EOC) exam required by the urban Catholic school and its larger system. However, Miss Hughes also uses subversive teaching to prepare her culturally and linguistically diverse students to contend with White supremacy embedded in the assessment by resisting normative text-centric approaches to reading.

White Supremacy Will Be on the Test

Miss Hughes teaches at Juan Diego High School,[1] a private Catholic school that accepts students from families living in poverty. Through donors' contributions, fund-raising, and a work-study program, the high school gives students access to a college preparatory curriculum. Student achievement data are used for accreditation decisions and to encourage donor funding, both of which are necessary to meet the school's mission and vision. Thus, Miss Hughes's curriculum is strategically designed to prepare students for an EOC exam.

The Dominance of New Criticism

The EOC is aligned with Common Core State Standards (CCSS) for Reading, which emphasize students' ability to draw understandings and gather information directly from complex and rigorous texts through close reading. Although the CCSS focus on process-oriented approaches to reading instruction, narrower guidelines for curricular development emphasize a text-centric approach to reading instruction that encourages readers to focus on the text itself without personal judgments, connections, or impressions (Newkirk, 2016; Thomas & Newkirk, 2011). Text-centric approaches to reading instruction reflect New Criticism, a literary theory that trains a reader's attention on a close, detailed reading of texts (Richard, 1956). This approach assumes texts have a stable meaning across spaces, time, and readers, making the texts more easily standardized and tested compared to other theoretical approaches to reading (Carillo, 2016; Macaluso, 2014).

The dependence on standardized assessment data from EOCs at Juan Diego is endemic of larger national trends in educational standardization rooted in quasi-experimental studies that value efficiency and effectiveness over meaningful engagement (Coffee et al, 2017; Delpit, 2006). Miss Hughes articulates the tension as "the balance against what I have to do because the school wants me to do it versus this is what my students need to be successful." Her concern is that if she does not get the balance right, students will not be prepared for a future of their choosing, and they will only be prepared to "pass a test." This is troubling when passing Juan Diego's EOC requires students to focus on New Criticism close readings of texts, readings that marginalize or erase her students' cultures and languages. Rather, the text reinforces Whiteness. Whiteness refers to a socially constructed and maintained ideology of beliefs, values, and characteristics that sustain White supremacy within society (Leonardo, 2013). Common characteristics of Whiteness include: "[a] an unwillingness to name the contours of racism; [b] the avoidance of identifying with a racial experience or group; . . . and [c] the minimization of racist legacy" (Leonardo, 2009, p. 32).

Whiteness is power-evasive even as it is powerful (Haviland, 2008). Text-centric approaches to reading can evade making their embedded White supremacy explicit.

For example, one of the four questions associated with Langston Hughes's poem "Mother to Son" (1922) on the EOC asks, "The speaker's use of dialect:" with four options to complete the sentence: "A. builds a level of suspense. B. adds comic relief. C. establishes authentic characterization. D. creates dramatic irony." The question positions the use of African American Language (AAL) as a dialect rather than as a language with its own syntax and grammar system (Boutte, 2008; Smitherman, 2006). Although all languages have dialects (Wolfram & Schilling, 2015), naming features of AAL as a dialect in this instance without naming other authors on the EOC, such as Henry David Thoreau, as having a dialect, recenters Whiteness while positioning AAL and its embedded dialects as an "other."

Although not the correct answer, the inclusion of option B "adds comic relief," further denigrates AAL by allowing a test taker to consider that the language is laughable. Students who speak AAL are "as one ever feel[ing] his . . . two-ness" against the white gaze within the proposed answers (Du Bois, 2015/1903), even as a text-centric approach to the question demands personal responses to the text be withheld. The correct response, "C. establishes authentic characterization," further implies that speaking AAL is universal across Black- and African American–identifying individuals since New Criticism posits a text's meaning is static over place and time. Thus, students who are non-AAL speakers are somehow "inauthentic" members of their racial communities. Although not explicitly stating its presence or power, embedded Whiteness within the question maintains White supremacy.

Subverting New Criticism

This question and others on Juan Diego's EOC diminish, distort, or erase the presence of race and linguistic diversity within works by authors of color through a text-centric approach, but that does not erase the texts' racial histories or the racial identities of the students reading the texts. The CCSS-aligned assessments emphasize text-centric approaches to reading that "insist on the existence of objectivity and, by extension, objective readings," which ultimately "depersonalize" the reading process (Carillo, 2016, p. 29). New Criticism, as a literary theory, claims neutrality, but claiming neutrality does not make any text or literary theory neutral—indeed, *no* text is neutral (Morrell, 2008). Refusal to acknowledge the historical, political, or cultural positioning of a text allows color-blind racism to remain unchallenged. Color blindness, the refusal to name or see race, implicitly and explicitly assumes there is something wrong with Black and Brown bodies because they are erased, unnamed, or ignored (Bonilla-Silva, 2006). When a text and its associated questions on a standardized test refuse to acknowledge race and other differences, it is complicit in color-blind racism and sustaining Whiteness as the objective standard students are expected to conform to (Milner, 2010).

Miss Hughes and her students did not create oppressive systems that protect white supremacy, but if she allows color blindness to silence discussions around differences and marginalization, she is complicit in allowing these systems to continue (Bonil-la-Silva, 2006; Lewis et al, 2007). Acknowledging this power, Miss Hughes pushes students to name differences in texts that span lifestyle, sexuality, gender, and race so that her students' identities are not devalued and erased in the process and so that their own silence does not perpetuate their oppression. In this chapter, we describe Miss Hughes's subversive teaching to challenge text-centric readings prescribed by the EOC, namely, how her students learned to apply layers of literary theory to read *with* and *against* dominant readings of EOC texts and questions.

Teacher Researchers

The authors of this chapter, Selena Hughes and Leah Panther, represent different po-sitionalities within Juan Diego High School. Selena identifies as a Black, able-bodied woman who had been teaching for five years prior to the school year described here. Leah identifies as a White, able-bodied Christian female. I was in my 10th year of teaching and a doctoral candidate when I approached Selena to collaborate on a re-search project on culturally sustaining pedagogies (Paris, 2012). We both engaged in participatory research over the course of a school year, which included regular conver-sations to challenge and decenter our own assumptions and biased understandings of the English canon, reading processes, and pedagogies. Working with racially, ethnical-ly, linguistically, and religiously diverse students, these necessary conversations chal-lenged Leah to acknowledge her own Whiteness and encouraged Selena, who often felt isolated because of her instructional practices focused on equity and justice. Collabo-ratively, we both worked, sometimes imperfectly, to recognize our own positionalities and power in the classroom: power to erase, sustain, or construct students' identities through the texts and pedagogies selected and used within the classroom. Within this collaborative environment, we sought to answer Alim and Paris's (2017) question:

> What if the goal of teaching and learning with youth of color was not ul-timately to see how closely students could perform to White middle-class norms, but rather was to explore, honor, extend, and at times, problematize their cultural practices and investments? (p. 3)

Across the school year, Selena prepared students for the required EOC by teach-ing the New Criticism, text-centric style of reading. However, she also critically cen-tered the valued languages, literacies, and selves of her students by teaching them to notice and resist the Whiteness inherent in the tests' questions. Miss Hughes layered literary theories in students' readings of texts as a subversive teaching practice so students were prepared to identify and name embedded structures on the EOC that devalued their dynamic linguistic and cultural capital (Alim & Paris, 2017; Rosa & Flores, 2017).

Teaching to (Disrupt) the Test

The following classroom vignette shows how Miss Hughes demonstrates her subversive teaching practice: She prepares students to read and respond to texts on a standardized assessment in both text-centric and critical approaches through a layering of literary theories (Borsheim-Black et al, 2014).

"This Is Manist": Layering Feminist Literary Theory

In the chapter's opening vignette, Miss Hughes asked students to summarize the stories depicted across three texts, name the characters, and identify patterns in the antagonists' actions before shifting to archetypal theory to help students name the pattern of predator, a pattern that served to distort White femininity and erase females of color in the texts. This opening peek into Miss Hughes's classroom served as the starting point for teaching and learning about feminist literary theory. The next week, Miss Hughes introduced students to the Bechdel test (Bechdel, 2008). This test was developed by cartoonist Alison Bechdel to create a conversation about feminism, or critiques of male normativity and dominance and the erasure of females, within media. Miss Hughes used a video to introduce her students to feminist literary theory using the test's four questions: Are there at least two female characters? Do the two women have names? Do they speak to each other? Is it about something other than a man? Miss Hughes has students practice the Bechdel test with the children's book *Mufaro's Beautiful Daughters* (Steptoe, 2001) before moving to an audio recording of the short story "The Yellow Wallpaper" (Gilman, 1892/1980). After students summarized the plot of the story and identified its central characters, Miss Hughes asked her students to analyze the story again: this time using an archetype from archetypal theory or the newly learned tools within feminist literary theory. In the following conversation, Janelle and Paula layer archetype and feminist literary theories to analyze the characters:

Janelle: If I had to choose one archetype, I think predator because the husband, John, he was like, he was dominating Jennie [the wife] [sic] I don't think that's feminist because it has to be two women. And the only women in the story are a maid, what's her? Mar-Martha? Martha who is like, the husband is her boss! That's not, she's not about to go [in Martha's voice]. I disagree with what you're doing so I quit. [regular voice] That's her job, right? So there's that. . . So there's two women. They're both being, he's [John] the predator, and he's, he's in control of both of them. So how, this isn't feminist. This is a man book or whatever you would, manist?

Ana: [laughing]

Paula: No, like, yeah to the whole predator thing, but she is, because
            she can't like, she don't have anyone to talk to so she, I don't
            know, makes someone? But it's like, that's her having some of
            that control, right? So yeah, I say this is feminist.

Janelle: [leaning forward smiling, hitting the palm of her hand against
            the desk] The woman in the wallpaper is her! It's not!

Leah: Paula, are you suggesting a woman in [a] relationship with a
            predator needs to, maybe not needs to, but might, uh, might,
            maybe metaphorically, split herself into different pieces?

Paula: [pause] I, I, well, I think Jennie did.

Janelle: Like, being different people when the man is around? [gives Ana
            a meaningful look]

Ana: [laughing]

Paula: Oh. [pause] Yea. Cause she, the wallpaper lady, she wasn't out
            when John came around.

Paula was able to use the Bechdel test and predator archetype to analyze the story noting the husband in the story "was dominating Jennie" in order "to have control over her." The vocabulary pushed her to consider the role of the woman in "The Yellow Wallpaper" as feminist agency: "that's her having some of that control." The layering of archetypal and feminist literary theories supported students' ability to name oppression, particularly male dominance, within the texts.

The layering of literary theories is akin to what Borsheim-Black et al. (2014) term critical literature pedagogy, a pedagogical approach to teaching canonical literature to interrupt embedded dominant ideologies. This includes "reading with" a selected text and "reading against" the same text to interrogate its implicit meanings. As students read *with* the text, they are asked to complete a New Criticism analysis, including summarizing, comprehending the plot, and analyzing an author's word choice. In Miss Hughes's classroom, that sounded like recognizing the patterns between protagonists in several texts, naming the characters in "The Yellow Wallpaper," and tracing character development in *Mufaro's Beautiful Daughters*. However, she does not stop there and asks students to read *against* the dominant readings. For Janelle and Paula, that meant using archetypal theory to recognize predatory behavior and using feminist literary theory to name patriarchal themes and female agency. The intentional layering of literary theories to teach reading prepared Miss Hughes's students to complete standardized assessments while also preparing them to name systems of oppression that are otherwise hidden under the false guise of neutrality (Macaluso, 2014).

The Ethos of Experience: Layering Rhetorical Analysis

In another example, Miss Hughes taught Patrick Henry's (1775) speech at the Virginia Convention to prepare students for a similar revolutionary-era text on the EOC. Henry's speech references slavery and freedom in figurative language, which did not reflect the reality of the enslavement of African peoples during the same period. Miss Hughes was troubled by the erasure and made the decision to teach Patrick Henry's speech alongside *The Interesting Narrative of the Life of Olaudah Equiano* (Equiano, 1789/2001) written by a formerly enslaved Black man and a contemporary of Patrick Henry. She explained:

> [W]hat's interesting is a lot of kids, Patrick Henry uses words like "slave." "We have to fight for freedom," or um, "either we fight for our freedom or we be enslaved." And the kids are like, "Oh, the British are going to enslave them" and they were thinking very literally. Y'know? This is a metaphor. Like, the British aren't going to put them in chains, but there's actual, real slavery happening so, and so we think about that. It's interesting when compared to Equiano where he's talking about actual, real slavery. This is not a metaphor anymore.

By intentionally pairing Equiano with Henry, students were prepared for similar questions on the EOC, such as analyzing the connotative and denotative meanings of terms through New Criticism readings, but students were also able to compare the same terms from two contemporaneous texts—one a counternarrative to the other. This put Henry's connotative references to slavery in contrast to Equiano's (1789) denotative reference, such as "Why are parents to lose their children, brothers their sisters, or husbands their wives? Surely, this is a new refinement in cruelty, which . . . thus aggravates distress, and adds fresh horrors even to the wretchedness of slavery" (p. 89). After comparing connotative and denotative meaning in both texts, Miss Hughes then asked students to consider the impact of the comparative pieces on Henry's ethos or credibility.

In this example, Miss Hughes explicitly taught rhetorical analysis as a literary theory to prepare students to identify the author's purpose, the historical and political context of the text, the audience, and how the author's identity, structures, language, and style may influence the former frames (Haas & Flower, 1988). Rhetorical analysis provides the language for students to discuss the patterns of text, structures, and language across one or more texts, encouraging intertextual connections that acknowledge the reader, the intended audience, and the author as functioning with a particular social, cultural, historical, and political context (Luke, 2012; Warren, 2013). The EOC required students to identify rhetorical devices, including ethos, pathos, and logos. Miss Hughes engaged students in rhetorical reading not only to meet these demands, but also for students to explicitly consider how the historical and political setting influenced the authors' use of ethos, eventually setting students up to critique its effectiveness. Miss Hughes perceived that including Henry's voice without challenging its minimization of racism and unwillingness to accurately name the contours of enslavement would have perpetuated his dominant ideology and positioned the narrative of history with the colonizer rather than the colonized (Domínguez, 2017). Students are not only prepared for the EOC, but also critique the author's work within its social, cultural, historical, and political context that stretches beyond "the four corners of the text" (Newkirk, 2016, p. 305).

Layered Theories to Take it There

In March, after six months of instruction on layering literary theories, Miss Hughes's American Literature course regularly reflected the goals she has for teaching and learning with youth of color. Her students were regularly exploring, honoring, and problematizing texts that reflected both dominant and nondominant communities. For example, one day Miss Hughes began class by asking, "Does the use of archetype limit cultural uniqueness or cultural expression?" while displaying two pieces of art: a stained-glass window from a Catholic cathedral titled *Mary, Comforter of the Afflicted* and a painting by Kehinde Wiley titled *Mary, Comforter of the Afflicted II.*

Within moments, three students were in the middle of an animated discussion. First, Joy explained:

> Okay, so you look at this stain glass thing or whatever, right? You've got this story. You have baby Jesus all happy and holy with his little glowy thing, you've got momma Mary all chill, Joseph on the side and these guys worshipping him, right? Okay, so I was saying they're all White, right? But over here [motioning to the left], no one's White.

Joy first completes the text-centric reading processes associated with the EOC: She summarizes the text, names the characters, and uses textual evidence to support her claims, citing "his little glowy thing" to support her inference that the baby figure represented Jesus. However, she immediately adds another layer to her description, naming the presence and absence of racial diversity. Joy rejected color blindness and named the difference in racial representation between the two images. Derrick added to her comment and extended it:

> You know what I just, I just noticed this. Look you've got the feathers, is that a Native American? . . . In the corner you have a Native American person, right? You've got the person in the blue thing, the way I see it

that's Muslim or whatever and then those kids, maybe that's the friends of the kid that just got shot or whatever and the man in chains down at the bottom, that's all enslaved people, so, you see? Each of these people they represented, the way I see it, they represent people that have been oppressed by . . . White people, right? [*sic*] So this is, this is a statement. I was saying, just before, I was saying the Jesus figure, right? You've got this baby over here just born and you got this boy over here, just died. [*sic*] So you've got like the beginning of Christianity and you've got the end of Christianity . . . that's what happened when Christianity like spread.

Derrick was able to name the various types of difference and oppression represented in Wiley's painting, such as religion, race, physical differences, socioeconomic status, and enslavement. In the process, he named and then rejected dominant readings of the stained-glass text that presented Christianity as a White, European, nonviolent force. He read *with* the texts and then *against* the texts, placing them within a historical and political conversation.

These vignettes represent the realization of Miss Hughes's goals for her students, which were much larger than a standardized assessment, and her agentive interpretation of the standardized assessment's requirements to meet these purposes.

Implications

Although Paula, Janelle, Joy, and Derrick do not represent every student in Miss Hughes's classroom, the conversations they initiated and sustained were evidence that Miss Hughes's reading instruction was meeting her goals of students reading *with* the texts on the mandated EOC and *against* them by using different literary theories to problematize and resist color blindness and erasure. To enact similar instruction, English educators must study the texts and types of questions that routinely appear on English assessments to consider which literary theories will best prepare students to meet various goals. Drawn from our own conversations, we offer these questions as a starting point for similar conversations:

- What content knowledge will students need to read the text (e.g., specialized language, intertextuality) and respond to the questions?
- What reading practices will students need to read the text (e.g. summarizing, using textual support) and respond to the questions?
- What dominant ideologies are embedded in the text and/or its questions (e.g. Eurocentrism, colorblindness, standard English)?
  - Do students have access to literary theories or tools to identify the dominant ideologies?
  - Do students have the language to name the dominant ideologies?

- ○ How will the literary theory and language be explicitly taught without giving up, sacrificing, or denigrating students' languages, literacies, or cultures?
- • What is the historical and political context of the text and/or its questions? The social or cultural context of the reader?
  - ○ Is the context provided?
- • Does it include an accurate and/or positive historical representation of the accomplishments, values, and beliefs of a culturally diverse population (Hollins, 2015)?

These questions reveal unconscious bias within the traditional New Criticism readings of English standardized tests. Once realized, educators are able to name and resist color-blind racism, Whiteness, and othering through the layering of literary theories within their own instruction.

Conclusion

Miss Hughes rejected the feigned neutral stance of mandated assessments and supported students' ability to name and discuss racism, sexism, religious oppression, and erasure of differences through the layering of literary theories. (Botzakis et al, 2014) similarly agree that standards and their associated assessments are, by nature, formulaic and narrow; they are not inherently bad but can reduce teaching to a checklist rather than one of the many complex tools at a teacher's disposal for curricular design. Miss Hughes made complex, agentive decisions about how to prepare her students for mandated assessments that were informed, but not governed, by the standards. By creating a foundation in the curriculum that valued her students' humanity, Miss Hughes explicitly built students' capacity to contend with White supremacy within mandated assessments.

Note

[1] Juan Diego High School is a pseudonym.

References

Alim, H. S., & Paris, D. (2017). What is culturally sustaining pedagogy and why does it matter? In D. Paris & H. S. Alim (Eds.), *Culturally sustaining pedagogies: Teaching and learning for justice in a changing world* (pp. 1–24). Teachers College Press.

Bechdel, A. (2008). *The essential dykes to watch out for.* Houghton Mifflin Harcourt.

Bonilla-Silva, E. (2006). *Racism without racists: Color-blind racism and the persistence of inequality in America.* Roman & Littlefield.

Borsheim-Black, C., Macaluso, M., & Petrone, R. (2014). Critical literature pedagogy: Teaching canonical literature for critical literacy. *Journal of Adolescent & Adult Literacy, 58,* 123–133.

Botzakis, S., Burns, L. D., Hall, L. A. (2014). Literacy reform and Common Core State Standards: Recycling the autonomous model. *Language Arts, 91*, 223–235.

Boutte, G. S. (2008). Teaching African American English speakers: Expanding educators and student repertoires. In M. Brisk (Ed.). *Language, culture, and community in teacher education* (pp. 47–70). Routledge.

Carillo, E. C. (2016). Reimagining the role of the reader in the Common Core State Standards. *English Journal, 105*(3), 29–35.

Coffee, A. C., Stutelberg, E. B., Clemets, C. H., & Lensmire, T. J. (2017). Precarious and undeniable bodies: Control, waste, and danger in the lives of a White teacher and her students of color. In S. Hancock & C. A. Warren (Eds.), *White women's work: Examining the intersectionality of teaching, identity, and race* (pp. 45–67). Information Age Publishing.

Delpit, L. (2006). *Other people's children: Cultural conflict in the classroom.* The New Press.

Domínguez, M. (2017). 'Se hace puentes al andar': Decolonial teacher education as a needed bridge to culturally sustaining and revitalizing pedagogies. In D. Paris & H. S. Alim (Eds.), *Culturally sustaining pedagogies: Teaching and learning for justice in a changing world* (pp. 225–246). Teachers College Press.

Du Bois, W. E. B. (2015). *Souls of black folk.* Routledge. (Original work published 1903).

Equiano, O. (2001). *The interesting narrative of the life of Olaudah Equiano.* Broadview Press. (Original work published 1789).

Gilman, C. P. (1980). *The Charlotte Perkins Gilman reader: The yellow wallpaper, and other fiction.* Pantheon Books. (Original work published 1895).

Haas, C., & Flower, L. (1988). Rhetorical reading strategies and the construction of meaning. *College Composition and Communication, 39*, 167–183.

Haviland, V. S. (2008). "Things get glossed over": Rearticulating the silencing power of whiteness in education. *Journal of Teacher Education, 59*, 40–54.

Henry, P. (1775, March). *Speech at the Virginia convention.* Virginia Convention. Richmond. Retrieved from https://avalon.law.yale.edu/18th_century/patrick.asp.

Hollins, E. R. (2015). *Culture in school learning: Revealing the deep meaning* (3rd ed.). Routledge.

Hughes, L. (2011). *Selected poems of Langston Hughes.* Vintage. (Original work published 1959).

Leonardo, Z. (2009). *Race, Whiteness, and education.* Routledge.

Leonardo, Z. (2013). *Race frameworks: A multidimensional theory of racism and education.* Teachers College Press.

Lewis, C., Enciso, P., & Moje, E. B. (2007). *New directions in sociocultural research on literacy.* Erlbaum.

Luke, A. (2012). Critical literacy: Foundational notes. *Theory into Practice, 51*(1), 4–11.

Macaluso, M. (2014). Trending bedfellows: The teaching of literature and critical approaches. *The English Journal, 104*(6), 78–80.

Milner, H. R. IV. (2010). What does teacher education have to do with teaching? Implications for diversity studies. *Journal of Teacher Education, 61*, 118–131.

Morrell, E. (2008). *Critical literacy and urban youth: Pedagogies of access, dissent, and liberation.* Routledge.

Newkirk, T. (2016). Unbalanced literacy: Reflections on the common core. *Language Arts, 93*, 304–311.

Paris, D. (2012). Culturally sustaining pedagogy: A needed change in stance, terminology, and practice. *Educational Researcher, 41*(3), 93–97.

Richard, I. (1956). *Practical criticism: A study in literary judgment.* Mariner.

Rosa, J., & Flores, N. (2017). Unsettling race and language: Toward a raciolinguistic perspective. *Language in Society, 46*, 621–647.

Smitherman, G. (2006). *Word from the mother: Language and African Americans*. Routledge.

Steptoe, J. (2001). *Mufaro's beautiful daughters*. Live Oak Media.

Thomas, M., & Newkirk, T. (2011). Can readers really stay within the standards lines? *Education Week, 93*(4), 28–29.

Warren, J. E. (2013). Rhetorical reading as a gateway to disciplinary literacy. *Journal of Adolescent & Adult Literacy, 56*, 391–399.

Wolfram, W., & Schilling, N. (2015). *American English: dialects and variation* (Vol. 25). John Wiley & Sons.

CHAPTER EIGHT

Inquiry Ignites! Pushing Back Against Traditional Literacy Instruction

JILL STEDRONSKY AND KRISTEN HAWLEY TURNER

A DECADE AGO, THE Common Core State Standards (CCSS) identified close reading as a fundamental skill of literacy. The creators of the standards defined close reading as focusing on "what lies within the four corners of the text" (Coleman & Pimentel, 2012, p. 4). This definition suggested a return to New Criticism, a literary theory that valued authorial intention above reader interpretation and influenced schools such as Jill's to adopt a rigid approach to teaching close reading. As an eighth-grade teacher of reading and writing, Jill experienced a dramatic shift away from reader response as her department revised its curriculum to meet the demands of the CCSS.

Her district's goal to increase standardized test scores that were associated with CCSS pushed instruction into formulaic, reductive patterns. To teach close reading, Jill was encouraged to *tell* her students the theme of a story, rather than having them inquire into the text itself. "Fear of failure" (Turner, 2010, p. 125) drove the lessons and curricular changes. To increase rigor, another call of the CCSS, the faculty added several classics to the curriculum. Although students struggled, fake-read, and Googled summaries of the books, Jill and her colleagues applauded that the students were reading demanding texts that would challenge their close-reading skills.

However, Jill began to notice that student writing about these books was formulaic; many relied on teacher-identified themes, standardized topic sentences, and simplistic outlines to help them write something that resembled an essay. As her district's test scores decreased, rather than increased as they had hoped, Jill questioned her practice. Through research and reflection, she developed a new philosophy: Close reading cannot live within a single text; it demands the reader bring personal beliefs, questions, and challenges to the text (Wilson & Newkirk, 2011).

Subverting the Norms of Close Reading

Although the idea of close reading was not new to literature studies, the CCSS made it central in middle and high school English language arts classrooms. However, the limited definition embedded in CCSS did not fully capture the essence of reading closely. Culler (2010) argued that close reading, as a practice, is not clearly defined, although scholars of literature, regardless of their theoretical stance, agree that it is necessary. Likewise, Jill agreed that close reading is an essential skill. Students need to learn "deep sustained reading" (Wilson & Newkirk, 2011, para. 3), or what Newkirk (2010) has called *slow reading*, which allows them to savor texts, "returning to passages that sustain and inspire" (para. 13). She concurred with Beers and Probst (2017), who said, "The most important thing we do with our children is to ask them to consider how they might have revised their thinking as a result of reading" (p. 162). Therefore, Jill vowed to disrupt the notion of close reading in her classroom—to make it an opportunity for students to examine themselves within the world. To do so, she needed to subvert the norms that had been adopted by her school.

As a teacher consultant for the National Writing Project, Jill's beliefs stand in direct contrast to the idea that close reading is, by itself, a fundamental skill worthy of test prep activities. Instead, Jill believes that to develop critical thinkers, she needs to engage her students in reading and writing that ignites their passions and reorients their thinking beyond their own experiences. Her experience in the classroom, coupled with her research, has led her to articulate the following values:

- Students must do projects for an authentic audience that will have some kind of impact on the world (Achor, 2010; Frankl, 2006; Pink, 2012).
- Reading and writing skills should be taught in the context of authentic work (Achor, 2011; Frankl, 2006).
- Authentic inquiry does not begin with a thesis statement but with an exploration that takes time (Kuhlthau et al, 2015).
- Inquiry requires deep reading and critical thinking (Daniels & Ahmed, 2015; Kuhlthau et al., 2015).
- Students must have choice and direct their own learning to challenge themselves (Beers & Probst, 2017; Daniels & Ahmed, 2015; Pink, 2012).

Her stance means that she must subvert the traditional practices that permeate her district. She accomplishes her goals by making authenticity and inquiry the cornerstones of her instruction. The remainder of the chapter details Jill's focus by (a) describing critical moves she made to put readers at the center of her classroom and (b) sharing her big-picture mind-set as she conceptualized an entire year of inquiry.

Seeking Authenticity

Jill made two important decisions in her quest for authenticity: (a) She abandoned the common, required texts, and (b) she shifted to a gradeless classroom. Both of these moves required Jill to take a stand in her practice. Just as she knew that grades could potentially limit curiosity and creativity for her students who always wanted to earn an A, she also knew that giving students *real* choices in the texts they read could inspire more critical and close reading than any list of texts selected by adults.

Although the district curriculum mandated required texts and asked all teachers to provide students with a "similar" experience, Jill's research found that choice was essential (Beers & Probst, 2017). If she wanted to offer an authentic experience, she needed to abandon the prescribed curriculum created by adults who believed *their* choices should be the children's choices. Although her colleagues argued against her that children did not know what they needed, Jill held her ground. She knew her department's mission: Advance students as readers, writers, speakers, listeners, and critical thinkers. She also knew that to advance her students, she needed to give them true choice in their reading.

Jill broke from her department's curricular mandates and began asking her students about what they wanted to read. She gathered information on their interests, their passions, and their curiosities. She shared short texts—poems, stories, news articles—as models of her own reading and opportunities to spark inquiry. At the end of each class, she asked students what they wanted to read the next day. She spent time in the evening finding texts that matched their desires. Soon, students were sending her reading material to share with the class, and eventually, each individual was able to select texts that engaged him or her and abandon texts that did not. Her eighth graders began to read authentically, acting like real readers who have the power to control their own reading lives. Jill became subversive, moving drastically away from the curriculum that other teachers were following.

Freedom from required texts was tempered by another traditional practice: grades. Students in her district chased the A, and Jill knew that to maintain an authentic environment, she would have to rethink her grading system. Her research and experience showed that motivation had to be intrinsic, not from a letter or number, and of course, she knew that real readers were not graded on their reading. Therefore, Jill decided to subvert another system at her school. Despite the fact that she was required to input grades and submit progress reports, she went gradeless.

Her students maintained weekly reflection logs where they discussed their learning, their struggles, and their wants and/or needs. Jill used the logs to make formative assessments as a space for conversation, as the starting point for conferences, and as the impetus for small-group or whole-class instruction. At the end of the quarter, students wrote letters to their parents describing their reflections, learning, and thoughts, and Jill wrote detailed progress reports in lieu of entering traditional grades. Assessment became part of learning rather than a reward or punishment. Through their reflections and goal setting, as well as Jill's close monitoring of them as individuals, students became better readers.

Jill's administrators and her students' parents understandably questioned her practice. Why was she not entering the required grades in the system? How could they know how their child was doing in comparison to peers without grades? Through open communication, justification of her practice based in research, and evidence of her students' growth, she was able to turn these questions into support of her practice. Some of this evidence came from improved test scores; however, Jill also maintained a "Student Lives" spreadsheet that contained an extensive, detailed list of students' skills, interests, past scores, struggles, and personal information. She used this information to write progress reports, converse with parents during meetings, and contribute to team meetings regarding individual students. Her subversion was supported by data. Jill knew her students better than she had in the past; the data she collected on each individual student showed that he or she improved in reading skills. She was helping them to build close-reading skills that they could transfer across texts of all kinds.

Igniting Inquiry

After committing to the two decisions described in the previous section (eliminating required texts and grades), Jill turned to the work of planning her curriculum. Curious by what intrinsically motivated students, Jill learned that all human beings' "richest experiences . . . come from when [they] are doing something that matters, doing it well, and doing it in the service of a cause larger than [themselves]" (Pink, 2012, p. 145). Jill knew that she needed to ask her students to do real inquiry into themselves and others and that close reading was an important tool in inquiry. However, she also knew that igniting inquiry could not happen through teaching close reading in a traditional way.

To truly ignite inquiry, value her students' interests, and develop skills of critical thinking through close-reading practices, Jill knew that she had to think beyond a single unit in terms of planning. Instead, she structured a yearlong inquiry to give students abundant time to read, discuss, and shift their ideas as they explored a topic. She wanted them to read deeply about questions that they developed, ones that mattered to them, and create products that reflected their learning—not ones that simply asked them to regurgitate facts from their research.

Her redesigned classroom became a place of experiences and growth, a place where skills were obtained because students had the desire to read and write. Jill served as guide, providing feedback on individual inquiries. She taught reading and writing skills in the context of her students' own work, not from a list of required content. Alongside this approach, Jill conceptualized the year as ongoing discovery, where students' interests led to questions that developed the curriculum. To spark their interest, thinking, and questioning, Jill shared her own inquiries, modeled her reading strategies, and invited them to suggest topics for the next day's conversations. Rather than units, Jill organized the year in five phases:

1. Developing a questioning stance
2. Sparking curiosity
3. Journey of exploration
4. Finding a focus and immersing deeply
5. Creating a product of learning

Developing a questioning stance

Jill began the year by guiding her students to develop a questioning stance, and through this stance, her students gained skills in close reading. On the first day of class, she invited students to brainstorm topics that interested them. By Day 3, Jill shared an article that she herself had read and thought aloud about the questions it raised for her. She asked the students to respond to her think aloud by writing their own questions on sticky notes. These sticky notes were the first in what became a wall full of curiosities that were sparked throughout the marking period. Each day, class ended with students writing ideas—some related to the conversation of the day and some suggesting future topics for reading.

This practice valued student voice in a way that challenged traditional instructional practices. Jill made it clear that she cared about her students' thoughts and questions. After setting this expectation of herself as a teacher, she turned to instruction in close-reading practices. Inspired by Beers and Probst (2016), she modeled critical reading through three primary questions that are transferable across texts: (1) What surprised me? (2) What has changed, challenged, or confirmed what I already know? and (3) What does the author think I already know? She taught these questions as the basis for responding to *all* texts—fiction and nonfiction, poetry and short story, social media and article.

Jill brought many texts to the class for common reading, all chosen in response to the input from the students each day. She also invited students to share texts with the group. Students practiced reading through the lens of the three questions individually and collaboratively, their reading always anchored with Jill's prompts about what questions their reading sparked. The simultaneous nature of prompting the students' own questions, alongside the reinforcement of transferable questions that could be asked of all texts, helped to establish a questioning stance among the young readers.

Sparking curiosity

The overarching goal of instruction was to help children find purpose so that they could guide their own reading and writing and, ultimately, inquire about topics that would help them to grow as individuals and/or to impact their communities. To explore their purposes, students created Ikigais (Kudo, 2018) and Vision Boards (Canfield, n.d.).

A Japanese concept, Ikigai is a *reason for being*, and this purpose sits at the intersection of four areas: passion, vocation, profession, and mission. To spark curiosity, Jill asked her students to explore the following questions connected to these categories: What do I love? What am I good at? What can I get paid to do? and What does the world need? As Jill worked toward her goals of reading, writing, speaking, and listening, the Ikigai became a tool for students to think, write, and share with others. Ultimately, it sparked questions that led students to reading material.

A second source of sparks for students came from vision boards. Vision boards are powerful tools that help students create a mental image of what they want their lives to be (Canfield, n.d.). To help students be reflective about who they are and who they want to be, Jill had each student keep a digital vision board from the beginning of the school year. Daniels and Ahmed (2015) noted that before children can question the world, "they question their own identity and grapple with the eternal adolescent question: Who am I?" (p. 18). Jill had her students begin with simple goals about school and their personal lives, but as they continued to read, they dug deeper into themselves. They saved quotes and images, set new goals for themselves, and began to map out meaningful future lives.

While students were exploring themselves, Jill continued to share her own reading, which sparked her own curiosity. She used a variety of articles and the United Nations Sustainable Development Goals to invite conversation and exploration—and more sticky notes on the walls. Through structured conversations, students began to connect the growing wall of questions to their own purposes. In some cases, they self-organized into groups that began to explore similar topics. In other cases, they found, perhaps for the first time in their education, a chance to explore a topic that truly mattered to them.

For example, Matias was fascinated with the Bermuda Triangle. He tackled complex texts, and in a conference with him, Jill suggested he utilize a close-reading strategy that was helpful in breaking down these unfamiliar texts. She modeled how to illustrate the passages that were most difficult. Matias found this strategy extremely helpful, and his illustrations became such an important part of his inquiry that he ended up using them in two of his final products: an article and a TED Talk. Matias, like his peers, was becoming a better reader because he was engaged in the texts he was reading.

Journey of exploration

Embracing a year of inquiry required that students have time to explore many different texts and time to think, write, reflect, and discuss. Jill had to be flexible. Students needed to be able to formulate questions about the world and themselves and be encouraged and permitted to change focus. True inquiry into any curiosity had to follow its own path, not the one the teacher created based on a structure of marking periods and grades. Students tracked their explorations by drawing mind maps. The maps helped them to see how real inquiry worked, and they discussed their individual journeys in small groups to clarify thoughts and narrow ideas they wanted to explore further. They had the freedom to let their reading and questioning alter their intended path—and they loved it.

Zoe was a passionate musician who lived in a home filled with music. It was not a surprise, then, that she started her explorations about the history of musical instruments. However, about halfway through the school year, Zoe's curiosity led her down a new road, one that was sparked by the close reading skills she had been developing. Because she started to read using the questioning stance Jill had taught, Zoe became critical of the textbook she was using in her social studies class. Shocked that she had previously accepted so much of the information in nonfiction (text) books as truth, Zoe now understood close reading meant she also needed to be critical of the source. Her inquiry path shifted dramatically, but she was engaged. She began her new inquiry into researching and reading about bias in textbooks. Excitedly, Zoe created a survey which she e-mailed to the assistant superintendent of curriculum. She requested access to the entire student body so that they could take her survey about textbooks and possible biases. Zoe organized her data into pie charts to communicate her results in a TED Talk. She also felt compelled to share this information with the assistant superintendent of curriculum so that the district might rethink the use of textbooks as the central source for some of its history classes.

Dedicating half the year to developing a questioning stance and identifying purposes and curiosities required that Jill subvert the prescribed curriculum. However, she knew that she was teaching important literacy skills and that her students were beginning to practice close reading in a way that transcended performance on a standardized test.

Finding a focus and immersing deeply

Eventually, with unbounded exploration, students began to settle into a question(s)—a curiosity that fueled their daily reading and writing. Guila's interests began with police brutality and the Black Lives Matter movement, but her curiosity shifted, and she ultimately settled into an inquiry related to abortion rights. She developed these questions: Why are people pro-life and why are people pro-choice? Which political parties are for and against abortion? Which religions allow abortions to be done? Which countries allow abortions? Similar to Guila, Sam was led by her curiosity from one topic to another. She moved from questioning why students in schools say the Pledge of Allegiance to asking how schools might affect the teenage brain. Her focused inquiry question became, "How can school labels affect a child?" Her final article was titled "The Genius and Insanity Link." With weekly inquiry circle discussions, conferences, mind mapping, writing, and workshopping, students were able to narrow their thoughts into a single question. However, they were *always* allowed to "disrupt" (Beers & Probst, 2017) their thoughts and shift their question to reflect their new findings.

They maintained daily logs (see Figure 8.1: Collin's Inquiry Log) to note the day's focus/question and jot down the day's work: reading, listening to videos, taking notes, conferencing, searching, and so on. They examined each text through the transferable questions that Jill had introduced them to earlier in the year and summarized their reading in a question, which ultimately fueled the next day's reading.

As part of their immersion, they wrote to advance their reading, writing, and critical thinking skills. They shared writing with peers for feedback and with Jill, who provided individual and small-group instruction in reading and writing based on the work her students produced. In keeping with Jill's new stance, they were not graded. This process helped students to narrow their curiosities into a single line of inquiry.

The questions they documented in their logs helped them to narrow their inquiries, and some students focused on a topic early in the process. Others traveled lengthier paths, allowing the reading sparked by one question to send them on a different journey. The process was messy, just like real inquiry can be, but for her eighth graders, it felt natural, not schoolish. As they learned, they became excited to share their learning. Uncovering what they wanted to share—and with whom—further narrowed their focus and allowed them to immerse deeper into the research.

Creating a product of learning

In Jill's desire for authenticity, she knew her students' inquiries had to result in tangible, real products that had an impact on their lives. Therefore, Jill offered many possibilities for students to share their learning. Charlie, who had been collecting data via social media about teen pressure and depression, wanted adults to be aware of the consequences of depression on youth and felt this outlet would be a good match for his goals. He thought he could also be one of the speakers at his school's next Empowerment Day. Josie, on the other hand, decided to take her research public in a different way: She planned to stand outside of the local grocery story and convince people to stop using plastic bags.

To expand the opportunities for students to share their voices beyond the classroom community, Jill created a TED-Ed club. The club allowed the eighth graders to develop TED Talks. Collin, who had been studying badgers, immediately knew that he wanted to share with the world that a badger's immunity to snake venom might help humans create antidotes to snakebites. He cared deeply that people know about this

Figure 8.1.

Collin's Inquiry Log

Date	What I did this period	What I plan to do next
12/10/18	Looked up books on this topic	Read some of these books and find more and where they are located

Ideas I am exploring and questions or wonderings I am having:
I would like to learn about venom and venom resistance.

Date	What I did this period	What I plan to do next
12/11/18	Watched videos on self immunization and found out where some of the books I want are	Read the books and watch more videos

Ideas I am exploring:
Venom and venom resistance

Date	What I did this period	What I plan to do next
12/12/18	Found trusted sites and people that I could use during my research	Use these sites and people in my research

Ideas I am exploring:
Venom and venom resistance

Date	What I did this period	What I plan to do next
12/13/18	Watched a video on how venom worked and how it has a lot of medical advantages	Keep watching videos by this person

Ideas I am exploring:
Venom

Date	What I did this period	What I plan to do next
12/17/18	Watched a video about the honey badger because they are known for their resistance to venom	Finish the video

Ideas I am exploring:
The honey badger

possibility. Derek combined his love of writing poetry with the creation of a TED Talk to enlighten others about the harmfulness of cancer drugs.

As the children shared how they thought they could have an impact on the world with their learning, it sparked others. Guila, for example, decided to go to the board of education about changing the electives and subjects taught in middle school. Just as students' inquiry varied, so did their products of learning. Jill led her students in brainstorming exercises that identified authentic audiences and opportunities, yet the students' inquiries led them to newfound knowledge that inspired new ideas for sharing. This pedagogy connected close-reading skills to powerful public writing. Instead of close reading living within a single text, which is how it was traditionally taught, close reading became fuel for authentic inquiry and activism. Through subversion in her practice, Jill helped her students to become advocates.

Seeking Authenticity and Inquiry as Subversive Practice

As a teacher of language arts, Jill believed in the power of critical reading and effective writing. She knew that close-reading skills are important in literacy development. Yet she also recognized that traditional practices of teaching close reading, those that were predominantly influenced by a need to score higher on standardized tests, did not allow for authentic reading on the part of her students, nor did they encourage her students to engage meaningfully in inquiries that would help them to think deeply about themselves and the world around them.

To address this disconnect in her teaching, she made a decision to subvert the traditional practices that permeated her district. Her stance challenged the status quo, it ruffled her colleagues and administrators, it confused parents, and it inspired her students. With freedom from grades and permission to follow curiosities and abandon lines of inquiry, the young readers in her classroom flourished. Because students cared about their inquiry, they cared about their reading and their writing. Jill's students approached each day with vigor and were driven to search more accurately, to find varied resources, and find good, research-supported evidence. They sought books and wanted depth.

One student wrote in his letter of reflection, "The inquiry project made me develop many skills. During this, I learned how to judge a website and information, deciphering important parts of articles, and writing to a non-specialized audience." This student, like so many others, indicated a desire to continue the inquiry beyond the class—to continue to read and write in authentic and meaningful ways. Jill ignited a fire of curiosity in her eighth-grade class, and her students' learning resulted in their lives being changed. Additionally, Jill is confident that they have mastered the skills of close reading needed for authentic inquiry. To accomplish this outcome, Jill needed to trust in herself, to trust in her students, and to step away from traditional pedagogies. She had to rethink the purpose of close reading and connect it to real-world literacy practices. Through her own curiosity—through seeing her teaching as an inquiry in and of itself—Jill was able to transform her pedagogy and her students' learning.

References

Achor, S. (2010). *The happiness advantage*. Crown Publishing.

Beers, G. K., & Probst, R. E. (2016). *Reading nonfiction: Notice & note stances, signposts, and strategies*. Heinemann.

Beers, G. K., & Probst, R. E. (2017). *Disrupting thinking: Why how we read matters*. Scholastic.

Canfield, J. (n.d.). How to create an empowering vision board [Blog post]. Retrieved from www.jackcanfield.com/blog/how-to-create-an-empowering-vision-book/

Coleman, D., & Pimentel, S. (2012). Revised publisher's criteria for the Common Core State Standards in English Language Arts and literacy Grades 3–12. Retrieved from http://www.corestandards.org/assets/Publishers_Criteria_for_3-12.pdf

Culler, J. (2010). The closeness of close reading. *ADE Bulletin, 149*, 20–25. doi:10.1632/ade.149.20

Daniels, H., & Ahmed, S. K. (2015). *Upstanders: How to engage middle school hearts and minds with inquiry*. Heinemann.

Frankl, V. E. (2006). *Man's search for meaning*. Beacon Press. (Original work published 1946).

Kudo, A. (2018). *My little Ikigai journal*. St. Martin's Press.

Kuhlthau, C. C., Maniotes, L. K., & Caspari, A. K. (2015). *Guided inquiry learning in the 21st century* (2nd ed.). ABC-CLIO.

Newkirk, T. (2010). The case for slow reading. *Educational Leadership, 67*(6), 6–11. Retrieved from http://www.ascd.org/publications/educational-leadership/mar10/vol67/num06/The-Case-for-Slow-Reading.aspx

Pink, D. H. (2012). *Drive: The surprising truth about what motivates us*. Riverhead Books.

Turner, K. H. (2010). Fighting the fear of failure: Resisting the effects of THE TEST in a thinking-based writing class. In D. M. Moss & T. Osborne (Eds.), *Critical essays on resistance in education* (pp. 125–141). Peter Lang.

Wilson, M. & Newkirk, T. (2011). Can readers really stay within the standards lines? *Education Week, 31*(14), 28–29. Retrieved from https://www.edweek.org/ew/articles/2011/12/14/14wilson.h31.html

CHAPTER NINE

"Climb Into Their Skin": Whiteness and the Subversion of Perspective

ANNA MAE TEMPUS AND CAREY APPLEGATE

HE WALKED IN LATE, and he walked in wearing the flag of the Confederacy, a long-dead racist project seeing its resurgence, apparently, in the White youth of Wisconsin. Several students exchanged looks as he found his seat and turned his attention quietly to me.

It was 10 minutes into class and a month into my first year of teaching. I, Anna Mae, was 22 years old, just six years older than this student. We had several things in common, most obviously our race; his White freckled hands resembled my own, as did his blue eyes. When we chatted about upcoming assignments, our accents and slang were the same. But it was his choice of attire that day that opened a chasm between us; I was suddenly overwhelmed with the lifetimes of horrific pain and boundless fear that went into making this symbol of the Confederacy something so easily wearable on a T-shirt.

I had a choice between silence and action. Silence meant looking away, enveloping myself within my White privilege, and exercising unity with my fellow White teachers who had also looked away from him that day. This silence, I recognized in that moment, was a weaponized tool of White supremacy.

My conversation with him was not perfect. Attempting to appeal to his humanity, I said, "Perhaps you don't realize how other students might now view you as someone who hates them, as someone who wants to see them hurt. Wearing this may cause others to feel afraid in this building, where they should be safe." Throughout the conversation, my student was quiet. He did not respond in anger or defiance, but at this comment, he lifted his chin and asked me slowly, "How could something *I* wear cause *them* to feel *unsafe*?"

Although this question was likely meant as a rhetorical stop to the conversation, I sensed a kernel of sincerity behind it. This student clearly had not had the opportunity to grapple with his place in the world and its context. His perspective, that of a White middle-class boy, had not just been centered on conversations in and out of the classroom but also allowed him to escape and neglect his own position in history. This continual centering of his White perspective is what empowered him to wear what he wore and to ask what he asked. Personally, I believe he likely knew he would receive pushback. I just do not think he ever expected it from someone who looked like us.

Traditional Explorations in Teaching Perspective

Racism is a structure, not an event.
—Kauanui (2016, p.1)

A short search online for how one might teach perspective in literature reveals myriad unit plans, activities, and how-to guides. Scholastic and Prestwick in-house bloggers offer helpful objectives and inquiries in articles, and English language arts teachers across all grade levels post to pages such as Teachers Pay Teachers with handouts tackling point of view in everything from *Macbeth* to Angie Thomas's 2017 young adult novel *The Hate U Give*.

Dissecting and evaluating point of view are two of those major foundational skills and for excellent reason. Examining point of view challenges students to understand characters and narrators complexly, as well as analyze how plotlines, style choices, and content are shaped through perspective. Teaching this at the high school level can be deceptively simple. It frequently involves reading short stories, quizzes on first- or third-person narratives, and perhaps even discussing "unreliable" narrators. Due to a Eurocentric literary canon, much of the conversation around style and content is shaped around a White identity, even when the characters are not overtly racialized.

Subverting the Teaching of Perspective

Regrettably missing from our dialogue with students is how our White-centered literary canon can create gaps in this type of instruction. First and foremost, a lack of fully developed and nuanced Black and Brown characters in traditional classroom texts means that students are continually learning about point of view through the lens of white people. Rudine Sims-Bishop (1990) wrote famously on the theory of windows, mirrors, and sliding glass doors, positing the idea that children need a variety of perspectives in literature to receive a fuller view of the world. However, simply plugging in texts that feature characters of color without providing students fuller context and tools with which to analyze the purpose of race within all stories does a disservice to our students' growth. "Dominant narratives," writes sociolinguist Dr. Lamar Johnson (2018), "often sustain whiteness, white supremacy, and anti-blackness by privileging the stories and voices of white people" (p. 113). To teach perspective traditionally, by which I mean not acknowledging the role race plays in perspective and in the narratives we teach, is to uphold White supremacy in our classrooms.

In 1996, the National Council of Teachers of English and the International Literacy Association (NCTE/IRA, 1996) jointly published a list of Standards for the English Language Arts, the first of which is that

> students read a wide range of print and non-print texts to build an understanding of texts, of themselves, and of the cultures of the United States and the world; to acquire new information; to respond to the needs and demands of society and the workplace; and for personal fulfillment. Among these texts are fiction and nonfiction, classic and contemporary works.

Although this standard creates space in the English classroom for perspectives beyond the canon, it does not explicitly call for critical readings of those texts or, in fact, any interrogation of dominant narratives. Strictly speaking, students could read a wide range of texts and still miss out on a wide range of perspectives. The act of *centering* diverse voices and experiences allows students into a better understanding of different contexts and perspectives through textual analysis. In other words, it is not just important that a novel include people of color; that those people of color are representative of a variety of different experiences—not simply representative of stereotypes or literary tropes—is also critical. In other words, including a variety of diverse voices in the curriculum is not only essential; there is also power in the voices and agency of those characters within narratives.

Taking an actively anti-racist stance in the English language arts classroom involves helping students navigate perspective through a wide variety of texts and contexts. As part of this process, we can incorporate several of the key principles from Critical Race Theory: race as performance, counter-storytelling, the centrality of lived experiences and experiential knowledge, a consciously social justice–driven agenda, intersectionality, an understanding of social constructions, and the myriad ways that historic events (such as slavery and colonization) influence each of these elements (Ladson-Billings, 2013; Ladson-Billings & Tate, 1995; Lynn & Dixson, 2013; Tatum, 2016). We also draw lessons from critical Whiteness studies scholarship, interrogating our own intersectional subject positions as White female teachers who have benefited from White privilege and the system of racism while also having to navigate other imbalances in power and position (Berchini, 2016; Matias

& Mackey, 2016). We acknowledge that the reluctance of White teachers such as ourselves to speak frankly about racism maintains White power and supremacy. Using a race-conscious framework during critical analysis exercises helps us *and* our students decentralize White perspective as the cultural standard. Furthermore, asking students to make connections between the texts we read and their own experiences helps them gain a deeper understanding of the texts, themselves, and the world we live in.

Teacher Positionality

As a young teacher having grown up in rural Wisconsin, my experience with race was shaped by many of the same factors that affect my students: Because of the severe lack of diversity outside of our major cities, my childhood understanding of other cultures as informed by race was developed through media. Furthermore, my own racial development was quite stunted due to the blind spot inherent to a culture that centralizes and does not question Whiteness. My coming of age was defined by experiences afforded to me through those privileges. For example, I was a reader from a young age, once checking out so many books from our local library that they disqualified me from their youth reading program. Although that detail may cause a sympathetic chuckle, it reveals three aspects of my childhood. One, my local neighborhood had a flourishing public library branch fed by sufficient tax dollars and the support of the surrounding community. Two, I had reliable and safe transportation to and from my library via my trusty bike and safe roads. Three, I had enough free time and stability at home, uninterrupted by caring for family members or working with my parents to pay our bills, that I could read a ridiculous and fortifying amount of literature.

But my racial privilege goes deeper: I saw myself reflected in the eyes of my local authority figures, in my teachers, and in the authors and characters of the books we read. I watched as those who looked, spoke, and joked like me ran their own businesses, became magical wizards, and won the hearts of their communities. Doubting my ability to do and be the same never occurred to me.

Now, as a public school teacher working in a district not two hours from where I sat as a public school student, I frequently grapple with how my privilege creates an unearned but ever-present platform from which I can enact change, whether for the good of my marginalized students or otherwise. In my public school setting, I am given certain freedoms within my work: I can choose the methodology with which I teach certain concepts, I can set the pace necessary for my students to learn those concepts, and I can bring my concerns to the curriculum team and trust I will be heard. However, like many other public schools, the texts my students read, the learning outcomes we assess, and the method of assessment are prescribed to me. Although I actively work against the systems at play through advocacy work in Washington, D.C., as well as local school board meetings, I must tackle the ongoing prompt of "How can I actively disrupt and subvert the curriculum given to me in order to dismantle the White supremacy inherent in this structure?"

In many ways, my privileges create openings for me to be able to do this work. I am, along with every other White teacher, able to spend my privilege by using my voice to push back against the forms of education that would otherwise seek to dominate my students. As I work to carve out a space in my classroom for marginalized and silenced student voices to develop and effect change, I must be constantly aware of how my Whiteness, affluence, and other points of privilege affect how my own voice is heard.

As perspective is inherently tied to identity, English language arts classrooms that subvert this standard have the potential to become radical sites of racial justice, even when they are subjected to prescribed curricula. When I think back to my own high school learning experience, I can easily spot the moments where a conversation on race would not have just been fruitful for our learning but also absolutely crucial to a better understanding of our world and of ourselves. And truly, few better examples exist for how conversations on perspective in literature *can be* than the second-most assigned text (Stotsky, 2010) in America in 2010: *To Kill a Mockingbird* (Lee, 1960).

The Approach

Teachers across America write op-eds on, host productions of, and continually teach this text that offers a look at the American justice system. For those of us unfamiliar with this text, a brief summary: A young White child of a lawyer in 1930s Alabama plays witness to the trial of a disabled Black man, Tom, falsely accused of raping a White woman in town. As the novel builds toward its climax of Tom's lynching in prison, our young protagonist learns lessons about kindness and empathy. As an American text with easy-to-determine themes, metaphors, and perspectives, it presents palatable inquiries into the fabric of our society while still coddling its majority White readership.

Traditional explorations of *Mockingbird* (Lee, 1960) frame it as a coming-of-age novel for the protagonist Scout, and thus, dissections of perspective often focus on her childhood and the loss of her innocence. Many of these interpretations of *To Kill a Mockingbird* (Lee) frame the narrative through Scout's White gaze, which "frames Atticus Finch, a White man, as the hero and frames Tom Robinson, an African American man, as the helpless, crippled victim. The plot . . . centers on Atticus Finch as the antiracist savior who defends Tom Robinson in court" (Borsheim-Black, 2015, pp. 418–419). As with other White-savior tropes, the narrative relies on the perspective of the White characters to drive the audience's understanding of the plot; as readers, we understand the story through the perspective of Scout and, by extension, Atticus. We rely on their understandings of race and class in this small southern town to decode the events surrounding the trial; in this narrative, Atticus is the hero of the story. "These [White-savior] stories have more to do with establishing the morality of White characters than with the lives and experiences of characters of color" (Borsheim-Black, 2019, p. 10). While taking the time to understand the protagonists is valid, a discussion of this novel that lacks considerable forays into the perspectives of the Black and Brown characters does a disservice to all students. It reinforces, perhaps subconsciously (or sometimes consciously), the lesson that White folks' ways of thinking, writing, and being are the *only* valid and important ways to understand a text and the world beyond it. Reaching students solely through a White point of view is an excellent way to ensure our students only understand the world through that perspective:

> *Teaching about white supremacy, whiteness, and anti-blackness is not for the faint of heart* . . . ELA teachers committed to this vision should engage youth in humanizing racial dialogue. (Johnson, 2018, p. 109)

In my unit on *Mockingbird* (Lee, 1960), students work toward contextualizing the novel in order to better understand Black perspectives in the novel. Two particular supplementary texts not only provide historical background but also allow an analysis of point of view to form. Marilyn Nelson's (2009) heartbreaking crown of sonnets titled *A Wreath for Emmett Till* is a reading regarding 14-year-old Till's brutal murder in 1955. After allegedly whistling at a White woman, he was viciously beaten, and his murderers were found not guilty by an all-White, all-male jury. This counterstory (Borscheim-Black, 2019) facilitates an invaluable discussion on how Whiteness worked within the judicial system to uphold the interests and freedoms of White defendants over Black victims. Because the crown of sonnets is written as an elegy from Nelson, a Black woman speaking from the 21st century to Till, a Black boy in the 20th century, it provides an excellent resource to discuss how the text was shaped through Nelson's perspective and identity as well as Till's. When connecting it with *Mockingbird* (Lee), students are then challenged to ask critical questions of Lee as author and Scout as narrator: How does Lee's identity as a White woman affect how this text was shaped? How does Scout, as narrator, limit our understanding of what is truly a Black man's story through her childlike naivete and Atticus's coddling?

Another text that can provide crucial disruption (Ebarvia et al, 2019) of the white-savior perspective in *Mockingbird* (Lee, 1960) is Nina Simone's (1965) performance of "Strange Fruit." Simone's incomparable voice and interview with a reporter provides a haunting overview of the deep trauma that comes from daily mistreatment paired with a near-constant fear of assault and death. And, rather than painting the common White moderate as a benevolent authority of the 1930s, it shines a light on the uglier truth: The White moderate as vindictive and murderous, able to not only lynch Black innocents but also view that as entertainment to be consumed.

After establishing a more accurate understanding of historical context through supplemental texts, my students then participate in an activity which further disrupts their preconceived notions of institutionalized racism. Using actual court cases from throughout the United States from the late 1800s to 2012, the students act as a current-day jury, discuss the charges, and provide me with their verdicts. In each of these cases, an obviously innocent Black defendant was always found guilty by an all-White jury and either executed by the state or lynched. My students are given the bare-bones information of the case presented before the jury, excepting the time period or the races of the individuals involved. Inevitably, as they listen to the details, my students realize that each of the defendants *must* be found innocent. After the activity is over, I read the details of each case aloud. With the first few taking place pre-1970s, my 15- to 16-year-old students find the results obvious as they catch on. However, with the last few, the latest ones, they begin to shake their heads. It serves as a natural point of inquiry for these young adults—they begin asking the questions we later turn into our Essential Questions of the unit: "How is this type of racism legal?" "What culturally allows the juries to behave in this way?" and "What can we do about it all?" These questions are disruptions of the curriculum that happen naturally when we create this kind of space for student voices to come through.

Here is a temptation to end the disruptions, as students are able to speak confidently about the racism of the 1930s. Therein, naturally, lies the danger. Especially in the context of my own room (a northern state with a long progressive history and an 86.2% White population), there is a distinct sense of here and there, of now and then—a line we can comfortably draw between ourselves as northern White folks and those *others*, the southern, racist, "White trash" *others*. Thus lies the issue with the safety of *Mockingbird* (Lee, 1960): when we teach it without continual disruption, students are unable to draw distinct connections to their own world and their own lives, finding within themselves perhaps some of Scout's uncomfortable, idle ignorance or even Bob Ewell's intentionally cruel and parasitic bigotry. Unless taught with the distinct intention to disrupt frequently, *Mockingbird* will remain a pillar of complacent racism in the guise of progressivism. Instead, we must find places throughout the text where we can challenge our students to question whose voices are centered in what conversations, whose perspective is being pushed aside, and whose power is facilitating that positioning. By centering and uplifting the voices of characters of color in our texts, not only do we provide our students with a more accurate and justice-focused understanding of the text, but we also give our students the tools with which to examine the work and themselves on a far deeper level than before.

For example, in Chapter 12 of *Mockingbird* (Lee, 1960), Calpurnia, the family maid and de facto matriarch, takes Scout and her brother to her Black church. Black churches were, as students learn, founded not just as a direct result of segregation but also purposefully as a sacred space of worship and community for Black folks, especially in the South. In this scene, Lula, one of three major Black women named in the entire book, flatly and bluntly tells Calpurnia that she "ain't got no business bringin' white chillun here" (Lee, 1960, p. 63). This is a common point of discussion for the novel, as it is often painted as the first time Scout and Jem experience discrimination. This leads to the broader themes of empathy and connects clearly to Atticus's insistence that the kids attempt to "climb into [someone else's] skin and walk around in it" (Lee, 1960, p. 16). However, a reading of this scene does not and cannot simply end with a pseudo-sense of righteousness over the "hypocrisy" of this scene. Doing so provides students the opportunity to claim "reverse racism" and shut down, rather than engaging with, the text. Instead, I can use perspective as a tool in this moment to shut down the myth of reverse racism and bring my students to a better understanding.

I begin with a short journal activity, asking them to respond to the following prompt: "What is your 'sacred space'? Describe it in detail."

Answers to this question include everything from students' bedrooms, cars, lockers, or athletic fields. Sometimes, especially for my more rural students, it extends to a deer stand, hunting grounds, or a cabin. We share these answers with each other, laugh as we hear some of the outlandish explanations, and make connections as a community. As they finish their discussion, I write a second question on the board and let them absorb it: "What would happen if someone invaded that space that you did **not** want there? How would you handle the situation?"

This time the answers turn thoughtful. Students suggest a conversation to let the person know he or she is not welcome. "What if they refuse to leave?" I prompt. The answers become a bit more forceful: Threats, calling the authorities, or a punch to the face should do it. We discuss the importance of these spaces, why we commonly seek them out, and why we are so quick to defend them against invasion.

This short conversation sets us up for success during Chapter 12. Although some students might protest that Lula should not have been so aggressive toward the children, they are often very quickly answered by other students defending her actions. They insist that Lula, in fact, was not aggressive at all toward *the children* but to Calpurnia, whom she felt was the one allowing the disruption of Lula's sacred space. We invoke the power of rhetorical listening (Diab et al, 2013) when we center the voices of these two Black women rather than the hurt and confusion of our young White narrator. This short conversation helps us understand how Scout's perspective as a white child often gives readers a limited view of the novel's events. By thinking critically about how point of view has shaped the style and content, my students have pushed past a passive reading that allows the rooted White supremacy behind the text to go undisturbed (Diab et al., 2013).

Conclusion

Uninterrogated Whiteness provides a building block to White supremacy through a continual centering of the dominant perspective. Race conversations need to be not only at the forefront of texts such as *Mockingbird* (Lee, 1960) but any text we teach in the modern English language arts classroom as well. Through the lens of perspective, educators can challenge the assumptions of white authors and narrators, including the ways in which a White savior is continually celebrated and centered throughout our popular literature. Texts such as *The Green Mile* (King, 2001), *The Help* (Stockett, 2011), and *Freedom Writers* (Gruwell, 1999) uphold these tropes and systems of power and without a subversive reading, the voices of the characters of color in these and other media will continue to be marginalized and silenced. Our Black and Brown students deserve to not just see themselves in the media we force them to consume but to also be given the tools to "critique, rewrite, and dismantle the damaging narratives that mainstream media has written about them" (Baker-Bell et al, 2017, p. 124).

Antiracism, like any worthwhile ideological commitment, resists simplicity and ease. The work is never done. And so it goes with subversive teaching: It is so much more than the texts we read or do not read. In a modern age of education in which more and more choice is taken away, teachers are often left with a prescribed curriculum that does not accurately reflect the experiences of the students before them. It is therefore not simply the right of the teacher but also our duty to subvert the traditional standards of our disciplines in order to disrupt the White supremacy lurking behind them. We must push back from the inside of these systems of power. Additionally, the role of a primarily White teaching force is to speak directly to our White students about the trauma and marginalization their Black and Brown counterparts face that comes from the racism inherent in our educational system.

Equity work is always incomplete and involves always striving. (Diab et al, 2013, p. 26)

Thus, when a White student walked into my classroom on a chilly October morning wearing a Confederate T-shirt, I recognized the power I can wield in an ongoing battle against White supremacy. This work is vital and radical, and a lack of dedication to it can result in complacency with a status quo that actively works to dominate our students. Without it, we often reinforce the negative and outright toxic ideologies presented in the texts our kids read. I see my student in the eyes of the students of Baraboo, Wisconsin, who in 2018 flashed a Nazi salute on the steps of their county courthouse before their high school prom.

If we wish for our students not just to walk away from our classrooms with a more complex comprehension of the world and the many tensions that exist within it but also to enact systemic change to create a better, more socially just world for all, we must then take the responsibility as their educators to provide them the tools with which they can engage in that paradigm-shift. Anti-racist work is ongoing, and the role of public school teachers within that remains a crucial one as we carve out a space which disrupts, subverts, and dismantles White supremacy within our classrooms, within ourselves, and within the world beyond.

References

Baker-Bell, A., Butler, T., & Johnson, L. (2017). The pain and the wounds: A call for critical race English education in the wake of racial violence. *English Journal, 49*, 116–129.

Berchini, C. (2016). Structuring contexts: Pathways toward un-obstructing race-consciousness. *International Journal of Qualitative Studies in Education, 29*, 1030–1044.

Borsheim-Black, C. (2015). "It's pretty much White": Challenges and opportunities of an antiracist approach to literature instruction in a multilayered White context. *Research in the Teaching of English, 49*, 407–429.

Borsheim-Black, C. (2019). *Antiracist literature instruction: Addressing racism through literature in White schools*. Teachers College Press.

Diab, R., Ferrel, T., Godbee, B., & Simkins, N. (2013). Making commitments to racial justice actionable. *Across the Disciplines, 10*(3). Retrieved from https://wac.colostate.edu/docs/atd/race/diabetal.pdf

DiAngelo, R. (2018). *White fragility: Why it's so hard to White people to talk about racism*. Beacon Press.

Ebarvia, J., Germán L., Parker, K. N, Torres, J. E. (2019). *#DisruptTexts*. Retrieved from https://disrupttexts.org

Gruwell, E. (1999). *The Freedom Writers Diary: Their Story. Their Words*. Broadway Books.

Johnson, L. (2018). Where do we go from here? Toward a critical race English education. *Research in the Teaching of English, 53*, 102–124.

Kauanui, J. K. (2016). "A structure, not an event": Settler colonialism and enduring indigeneity. *Lateral 5*(1). Retrieved from https://csalateral.org/issue/5-1/forum-alt-humanities-settler-colonialism-enduring-indigeity-kauanui/

King, S. (2001). *The green mile*. Signet Books.

Ladson-Billings, G. (2013). Critical race theory—What it is not! In M. Lynn & A. Dixson (Eds.), *The handbook of critical race theory in education* (pp. 34–47). Routledge.

Ladson-Billings, G., & Tate, W. (1995). Toward a critical race theory of education. *Teachers College Record, 97*, 47–68.

Lee, H. (1960). *To kill a mockingbird*. J. B. Lippincott & Co.

Lynn, M., & Dixson, A. D. (Eds.). (2013). *Handbook of critical race theory in education*. Routledge.

Matias, C. E. and Mackey, J. (2016). Breakin' down Whiteness in antiracist teaching: Introducing critical Whiteness pedagogy. *The Urban Review, 48*, 32–50.

NCTE/IRA standards for English/language arts. (1996). Retrieved from http://www.ncte.org/standards/ncte-ira

Nelson, M. (2009). *A wreath for Emmet Till*. Houghton Mifflin.

Shakespeare, W. & Raffel, B. (2008). *Macbeth*. Yale University Press. https://doi.org/10.12987/9780300138276. (Originally published 1606).

Simone, N. (1965). *Strange fruit* [Video file]. Retrieved from https://www.youtube.com/watch?v=cvwlPKCfkim

Sims-Bishop, R. (1990). Mirrors, windows, and sliding glass doors. *Perspectives, 6*(3), ix–xi.

Stockett, K. (2009). *The help*. Berkley Books.

Stotsky, S. (2010). Literary study in Grades 9, 10, and 11: A national survey. *Forum: A Publication of the ALSCW, 1*(4), 1–77.

Tatum, B. D. (2016). Teaching White students about racism: The search for White allies and the restoration of hope. In E. Taylor, D. Gilborn, & G. Ladson-Billings (Eds.), *Foundations of critical race theory in education* (2nd ed., pp. 278–288). Routledge.

Thomas, A. (2017). *The hate u give*. Harper Collins.

CHAPTER TEN

Making a "Safe" and Subversive Space for Students' Lives Through Open Mic

CAROLINE T. CLARK AND JILL M. WILLIAMS

As experienced English language arts (ELA) teacher-researchers, we understand the challenges of teaching *to* the standards and *for* social justice, all while maintaining "safe" spaces for student learning. We are equally aware, however, that the hegemony of whiteness[1] and heteronormativity in K–12 education makes "safe" a loaded, inequitable concept. Some teachers may not feel "safe" addressing "controversial" topics for fear of retribution, including possible job loss or simply loss of classroom control during challenging discussions. For students, feeling "safe" in school is even more ephemeral, especially for students who may not fit the invisible but ever-present norms of these spaces (see, e.g., Hope et al, 2015; Pascoe, 2007). This chapter responds to these tensions by focusing on Jill's (re)design of a districtwide, multicultural literature course, chronicling her moves to gradually subvert the usual curriculum and make space for students to bring stories from their own lives into the classroom.[2] Whether this was "safe" for everyone is arguable. What is clear, however, is that by holding space for students' stories, Jill subverted the ELA curriculum-as-usual and, in particular, the multicultural literature course by adding a cultural studies perspective and Open Mic. In doing this, Jill created a venue in which she and her students could safely practice having discussions that mattered to them while also addressing an expanded set of ELA content standards in deeper, more meaningful ways.

We begin by articulating our own positionalities and examining how these both shape and limit the work we do as scholar-educator-activists. Next, we describe Jill's teaching and how she forwarded her goals for social justice while also covering the required ELA standards particularly through her (re)design of a multicultural literature course and the addition of a new course assignment, Open Mic. Finally, we argue that, through Open Mic, Jill created a subversive opening in her classroom where stories from students' lives were taken up as serious texts for study and that, through this assignment, Jill was able to advance equity and question privileged school and societal norms while also engaging students in required ELA content.

Our Positionalities

Both of us are white, middle-age, cisgender, middle-class women, one bisexual (Caroline) and one straight (Jill). Both of us are also experienced ELA teachers. Prior to meeting in 2000, Caroline taught in K–12 public schools for five years, and Jill had been an ELA teacher for three years. When we first met, Caroline was a professor at a nearby university where Jill was taking graduate courses. We connected through our shared 12 years in a teacher inquiry group committed to supporting sexual and gender diversity in schools (see, e.g., Blackburn et al, 2018; Blackburn et al, 2010), and through our work as English teacher-educators. Jill served as a mentor teacher to students in the licensure program that Caroline coordinated, and in her role, Caroline had observed interns in Jill's school numerous times. Ultimately, Jill completed her PhD in 2012 with Caroline as her doctoral co-advisor. In 2014, Jill left her classroom to become the district curriculum coordinator for secondary ELA and social studies.

We know that our whiteness, social class, cis-identities, and academic degrees—and their intersections—grant us privilege (Collins & Bilge, 2016). We also know these privileged identities, if left unchecked, may limit our insights and foreclose our understandings of "safety" and "subversion." As Castagno (2008, p. 315) notes, white educators' desire for "comfort and ideological safety" often limits their willingness to engage in discussions of race or practices that disrupt the status quo. Although our awareness of privilege is no guarantee we will avoid the pitfalls and blind spots of our positionings, we believe that our histories of working to combat homophobia and heteronormativity in schools and our ongoing efforts to practice "cultural humility" as researchers (Quigley, 2016, p. 26) can act as guardrails, helping us name and own our epistemological limits.

Jill's Teaching

Even before we collaborated on this study, Jill had long been an advocate for social justice. She was the advisor to her school's Gay Straight Alliance (GSA) and actively worked to incorporate multiple perspectives into her English curriculum (Smith,

2007, 2010). Although her district was large and diverse in terms of race, ethnicity, and social class, her high school had no GSA until she agreed to advise one. Advising the GSA gave her insights into what kinds of stories were valued in her school and which ones were not. She found that LGBTQIA+[3] people were everywhere in the school community, but their stories and experiences were completely missing. As Jill puts it, "We had signs up about community and safety all over the school and yet this whole group of people was being made to feel invisible." These experiences laid the foundation for Jill's (re)design of an elective ELA course, Multicultural Literature, for juniors and seniors in her district.

The Traditional Multicultural Literature Course

Originally, the course took a tourist approach (Brauer & Clark, 2008) to learning about "other" cultures, providing windows for white students and the occasional mirror for students of color (Bishop, 1990). The curriculum was strictly print-text-focused and conventional, organized around different genres (e.g., Multicultural Drama, Multicultural Poetry, etc.) and aimed at exposing students to different cultural groups (e.g., Jewish, African American, etc.) in isolation from one another, a format that reflects how many such courses are organized nationwide (Stallworth et al, 2006). As an experienced ELA teacher in the district, Jill was involved in the original design of the course, which fulfilled a significant need to bring more diverse literature into the overall ELA curriculum. Despite being traditional and conventional, Jill was "on board" with teaching the course as it was originally conceived because she recognized the value of providing diverse students opportunities to see themselves in course texts. That said, she also recognized the limitations of the course and worked more subversively and incrementally on its (re)design.

Small, subversive steps for change

From the outset, Jill recognized that some features of the course, like the English standards more generally, "still seemed affixed to ideas that reflect a narrow slice of the world" (Kirkland, 2008, p. 70). When she initially taught the course, Jill maintained its original title and format but eschewed the preferred course textbook that reflected the problematic topics and structures described earlier. Instead, Jill used the textbook as a supplement and wrote small grants to purchase class sets of books that provided more complex and overlapping representations of cultural diversity. These included *The Color of Water: A Black Man's Tribute to His White Mother* by James McBride (1995), *A Yellow Raft in Blue Water* by Michael Dorris (1987), and *Montana 1948: A Novel* by Larry Watson (1993).

Next, Jill gained districtwide approval to change the name of the course to Cultural Studies in Literature. This move provided a small opening in the curriculum, allowing Jill, and other ELA teachers in the district, to move beyond a strict focus on literature at the expense of exploring literacy more broadly (Willinsky, 1991). With this opening, Jill brought more texts and media into the classroom, including film, music, and children's picture books, creating opportunities for what Scholes (2011) describes as "comparative textuality," which "embodies a more spacious idea of literacy than a concern with literary works alone" (p. 139). As the course and her experiences teaching it evolved, Jill proposed a new course description that reflected the expanded texts and conversations the course was affording to her students and her, one that is still reflected in the district's course description guide today:

> This course requires students to develop understanding of the social role of local and global texts, such as literature, film, music and mass media through multiple perspectives as well as recognize their influences on identity, culture, socioeconomic status, politics, and ideology. Units of study may include topics related to race, ethnicity, gender, religion, and sexual orientation. Mature language and content may be encountered through various texts. This course counts as 1.00 English credit toward graduation. (Hartville[4] City Schools, 2018, p. 32)

Meeting the standards

Across her 17 years of teaching, Jill saw standards as the minimum and assumed that she would "hit them" regardless of what texts she used. As she revised this course, however, her attitude toward the standards began to shift. In the Multicultural Literature course as it was originally conceived, for example, the covered standards focused mainly on reading literary fiction and writing in response to literature. For example, the course consistently hit the Ohio Learning Standards for the English Language Arts for Reading Literature in Grades 11 and 12 (Ohio Department of Education, 2017), which require that students identify two or more themes and analyze their development over the course of the text (RL.11-12.2). In both the earlier and the later version of the course, these standards were covered.

Even as the course changed from a multicultural to a cultural studies focus, however, many other ELA standards were only peripherally addressed or left uncovered, particularly ones related to Speaking and Listening, which require that students be able to initiate and participate effectively in a range of collaborative discussions on a grade-level topics, texts, and issues (SL, 11-12.1), and ones related to language, which require them to understand language use in different contexts and make effective communication choices when speaking, reading or listening (L.11-12.3).[5] Moreover, still missing from the course was any attention to self-reflection, whiteness, gender, sexuality, and intersectionality or any of the related privileges and oppressions that often map onto these identities, both personally and systemically. Although some of these were named in the new course description, cited earlier, because these were recommended (i.e., "may include") but not required, many of these issues were still absent from the course. Equally absent was attention to multimedia platforms and places beyond the classroom, such as work, where students often negotiated and navigated diversity in their lives.

Subverting the Curriculum Through Open Mic

Although the district, as a whole, had adopted the revised course as an ELA elective for juniors and seniors, Jill was not satisfied that it was adequately meeting the needs of students. As the GSA advisor, she recognized that many topics and texts related to the lives of LGBTQIA+ students were still absent from the curriculum. She also knew that many teachers in the district were reluctant to bring these texts and topics into their teaching because they feared potential repercussions from parents, administrators, and colleagues or felt they simply did not have the skills or know-how to manage discussions with students (Clark & Blackburn, 2009; Blackburn et al, 2018). Aiming to further expand the topics and openings that were available to students, Jill introduced a new assignment to the course, Open Mic. Jill first added Open Mic in the autumn semester of 2009. Caroline then spent spring semester 2010 observing Jill's Cultural Studies in Literature course, engaging with students, collecting student work, and videotaping class, including all the Open Mic sessions. These data inform the account and analysis that follow.

Introducing Open Mic

When she first added Open Mic to her course, Jill made it a required assignment on her syllabus, describing it as "an opportunity to SPEAK to the class about your ideas and interests and to listen to the ideas and interests of your classmates." Open Mics entailed an oral presentation on some topic, text, or issue, followed by a full class discussion led by the student. Additionally, students had to submit a "thorough, typed rationale" for their Open Mic, explaining why they presented what they did and how they saw it fitting into the course. There were no time parameters for how long a presentation lasted or topic requirements or constraints, provided it somehow fit into the "cultural studies" aims of the course and was reasonably school-appropriate. Each student was required to complete two Open Mic assignments during the semester. Typically, all Friday class sessions were dedicated to students' Open Mics. Jill's decision to allocate this amount of class time for Open Mic was subversive in and of itself, as she resisted the typical pressure to cover the curriculum standards at the expense of an important opportunity for student learning (Crocco & Costigan, 2007). And, once this time was set aside, more opportunities for subverting the conventional multicultural literature course followed.

Through Open Mic, a wide array of new texts were invited into the classroom. Some students brought in humorous texts, satires, and other cultural commentary related to race and intersectionality, including video sketches from *The Dave Chappelle Show*, print comics such as *The Boondocks* by Aaron McGruder, and blog posts from the Black Jewish radio host Jay Smooth. Others wrote original stories or poems that addressed a key theme of the course or extended a scene from a shared novel, read these aloud, and discussed their writing with classmates. And some just posed a question, as when Devon, a light-skinned, cisgender, straight Black youth, after reading "A Letter to Harvey Milk," by Leslea Newman (1988) described his earnest wondering about the question, "Is being gay a choice?" and opened the space for discussion and debate with his classmates.

Initially, however, Open Mic was not universally embraced or even understood. As Jill noted, some students "clicked" with the assignment right away and would have a long list of texts to share, while others struggled to generate a single topic or text. Students also wondered how their topics and texts even connected to the course, with many stating, "I don't know what to do!" or asking, "Is this okay? Is this allowed?" To help these students build confidence in their choices, Jill modeled Open Mics that included YouTube videos and poems. She also encouraged students to make purposeful connections with other assignments in the class or with other classes they were taking that semester. Jill also subverted typical notions of ELA assignments by allowing students to "repurpose" papers to meet the Open Mic requirements. When she first introduced Open Mic, Jill was surprised that students expressed concern about using prior work from another class to fulfill the assignment. Jill allowed students to reanalyze or re-present completed assignments but required that they add the lenses of "cultural studies" to this prior work and explain how doing so changed or added to their original work. Providing support for students to make connections to prior assignments and other courses was a good way to support students who initially struggled with the concept of being able to choose their own texts. Not insisting that all texts be 100% newly created and specific to the class was a supportive, subversive move. Although some ELA teachers might see this as a form of "self-plagiarism," Jill allowed it, recognizing that, for her students, having a safe, supportive space in which to practice using a cultural studies lens was more important, in this instance, than having them create a wholly original piece.

Making space for students' lives through Open Mic

As students gained experience discussing literature and other texts through a cultural studies lens, more students brought personal stories from their lives into the classroom. As the spring semester progressed, these stories dominated the Friday sessions. For example, Brenda, a tall, dark-skinned Black girl with shoulder-length hair and glasses who was a frequent contributor in class, focused her Open Mic on an experience from her job working as a cashier at a grocery store when she was directed by her supervisor to treat a "foreign" shopper differently from a white shopper. When a "foreign" male shopper came to Brenda's lane to purchase 30 cases of Coke, more than a dozen cartons of orange juice, and "like, a hundred" cans of tomato paste, Brenda's supervisor stepped in to tell her that the store had a six-item limit per sale policy. After the man left, her supervisor said the policy was needed because "foreigners are taking our products and selling them at their own markets for a profit." When a subsequent white female entered Brenda's lane with more than a dozen containers of yogurt, and Brenda asked her supervisor if the six-item limit applied, her supervisor said, "No, she's fine." After her shift, Brenda spoke to her manager and asked, "That's a little bit racist there, don't you think?" The manager asserted that "they *are* taking our products and selling them for a profit," but Brenda reasserted that she did not think it was fair because "how do we know the white lady wasn't doing the same exact thing?" and called the practice "stupid." Brenda was written up for her comments by her manager.

Brenda's story was interrupted once, by Jill, who asked how her manager knew that customers were "foreign." Brenda shared that this was, in part, because they spoke different languages but also because her supervisor "said so." When Brenda reached the point in her story where the manager said she should ring up the white customer, a male classmate softly exclaimed, "Whoa." At the conclusion of Brenda's story, Jill asked the class, "What questions—what are you guys thinking about?" A white female student, Lara, asked, "What if the people are like buying a ton of stuff, and spending their own money, and they're gonna go donate it to a soup kitchen?" Brenda nodded in agreement, adding, "Or, like, and then the guy had come back in later with his wife and his kids?" Jill asked other students how they would have responded if they were in Brenda's shoes, leading students to debate when they would speak up for others, why, around what issues, and with what consequences. Brenda's Open Mic, including her opening story and students' subsequent discussion, lasted more than 15 minutes and ended with students loudly applauding the exchange.

Next up was Zeke, a white male student with brown hair flopping forward, half-covering his glasses—a gray plaid scarf wrapped loosely around his neck. Zeke was generally a quiet student who rarely contributed to large class discussions. Announcing to the class, "I play Xbox a lot," he shared his experiences with "Xbox prejudice" and how people act in online spaces. After defining the word *stereotype*, Zeke shared that "knowing this and having a moderately firm grasp on the open ignorance of people on the Internet," he usually likes to play into "people's assumptions" to see how they react. Zeke described using "different voices" as he spoke to other players using the game's microphone function. Zeke demonstrated a range of voices for the class, including his "nerdy white dude" voice; his "Eddie Murphy-sounding guy"; his "Pedro-sounding guy, like from *Napoleon Dynamite*"; and his "super southern-sounding white guy." He shared that when he used these voices during the game, he was called "every slandering term from like every race. Like all of them, I've probably been called it." He concluded his sharing by reading, in part, from his write-up:

So, it's like, anonymity on the Internet is like, it's as freeing as it is, like, I worded it here, "a battlefield for mindless slander." And it's like, really the only place, like, that I really ever hear like real hate speech. And, so, that's it.

After his opening story, Jill asked Zeke for an example of how he knew participants were getting angry at the personae and not at him. He responded by sharing an experience of entering the game and speaking slowly, with accented English, as if he might be a native Spanish speaker. In response, another player called him a "wet-back" and "a bunch of racist stuff" and said, "Oh, you jumped the border." Zeke noted that he sees himself as just "a weird-looking white dude" but because other players hear a Spanish accent on Xbox Live, he's "getting called a bunch of racist stuff" as evidence that the vitriol he heard was focused at his accented English and the foreignness it conjured, not at him personally.

After he concluded, his classmates immediately shared their own stories of racism on Xbox Live. Students unanimously agreed that the N-word is easily the word they hear most often during the game. Jill probed as to why they thought this was happening, and a white, cisgender male student, Jamie, asserted that it is because "they know nothing[']s gonna happen." When asked about the age of other Xbox Live players who made these comments, Zeke said they "typically sound like really little kids, like 12" but that "even the 20-year-old-sounding guys will say something just ridiculously mean over nothing. Just because I'm talking differently." As the discussion continued, several female students shared that they "don't really play Xbox," but they like to talk on the microphone, leading to stories about overt sexism on the game, such as when Jenna, a white, cisgender female was called "a dumb bitch." Like Brenda, after 10 minutes of sharing his story and leading discussion, Zeke was met with resounding applause from his classmates.

Discussion and Implications

Brenda and Zeke provide just a glimpse of how Open Mic functioned in Jill's classroom. What is evident, we hope, is the sophistication of students' questions and analyses, the support and guidance offered by Jill, and the thoughtful responses provided by classmates. Across these two examples, we see how issues of race, discrimination, and prejudice permeate students' lives and the efforts they are making to understand these experiences in productive ways. Brenda's Open Mic created a space for her classmates to question what everyday racism looks like and to consider their own responses in similar situations, real or imagined. And Zeke, in effect, used his experiences with Xbox Live to conduct a study not unlike the work of sociolinguists examining discrimination based on race, ethnicity, and language in housing, job-seeking, and other domains (see, e.g., Lippi-Green, 2012; Massey & Lundy, 2001). We contend that these experiences not only meet the ELA standards but also exceed them, deepening students' study of language, literacy, speaking, and listening by connecting it to issues these young people will continue to encounter long after they leave Jill's classroom, reflecting what David Kirkland (2008) calls "a new English education." Both Brenda and Zeke recognized and analyzed themes of racism and discrimination in the text of their lives and, through their Open Mic stories, analyzed these texts (RL.11-12.2). In sharing these stories with their peers and teacher, they had to use language to clearly and compellingly convey their experiences (L.11-12.3) and then participate in a range of discussions, listening to other perspectives, responding to critical questions, and elaborating and extending their own thinking (SL, 11-12.1). Clearly, these standards were met.

We argue as well, however, that through her (re)design of the course and, in particular, through the addition of Open Mic, Jill also created a subversive opening in her classroom for advancing equity, questioning privileged school and societal norms, and engaging students more deeply and authentically in required ELA content. Although these choices posed potential risks for her, by making changes incrementally, over time, and through the district's official curriculum, Jill worked within the system to create a context that supported her choices, should she need it. Moreover, by making Open Mic an assignment that was student-driven, Jill had some degree of "cover" should anyone accuse her of bringing in "controversial" topics or content. Still, when Jill first taught the class, she felt like she had to close the door, especially during Open Mic. She worried about people who were not part of the class community entering the space and hearing students' stories without fully understanding the context. Interestingly, Jill was not the only one monitoring this; if the door was open during a sensitive discussion, students also closed the door *for* one another. Throughout the year, students seemed to understand and evaluate the potential risks and aimed to create a safer space for each other.

Jill and the students also had explicit conversations about context and "code-switching" when outsiders or administrators came to sit in the class. Here, Jill's aims were not to convey that controversial subjects were inappropriate; rather, she wanted students to understand that learning to share personal stories is hard work and takes time, practice, and support, as do unpacking, processing, discussing, and even listening to these stories.

Most important, through Open Mic, students' stories were centered and positioned as an important part of the curriculum. Their stories were just as worthy of study as any text that Jill gave them. For some students, this was a revelation. Most never knew these stories held value, except to them, and many, at first, did not see how they connected to school or the class. Ultimately, though, the rewards of Jill's subversive teaching far outweighed the risks. The texts of students' lives did not displace conventional ELA content and standards; they complemented and expanded them. The space afforded by Open Mic acted as a conceptual and literal jumping-off point for students that extended their study of ELA beyond the four walls of the physical classroom into the school, the community, their homes, and beyond.

Endnotes

1   In keeping with recent work on Critical Race English Education (Johnson, 2018), through this chapter we use upper case to reference Black and Brown and lower case to reference white/whiteness as a move to help dismantle and interrupt white supremacy.

2   Data for this chapter come from Caroline's observations and videotaping of Jill's semester-long ELA course in a comprehensive, public high school with a total enrollment of 1,624 students (67.4% white, 20% Black, 5% biracial, 3.9% Hispanic, 2.6% Asian, 0.1% Native American, and 0.1% Pacific Islander). There were 23 students enrolled in the course: 12 male students (9 white, 2 Black, 1 biracial) and 11 female students (9 white, 2 Black). All the students were cisgender, and none of the students identified openly as LGBTQIA+.

3   We use the acronym LGBTQIA+ throughout this paper in reference to people's nonheteronormative identities. LGBTQIA stands for Lesbian, Gay, Bisexual, Transgender, Queer, Intersex, and Asexual, while the + stands for all of the other sexualities, sexes, and genders not included in these few letters. We use this acronym to be as inclusive as possible of the sexual identities that students have expressed in our work across the years. However, in discussions of curriculum, we use LGBT-inclusive.

4   Hartville is a pseudonym.

5   To see the entire set of Ohio ELA Learning Standards, go to http://education.ohio.gov/getattachment/Topics/Learning-in-Ohio/English-Language-Art/English-Language-Arts-Standards/ELA-Learning-Standards-2017.pdf.aspx?lang=en-US.

References

Bishop, R. S. (1990). Mirrors, windows, and sliding glass doors. *Perspectives: Choosing and Using Books for the Classroom, 6*(3), ix–xi.

Blackburn, M. V., Clark, C. T., & Schey, R. (2018). *Stepping up!: Teachers advocating for sexual and gender diversity in schools.* Routledge.

Blackburn, M. V., Clark, C. T., Kenney, L. M., & Smith, J. M. (Eds.). (2010). *Acting out!: Combating homophobia through teacher activism.* Teachers College Press.

Brauer, L., & Clark, C. T. (2008). The trouble is English: Reframing English studies in secondary schools. *English Education, 40,* 293–313.

Castagno, A. E. (2008). "I don't want to hear that!": Legitimating Whiteness through silence in schools. *Anthropology and Education Quarterly, 39,* 314–333.

Clark, C. T., & Blackburn, M. V. (2009). Reading LGBT-themed literature with young people in classrooms: What's possible? *English Journal, 98*(4), 25–32.

Collins, P. H., & Bilge, S. (2016). *Intersectionality (key concepts).* Polity Press.

Crocco, M. S., & Costigan, A. T. (2007). The narrowing of curriculum and pedagogy in the age of accountability: Urban educators speak out. *Urban Education, 42,* 512–535.

Dorris, M. (1987). *A Yellow Raft in Blue Water.* Henry Holt and Company.

Hartville City Schools (2018). High School Course Description Guide, 2017-2018. Retrieved from https://www.hartville.k12.oh.us/docs/district/depts/22/17-18%20course%20desc%20guide.pdf?id=561549.

Hope, E. C., Skoog, A. B., & Jagers, R. J. (2015). "It'll never be the White kids, it'll always be us": Black high school students' evolving critical analysis of racial discrimination and inequity in schools. *Journal of Adolescent Research, 30,* 83–112.

Johnson, L. L. (2018). Where do we go from here? Toward a critical race English education. *Research in the Teaching of English, 53,* 102–124.

Kirkland, D. E. (2008). "The rose that grew from concrete": Postmodern Blackness and new English education. *English Journal, 97*(5), 69–75.

Lippi-Green, R. (2012). *English with an accent: Language, ideology, and discrimination in the United States* (2nd ed.). Routledge.

Massey, D. S., & Lundy, G. (2001). Uses of Black English and racial discrimination in urban housing markets: New methods and findings. *Urban Affairs Review, 36,* 452–469.

McBride, J. (1995). *The Color of Water: A Black Man's Tribute to His White Mother.* New York: Penguin Group.

Newman, L. (1988). "A letter to Harvey Milk." In *A letter to Harvey Milk: Short stories* (pp. 25–28). Firebrand.

Ohio Department of Education (2017). Ohio's Learning Standards: English Language Arts. Retrieved from https://education.ohio.gov/getattachment/Topics/Learning-in-Ohio/ English-Language-Art/English-Language-Arts-Standards/ELA-Learning-Standards-2017.pdf.aspx?lang=en-US.

Pascoe, C. J. (2007). *Dude, you're a fag: Masculinity and sexuality in high school.* The University of California Press.

Quigley, D. (2016). Applying "place" to research ethics and cultural competence/humility training. *Journal of Academic Ethics, 14,* 19–33.

Scholes, R. (2011). *English after the fall: From literature to textuality.* University of Iowa Press.

Smith, J. M. (2007). *Montana 1948*: Crossing boundaries with queer theory. In A. O. Soter, M. Faust, & T. C. Rogers (Eds.), *Interpretive play: Using critical perspectives to teach young adult literature* (pp. 161–171). Christopher-Gordon.

Smith, J. M. (2010). Overcoming an identity of privilege to support LGBTQ inclusivity in high school. In M. V. Blackburn, C. T. Clark, L. M. Kenney, & J. M. Smith (Eds.), *Acting out!: Combating homophobia through teacher activism* (pp. 114–126). Teachers College Press.

Stallworth, B. J., Gibbons, L. & Fauber, L. (2006). It's not on the list: An exploration of teachers' perspectives on using multicultural literature. *Journal of Adolescent & Adult Literacy, 49,* 478–489.

Watson, L. (1993). *Montana 1948*. Milkweed Editions.

Willinsky, J. (1991). *The triumph of literature/The fate of literacy: English in the secondary school curriculum.* Teachers College Press.

CHAPTER ELEVEN

The Responsible Change Project: Subverting the Standardized English Language Arts Curriculum

HEATHER COFFEY AND STEVE FULTON

As the American public school population has become more ethnically, linguistically, and socioeconomically diverse, the English language arts (ELA) curriculum has become more standards-driven with a focus on high-stakes testing. Although national policies such as the Every Student Succeeds Act (ESSA, 2015) claim to have provisions for "[a]dvanc[ing] equity by upholding critical protections for America's disadvantaged and high-need students," state and local policies and testing structures negate this provision and are detrimental to students from marginalized groups and those living in poverty. Resulting from this continued path toward standardization, justice-oriented educators have made it their mission to create curriculum that challenges standards models and engages students in high level critical thinking and social action (Butin, 2003; Coffey & Fulton, 2018; Conklin & Hughes, 2016). These subversive models of teaching enable justice-oriented educators to advocate for students in ways that help them recognize their value while maintaining academic rigor and challenging them to think critically. We argue that teachers can engage students in subversive or *critical* pedagogies that encourage students to critique the status quo and reject mundane, standardized curriculum that serves to sort and place them in society (Postman & Weingartner, 1969). Subversive teachers leverage the state standards without narrowly focusing on a traditional ELA curriculum of formulaic writing instruction, close reading of irrelevant texts, and teacher-directed lessons that are disconnected from students' lived experiences.

Unfortunately, scripted curriculum dominates classrooms across the nation (Ladson-Billings, 2017), leaving little room for teachers to design their own lessons. Steve, a 17-year veteran of the ELA classroom at North Community Middle School (NCMS), has taught through the years of teacher-developed lessons and scripted curriculum in a state that has quarterly benchmarks and end-of-grade testing that is punitive for students and teachers. Steve has witnessed a definite change in the amount of freedom he and his colleagues have had to assess the learning needs and differentiate the curriculum. Steve actually became disappointed and disenchanted with teaching for a while; however, his perspective changed when, upon his district's adoption of *Understanding by Design* (Wiggins & McTighe, 2005), his superintendent and his principal encouraged teachers to design their own curriculum—as long as it included two guiding principles: (1) a focus on teaching and assessing for understanding and learning transfer and (2) a curriculum design that planned "backward" from the end objectives with an increased focus on explicit standards-based instruction.

Teachers at Steve's school were, at first, cautious of the new planning model; however, they rewrote and implemented the curriculum. They followed the guiding principles, and they developed a powerful framework that wove social justice and activist texts throughout the activities and lessons, all while maintaining the rigorous state standards. Because school district administrators trusted the professional knowledge and talent of their teachers, this labor of love resulted in a horizontally and vertically aligned standards-based curriculum. Upon conclusion of this task, Steve and his eighth-grade ELA colleagues had developed The Responsible Change Project (RCP), a comprehensive justice-oriented curriculum with inquiry at the core. Combining the standards-based state curriculum with the freedom to utilize culturally sustaining pedagogies (Paris & Alim, 2017), the RCP is a yearlong unit of study that includes nontraditional young adult literature, the exploration of the relationship between the real world and the figured world of school, and a space where students research and develop solutions to problems within their communities.

The RCP also incorporates the College, Career, and Community Writing Program (C3WP), developed by the National Writing Project (NWP), which has been implemented with fidelity in middle and high schools across the nation for the past five years. NCMS adopted C3WP, and Heather provided professional development around the central components of the program, which include writing recursively, developing nuanced claims, and considering one's place in complex conversations.

Although the community-based activist project was not an original component of C3WP, multiple school sites around the nation use C3WP as a platform for students to address issues of concern within their communities. Building on the mission of the NWP, C3WP engenders classroom spaces where students become skilled writers and active participants in their local and global communities. At NCMS, the

C3WP provides a strong writing curriculum as a foundation for leveraging the work the eighth-grade ELA teachers envisioned happening. First, it supported students in developing the practice and habits of mind that underlie critical reading, argument writing, and considering multiple perspectives. It also provided a yearlong framework for teaching lessons that align with the state standards, something Steve uses to guide his work in developing the curriculum through the Understanding by Design process (Wiggins & McTighe, 2005). Although the RCP meets the goals of the traditional ELA expectations, it also subverts it by incorporating young adult literature that sheds light on social problems, such as police brutality, human trafficking, discrimination, and poverty. Furthermore, the curriculum challenges these students to learn multiple sides of the issue and to promote solutions from the perspective of the very people who are being marginalized.

Subverting Standardized Curriculum Through Development of an Activist Mind-Set

The RCP progressively engaged students in scaffolded instruction to support critical reading, writing, and developing an activist mind-set. The progression included social justice inquiry, reading, informal and formal research-based writing, service-learning, TED Talk-style presentations, and teacher-facilitated discussions and reflections. Students consulted primary documents, informational texts, and even social media to gauge the degree to which their concerns were related to the national conversation on the topic.

The stage was set for this progression early in the fall semester when students developed claims in response to reading several texts on national topics, such as immigration and gun violence. Students also read social justice–themed novels in small groups, identifying relevant social issues and analyzing the effects of power and privilege. Toward the end of the first semester, students read texts that addressed the historical context and complexity of modern racial injustice and created a piece of writing that made a clear claim and included appropriate evidence from the text to support that claim and develop an argument. Other skills students developed during the first semester included annotating texts, integrating source material into a piece of argument writing, developing a clear line of reasoning, and addressing opposing viewpoints. This sustained and recursive experience with argument, combined with discussion of a large number of modern social issues, prepared students for the next stages of the project. In the second semester, when the more direct work of the RCP occurred, Steve's students drew on what they learned during the first semester to identify meaningful social issues to inquire into with the purpose of enacting change.

Crafting a Justice-Oriented ELA Curriculum

In this next section, we describe how Steve and his co-teachers were able to subvert the traditional eighth-grade ELA curriculum to empower students to make change in their communities. The state standards for ELA instruction require students to be able to make inferences when reading literature, to cite specific evidence when reading and respond-ing to informational texts, to write arguments for a particular audience, and to integrate and evaluate information presented in diverse media and formats. Prior to engaging students in RCP, teachers at NCMS found it difficult to effectively and meaningfully engage students in all standards; however, upon conclusion of the unit, the teach-ers realized that they were able to more purposefully and thoroughly teach all the standards through the RCP. In what follows, we describe both the curriculum and the student learning outcomes from the first iteration of this justice-oriented, teach-er-developed curriculum.

Steve and Heather: Building a university–school partnership

The authors of this chapter include Steve, an ELA teacher with 17 years of experience at the middle school level, and Heather, an English methods professor at a large public university in the southeastern United States. Steve and Heather met more than 10 years ago when Steve was enrolled in Heather's graduate-level ELA methods course. Having recently completed a doctorate in education reform, Heather's research re-volved around critical literacy and urban youth communities. Steve, a practicing teach-er completing his Master of Arts in English Education, was a member of a captive audience of motivated middle-grades ELA teachers seeking to improve their practice with innovative teaching ideas.

They continued working together after that initial contact in that graduate methods course, as Steve was always willing to have an extra hand in the class-room and Heather wanted desperately to keep one foot in classrooms similar to the one she taught in years before. Historically, at Steve's school, research has been a primary focus of eighth-grade ELA curriculum, and Steve often uses this oppor-tunity for encouraging students to develop research-based projects driven by their interests. He really loves when these ideas and projects extend beyond the walls of the school. Steve's instructional decisions are rooted in the equity mind-set he has developed over the course of his teaching career. Experiences in both graduate courses (English methods, in particular) and his work with the NWP inspired the development of an asset mind-set focused on a pedagogy reflective of constructivist theory and student-directed interests. Steve has taught in the same community for the past 16 years and lives less than a mile from the school. He knows the culture, the population, and the local issues that are present. He does not approach activist work with his students as something that he is doing to, or even for, them; instead, his focus on progressive local change and developing students' sense of agency is in all their shared best interests.

Steve's rationale for subversive teaching

When Heather initially asked Steve about his interest in this justice-oriented teaching model, he explained that he grew up in a midwestern state in a city that was mostly White and middle class. When he came south to teach in this small town, he was presented with a diverse population of students with which he had no experience. Steve learned quickly that establishing a learning environment that was relevant and engaging required him to value the funds of knowledge (Gonzalez, Moll, & Amanti, 2006) students brought with them. Steve recognized the need to adopt a dialogic approach that involved listening to students, respecting their histories and perspectives, and establishing a community where knowledge was built through negotiation. Steve was continuously exploring ways to empower his students and to be more thoughtful about how to incorporate both local and national current events into his classroom. He wanted to ensure students' concerns were represented and valued, conflicting views would be discussed, power structures could be analyzed, and the agency to enact change could be cultivated.

At first, Steve felt isolated because, aside from being an outsider, teachers in this small mill town were not having conversations about critical literacy and empowering students to be activists. Over time, he developed roots in the community and became a familiar part of it, which is likely one of the most influential reasons why he is able to do this work. Steve's experience with the NWP, coupled with a real interest in the success of his students, brought about a deeper understanding of constructivist teaching practices in action. This established community of teachers was empowering because they deeply understood his rationale for this pedagogical approach. This is where Steve's journey into justice-oriented and subversive teaching began.

School and community context

The students at Steve's school are incredibly diverse with the population almost evenly split between Hispanic, African American, and White students, with a small population of Asian and multiethnic students. Although there are students from middle- and upper middle-class socioeconomic groups, 76.9% of students are eligible for free and/or reduced-price lunch. The town in which the school is located has definitely felt the changing global economy as it was once home to the world's largest textile mill. In 2003, when the textile mill filed for bankruptcy, more than 4,000 people lost their jobs overnight, thus changing the course of history for the town. Many of the residents, once employed by the mill, were only experienced in skilled blue-collar work required by the industry. This misfortune still influences the economy of the town and has caused ripple effects in the areas of crime, poverty, and joblessness. Despite the negative outcomes from the closing of the world's largest mill, the town has held tightly to its sense of community and identity as a small town, providing opportunities for families to build on their assets.

Developing an Innovative, Justice-Oriented Curriculum:
Why Responsible Change?

When reflecting on that first iteration of the RCP, Heather and Steve realized that by creating the RCP as a way to address standards, they were actually undermining standardization. In fact, by offering students texts that critiqued systems of inequality (e.g., *Dear Martin*, Stone, 2017; *The Absolutely True Diary of a Part Time Indian*, Alexie, 2007; *The Hate U Give*, Thomas, 2017), students developed standards-based skills while also gaining awareness that school curricula have meaningful implications. Similarly, while providing space for developing curricular skills around topics of interest, students engaged more deeply with these topics that are often considered taboo in a classroom. These are the ways that the traditional, standardized curriculum was subverted and students engaged in social and political discussions while improving their writing and communication skills. The following section provides powerful examples of the work that emerged from the RCP.

Tally and Destiny's experience

Tally and Destiny, two adolescent females who identified as Hispanic and African American, respectively, began the RCP curious about racial discrimination. As young women of color, they had experienced firsthand unjust stereotyping and microaggressions, and they noticed how race was a particularly divisive subject in their community. Through their research and writing, they noted how the demographics of the country are changing and concluded that because our country is growing more diverse, for youth to learn about tolerance and to develop sensitivity is particularly important. They planned to create buttons and T-shirts that promoted racial equity; however, when they could not find a way to finance the materials for their production, they decided in frustration to abandon their plan.

Steve encouraged them to consider other resources they could leverage to make positive change in their community. After discussing their real intent, they decided to invite the community into a dialogue about race to promote a deeper understanding of this complex issue that shapes our identity and interactions with others. Tally and Destiny then planned to start a diversity club at the school with the intention of using the organization as a platform to host these discussions. They made a presentation intended to promote the club, start conversations, and break down walls. They also got a principal at a local elementary school to agree to have them come speak to students. Days before their presentation, the principal contacted Steve and canceled because teachers at the school objected to the presentation, explaining that race was too controversial for fifth graders.

Tally and Destiny were furious. They were just about out of class time to work on the project, and they felt like they had gotten nowhere. Steve listened to their disappointment and shared their frustration but was not sure what they should do next. Destiny suggested reaching out to one of their seventh-grade teachers with whom they felt connected, and Steve encouraged Destiny to e-mail that teacher. She accepted their proposal. Both girls presented, and despite this small victory, the experience and frustration that came from trying to address this real-world issue in the school setting were far from what they anticipated. The process for Destiny and Tally was unique to them, but the challenges they faced and the need for problem solving when moving their ideas from concept-to-action in society were threads common to all students taking part in the RCP.

Throughout this semester-long process, Tally and Destiny developed skills from the traditional curriculum. Starting with a concern from their own lived experiences, they deepened their understanding through reading multiple informational texts. They drew on this reading to develop a more nuanced claim that was the basis for an argument, which was supported by multiple text-based sources. They wrote a research-based argumentative paper, per Steve's requirement, but the plan they crafted led them to compose multiple texts for authentic purposes and audiences. They captured ideas from their ongoing conversations on a Google Doc and carefully considered their tone and message in the e-mails they sent to the principal and school staff. They also considered the background knowledge and experiences of their student audience in the presentation they crafted. The skills and knowledge Tally and Destiny developed through this project completely supported the requirements of the standard curriculum; however, unlike many school assignments, they were writing for real audiences and real contexts.

Brian, Larry, and Stephanie's experience

Earlier in the year, a news story broke about a local couple arrested for running a puppy mill. The animals were mistreated and kept in horrible conditions. Two of Steve's students were enraged by this story—upset that this happened in their community and further disturbed when their research uncovered how common an occurrence it is. They met outside of school and designed a plan for taking action well before the class even began this part of the project.

On the first day of the project, these students presented Steve with their plan to host a rally in the state capitol (two hours away) along with a daylong conference, filled with speakers and workshop sessions. They were not sure what was going to happen at the conference but had a list of estimates from various hotels for hosting the event. Steve was impressed by their drive and commitment but knew this was something they could not attempt without significant adult and financial support. Not long after he began thinking about how to redirect this group to make their project more manageable and local, he got an e-mail from an angry parent concerned about the feasibility of requiring children to complete such an expensive project.

The next day, Steve met with the group and asked them to start over. Although their goal was admirable, he asked them to think more locally and to consider their research. How could 14-year-olds realistically address a need with limited access to money and transportation? Although they were deflated, Stephanie mentioned that, through her research, she learned that young children often did not know how to take care of pets or interact with pets they encountered in public. Stephanie proposed a training session for elementary-aged students so they could learn how to properly care for pets and interact with those of others. Stephanie drafted an e-mail to local elementary school principals to find an audience while Brian and Larry started planning the presentation on a Google Doc. The group heard back from a willing principal and, over the next several days, developed the presentation. The principal was part of the process, checking in on the group's planning document and slideshow. In the end, they successfully delivered their presentation to a room of 100 second graders. Although the group members were nervous, they felt that their message was heard, and these three eighth graders were empowered through what they had accomplished.

Like with Tally and Destiny's project, the group's project ended up being different from the initial conceptions and led to better understanding the scope of organizing events and limitations of being 14. It also provided them with a meaningful context to develop content knowledge. Creating this context subverts traditional standards-based instruction by creating the opportunity for the standards to be meaningfully applied. Throughout the process, Brian, Larry, and Stephanie were driven by their own motivation and had the opportunity to use literacy and the recursive process for authentic purposes through the application of all ELA strands—reading, writing, speaking, listening, viewing, and visual representation. They conducted additional research to fill in gaps of background information, scripted everything each person would say, and then revised for greater simplicity and interactivity. They edited images and video clips in their presentation to make them more concise and appropriate for young audiences. On their slideshow, they simplified text and placed more of a focus on visual elements to accommodate the reading abilities of their audience. And they rehearsed and provided each other with meaningful and honest feedback because of their shared investment.

How RCP subverts the ELA curriculum

Unfortunately, the RCP was not linear and neat like most students are accustomed to in school; instead, it challenged students to problem solve and then redirect and refocus when the plan did not meet reality. The work of the students in Steve's eighth-grade class satisfied what the state and district expected students to be learning, but in reality, if an outside observer had witnessed a single day of the process, he or she would not see uniform standards-driven learning. They would see students following their interests to do authentic work. Beneath the surface of the tidy curriculum documents, the curriculum was subverted through students engaging in controversial discourse, using the Internet and library to find resources to support their inquiry, and writing e-mails and phone scripts to communicate with adults in positions of power. All this newly developed knowledge, and the path taken to develop it, made the curriculum enticingly more meaningful for the students.

In her 2013 *English Journal* article "Subversive Acts of Revision: Writing and Justice," Heather Bruce challenges ELA teachers to "stop obedience to and silence in the face of oppressive and unjust systems let loose upon our schools, or teaching, and our students . . . we must claim English education for social justice" (p. 31). The crux of Bruce's argument centers around using Sonia Nieto's three components of social justice: (1) curriculum that is both rigorous and challenges deficit-minded approaches to teaching all students, (2) culturally responsive teaching materials that encourage a focus on student assets, and (3) a safe classroom environment where students feel empowered to critique social norms and develop agency. When combined, a curriculum developed around these elements has the potential to teach students how to read and write for real purposes, confronting the –isms in their communities. Bruce (2013) challenges teachers to be subversive, "blurring the line between teaching and activism" (p. 32). Essentially, through building the curriculum around writing arguments, making claims on the front end of the project, and then bringing in opportunities to read, write about, and discuss diverse texts, Steve increased possibilities for student choice centered on their interests and concerns later in the project, as Bruce (2013) suggests must happen in a subversive writing classroom.

The final component of the project required students to create a TED Talk-style presentation for an audience of peers and community members. Students passionately delivered spoken arguments, supported by their research and experiences with activism. Students found voice and personal relevance and provided commentary on their research and work as activists. Some students spoke with pride about the change their actions prompted in the community, while others simply did not experience the same degree of success. Similar to Destiny and Tally, many articulated how the experience taught them about the complexity of current issues and realities of doing activist work.

Implications and Conclusion

This exploration speaks to the risks, challenges, and rewards Steve takes and provides a rich description of how he challenges his students to take risks, conquer challenges, and reap rewards. Now, more than ever, we need research that shows practical applications of the ways that social contexts matter in teaching, learning, student growth, and in the development of equitable and just forms and systems of education. Steve and Heather take pride in the outcomes this curriculum has had for these students and in the positive response received from so many educators.

The greatest takeaways from implementing this curriculum over the past three years is that teaching for activism, and doing it well, is inherently messy and exhaustive. A deliberately ambiguous approach involves continuously communicating with students and trusting them to determine direction. Such uncertainty is unfamiliar in an institution that is known for following a predictable pattern of teacher-given instruction followed by an assessment. There is a learning curve in justice-oriented subversive teaching marked by the recursive process of questioning, dialogue, and reflection. Amid this learner-driven activist work, the course of direction often changes, making the end objective almost unrecognizable. The value of the process and resulting agency and empowerment are not fully understood and actualized until both the teacher and learner have the opportunity to reflect and celebrate at the end. Thus, the RCP will continue to be the crux of the eighth-grade ELA curriculum at NCMS and will evolve through each annual iteration.

Standardization in the form of scripted curriculum, benchmark testing, and other state and national initiatives are part and parcel of public education today. Therefore, it is up to those who want a high-quality, rigorous, meaningful curriculum to design and implement activities and lessons that support the standards. We argue teachers can subvert the traditional standards-based curriculum by exploring the needs and interests of students and focusing on the development of a curriculum that empowers students to examine how they matter. The RCP provides a strong example of a teacher-developed curriculum that not only engages students in high-interest, culturally sustaining pedagogies but also helps them develop necessary problem-solving skills and find agency.

References

Alexie, S. (2007). *The absolutely true diary of a part-time Indian*. Little, Brown.

Bruce, H. E. (2013). Subversive acts of revision: Writing and justice. *English Journal, 102*(6), 31–39.

Butin, D. W. (2003). Of what use is it? Multiple conceptualizations of service learning within education. *Teachers College Record, 105,* 1674–1692. doi:10.1046/j.1467-9620.2003.00305

Coffey, H. & Fulton, S. (2018). The Responsible Change Project: Building a justice-oriented middle school curriculum through critical service-learning. *Middle School Journal, 49*(5), 16–25.

Conklin, H., & Hughes, H. (2016). Practices of compassionate, critical, justice-oriented teacher education. *Journal of Teacher Education, 67,* 47–60. doi: 10.1177/0022487115607346

ESSA (2015). Every Student Succeeds Act of 2015, Pub. L. No. 114-95 § 114 Stat. 1177 (2015–2016).

Ladson-Billings, G. (2017). The (R)Evolution will not be standardized: Teacher education, hip hop pedagogy, and culturally relevant pedagogy 2.0. In D. Paris & H. S. Alim (Eds.), *Culturally sustaining pedagogies: Teaching and learning for justice in a changing world* (pp. 141–168). Teachers College Press.

Paris, D. & Alim, S. (Eds.) (2017). *Culturally sustaining pedagogies: Teaching and learning for justice in a changing world*. Teachers College Press.

Postman, N. & Weingartner, C. (1969). *Teaching as a subversive activity*. Delacorte Press.

Stone, N. (2017). *Dear Martin*. Simon & Schuster.

Thomas, A. (2017). *The hate U give*. Balzer + Bray.

Wiggins, G. & McTighe, J. (2005). *Understanding by design* (2nd ed.). Association for Supervision and Curriculum Development.

CHAPTER TWELVE

Disability as Pedagogy: Vulnerability as a Social Justice Tool

KATIE ROQUEMORE

I FIRST DISCLOSED MY disability during my freshman year of college. Even though I had been diagnosed with muscular dystrophy shortly before my 12th birthday, only those closest to me knew. When I began struggling to carry heavy textbooks and walk long distances across my college campus, I started using a mobility scooter. I did not so much disclose my disability as allow the scooter to announce it. No longer passing as abled meant that I was often treated differently by my peers, both those who knew me and those who did not. The stigma of being disabled, particularly young and disabled, was unimaginably hard for me. I quickly learned that my first task was to put others at ease, to show how despite my disability I was still "normal" (Goffman, 1963). I had only experienced my disability through a deficit lens—countless trips to specialist doctors had taught me that my disability was a defect and that I should hope one day there would be a cure (Clare, 2017; Shakespeare, 2018). Because I excelled in school and wanted to become a teacher, I minimized my disability experience to prove that I was capable of teaching despite my limitations. I internalized the shame and stigma of my disability and did not believe disability could be a positive part of my identity.

During my first year of teaching, I began realizing how wrong I was to minimize my disability identity. Through embracing my vulnerabilities, I could create a more inclusive classroom. Although I did not realize it, I was enacting disability pedagogy.

Disability as pedagogy centers the personal experience of disabled educators as models for resistance and justice in the classroom (Anderson, 2006; Pritchard, 2010). Although I did not have the language of disability pedagogy, I began making decisions in my classroom that centered the vulnerability of my disability. I rejected the myth of independence, accepted my limitations, and allowed students to do the same. This vulnerability and disability pedagogy became critical components of writing instruction in my classroom.

Traditional Research and Writing Practices

Argumentative and persuasive writing instruction is expected in ELA classrooms. Components of traditional argumentative writing include claims, evidence, and warrants, where teachers are expected to instruct students in reasoning skills and research practices (Howell et al, 2017). Many students' only exposure to argumentative writing comes in the form of the five-paragraph essay. The five-paragraph essay dominates ELA instruction, in part, because of its connection to standardized testing; students are taught to write this way for tests (Schwartz, 2014). Students learn that there is one correct way to write an essay with little room for creativity. At the school where I taught, the English department expected students to write research papers each year. During my first year of teaching, this meant requiring students to choose a topic related to a required text, conduct research using digital and print resources, and complete research notecards for each fact they find. When we adopted a new curriculum, this focus shifted slightly to include more student choice and what the district called "engaging scenarios."

The expectations of how to conduct research and write arguments did not shift. To meet the expectations of these traditional writing assignments, students often learn formulaic rules to writing that include the thesis as the final sentence in the introductory paragraph, a separate paragraph for each main idea, and at least three sentences per paragraph (Miller, 2010). The research unit plan I was supposed to follow asked students to explore the power that words, both spoken and written, have to persuade, motivate, and foster change. Students were supposed to analyze foundational U.S. documents that have themes of injustice, per the Common Core State Standards, and then research, write, and compete in a fake TED Talk competition about their topic. Students were expected to meet standards for reading informational texts and writing explanatory texts, such as being able to delineate and evaluate arguments and write texts that examine and convey complex ideas. The emphasis on claims, warrants, and evidence remained and did not allow for personal experience and emotion.

Activist Writing for Social Justice

As a new teacher, I was not confident to change the research paper assignments right away, but as I continued to explore disability as pedagogy, I realized I needed to change how I approached writing instruction. One spring, the school's only elevator broke down for more than 30 days. On days it was not working, I had to circle the school and move through the parking lot, around to the sidewalk, and across some grass to get to my classroom. Students noticed, and then they started asking questions. They recognized the injustice, not just for me but also for others in our school community who may need the elevator. Each day of the breakdown, students would ask me for an update. I could only tell them that it had been reported—that maintenance knew of the issue. Anderson (2006) writes:

> Teachers with disabilities engage the political by living with inaccessible buildings, attitudes, and policies. Colliding with these structures impacts personal experience: the self confronts social disablement with one's impairment. Teachers with disabilities live out a highly personal and embodied politics of resistance while serving as a guide to students in the classroom. (p. 375)

Eventually, students started writing e-mails to administrators in the superintendent's office. Their activism led to daily e-mail updates on the status of the elevator repair work and several apologies from people in high-ranking positions. Without their persistence, I do not think I would have gotten those updates and apologies. The elevator was repaired and operational within a week.

To me, it became clear that opening up to students about my disability and embracing my vulnerability were teaching them lessons in social justice and inspiring action. The e-mail campaign to district administrators was authentic, and students used writing skills to accomplish their goals. I wanted to embed this same type of social justice work in our class. Traditional writing approaches diminish emotion in favor of reason and factual evidence. Frustration and anger upon witnessing ableism and injustice prompted the students' action. My vulnerability became a tool to center social justice in writing instruction. Our district's push to have students read more informational texts and write research papers was one opportunity I had to subvert traditional reading and writing assignments.

Disability as Pedagogy for Subversion

I had not considered how my disability identity could be an asset to my teaching. My experiences in my teacher education program reinforced internalized ableism because disability was almost always situated as a problem. Although my teacher preparation courses focused on teaching for social justice and preservice teachers were expected to think critically about their identities and positionalities in the classroom, this identity work was limited to race, gender, socioeconomic status, and, at times, religious beliefs. Our professors did not include ability as part of our identities, and my peers and I were never exposed to positive disabled role models. Now

I understand that my experiences in teacher education and as a teacher are impacted by dysconscious ableism. Broderick and Lalvani (2017) explain that educators often have a limited understanding of how disability functions as a form of social oppression. Dysconsciousness is created by and supports normative ideologies and is characterized by "an uncritical habit of mind" that is learned through typical educational experiences (King, 1991, p. 135). Dysconscious ableism

> is a form of ableism that tacitly accepts and reproduces what Campbell (2009) refers to as the two core elements of ableism's regime: "the notion of the normative (and normate individual) and the enforcement of a constitutional divide" between abled and disabled identities. (Broderick & Lalvani, 2017, p. 895)

In teacher education practice, dysconscious ableism makes it challenging for teachers to understand ableist oppression and enact socially just, equitable, and liberatory practices.

I experienced dysconscious ableism in the taken-for-granted understandings of where disability belongs in education. Disability is typically synonymous with special education, so a disabled teacher forced my peers to confront "the notion of the normative." I learned that the only place disability exists in schools is in special education. I downplayed my limitations and vulnerability to seem more like my peers and less like students in special education, and I was often complimented for overcoming my disability or "not letting it hold me back." I believed that my disability was a negative part of me. However, openly disabled teachers engage the political and "live out highly personal and embodied politics of resistance" through their unique standpoint of social disablement (Anderson, 2006, p. 375). Disabled teachers are models of resistance, persistence, and support for students by "challenging the animosity of dominant cultural beliefs of disability" and enacting pedagogic justice (Pritchard, 2010, p. 43). Disability as pedagogy welcomes the disabled body into the classroom as it is.

After I had been teaching for several years, I learned that there are varied theories of disability. The most prominent is the medical model of disability that views disability as an individual deficit. It is the model that most medical, rehabilitative, and special education practices utilize. In this understanding of disability, my muscular dystrophy was the problem, not an inaccessible built environment. This model focuses on cure and rehabilitation or training to make disabled bodies and minds perform more like typical bodies and minds. Social models of disability, however, theorize that disability is socially constructed, and disabled people face discrimination and oppression because of their environments. Early social model proponents focused mainly on physical disability. For wheelchair users, like me, aspects of an environment—buildings with stairs, narrow doorframes, and small restrooms—are what disable, not bodily limitations. Empowered by the social model of disability, I sought out disabled bloggers and activists and learned more about disability justice. When I began to reframe my experiences as a disabled woman through a social justice lens, my entire world shifted. I realized that my body was not the problem and that I could use my experiences to build authentic relationships with students. This meant sharing my experiences with ableism, like the slow response to the broken elevator, and reframing my vulnerability as an asset. I found that I could best model this through writing with students.

Vulnerability and Social Justice Writing

When it was time for the research paper unit, I knew I wanted to change aspects of the district plan that culminated in a fake TED Talk competition. I decided to remove the competition but keep the public speaking element. This required students to conduct research on a social injustice, write an argumentative paper, and make decisions to transform the written word to a spoken presentation. Students would pick topics that mattered to them and present to the class. As a class, we would brainstorm injustices, and then using my experiences as a disabled woman, I would model each step of the project by writing a talk about ableism. Students suggested injustices you might expect, such as pollution and cosmetic testing on animals. However, students also suggested topics from their own lived experiences. One student spoke about the bias of the court system toward mothers in custody proceedings—she rarely gets to spend time with her father.

Once students chose topics, we analyzed TED Talks as informational texts—subverting the notion that print texts are the only texts used in English classes. Instead of focusing on many different injustices (as the prescribed unit plan suggested) as a class, I decided to focus our class analysis on a single injustice—modern slavery. This allowed me to model research and analysis on a single topic—what students would do for their TED Talks—and include the whole class in the process. In addition to reading speeches, news reports, and documents from the United Nations on human rights, we watched a TED Talk by photographer Lisa Kristine, who traveled the world photographing people currently enslaved. From miners in the Congo to the textile industry in India to sex slaves in Nepal, she bears witness to modern slavery by photographing portraits.

As a class, we analyzed how Kristine wove together her photographs with factual information to create an argument to end modern slavery and support the nonprofit Free the Slaves. Although Kristine mentions that modern slavery also exists in the United States, her talk focused on the global scope of modern slavery. I wanted students to explore how the injustice of modern slavery was an issue in their own community. I asked a local sheriff, who was married to another teacher at our school, to come speak about human trafficking in our community. He was one of the first sheriff deputies in our state to be trained for a special task force that identified and responded to human trafficking. Students sat enthralled as he explained that the three most common sites he finds human trafficking occurring are restaurants, nail salons, and brothels. Even though we had researched modern slavery as a class, it was not until our guest shared real-life examples from our city that students could bridge our research to our lives.

To provide another example of a TED Talk and share more about my topic with students, I shared with the class Stella Young's (2014) "I'm Not Your Inspiration, Thank You Very Much" talk. As part of our analysis, we looked for elements such as a hook, narrative, evidence, visual, and call to action in her talk. Young's talk introduced students to the social model of disability and to the idea of "inspiration porn." She gives examples of common images we see on social media—a girl with no arms using her mouth to hold a pencil and draw—to explain inspiration porn. Images such as this one are created not only to make able-bodied people feel inspired but also to objectify disabled people. Her talk is funny and easy to understand. It allowed me to bring up ideas such as inspiration porn with my students and include my own experiences. Her talk also modeled how students could write and present on an injustice while using humor. Young talks about the "Big Lie" we have been sold about disability—that it is a tragedy—and our class was able to think about how narratives shape other injustices.

Using the ideas from Young's talk, I modeled for students each part of the writing process. Young's hook was a humorous story about the time when she was 15 and a community member wanted to nominate her for a community achievement award. Her parents insisted she had not achieved anything. She says,

> I went to school, I got good marks, I had a very low-key after school job in my mum's hairdressing salon, and I spent a lot of time watching *Buffy the Vampire Slayer* and *Dawson's Creek*. Yeah, I know. What a contradiction. But they were right, you know. I wasn't doing anything that was out of the ordinary at all. I wasn't doing anything that could be considered an achievement if you took disability out of the equation. (Young, 2014)

For my own hook, I wrote about a time that a stranger tried to put my coat on for me without asking and ignored my repeated assurances that I could do it myself. As a class, we talked about how using an emotional narrative can be one strategy to hook your audience. Whereas Young used humor, I tried to write my hook in such a way to capture my frustration. Crafting a hook in this way also incorporated evidence in the talks. I had found an engaging way to model writing for my students (they had questions and comments about my experience), and, I believe, it empowered them to share their own vulnerabilities.

Vulnerability is a shared human experience. The ways that being disabled exposed my vulnerabilities to students strengthened our relationship. It also shaped how I came to believe in the goals of social justice education. To understand our vulnerability is to understand our privileges and oppressions. To understand our vulnerability is to understand what it means to belong. Disability as pedagogy is one way to subvert traditional, oppressive educational norms. Not every teacher will have a disability identity, but we all can learn to express our vulnerability in ways that build a classroom community.

References

Anderson, R. C. (2006). Teaching (with) disability: Pedagogies of lived experience. *Review of Education, Pedagogy & Cultural Studies, 28*, 367–379.

Broderick, A., & Lalvani, P. (2017). Dysconscious ableism: Toward a liberatory praxis in teacher education. *International Journal of Inclusive Education, 21*, 894–905.

Campbell, F. (2009). *Contours of ableism: The production of disability and abled-ness*. Palgrave Macmillan.

Clare, E. (2017). *Brilliant imperfection: Grappling with cure*. Duke University Press.

Goffman, E. (1963). *Stigma: Notes on the management of spoiled identity*. Prentice-Hall.

Howell, E., Butler, T., & Reinking, D. (2017). Integrating multimodal arguments into high school writing instruction. *Journal of Literacy Research, 49*, 181–209.

King, J. E. (1991). Dysconcious racism: Ideology, identity, and the miseducation of teachers. *Journal of Negro Education, 60*, 133–146.

Miller, J. (2010). Persistence of the five-paragraph essay. *English Journal, 99*, 99–100.

Pritchard, G. (2010). Disabled people as culturally relevant teachers. *Journal of Social Inclusion, 1*(1), 43–51.

Schwartz, L. H. (2014). Challenging the tyranny of the five-paragraph essay: Teachers and students as semiotic boundary workers in classroom and digital space. *Literacy, 48*, 124–135.

Shakespeare, T. (2018). *Disability: The basics*. Routledge.

Young, S. (2014). *I'm not your inspiration, thank you very much* [Video file]. Retrieved from https://www.ted.com/talks/stella_young_i_m_not_your_inspiration_thank_you_very_much?language=en

CHAPTER THIRTEEN

Gender Bending the Curriculum: Queer Approaches to Teaching Shakespeare

RYAN BURNS AND JANINE BOISELLE

IN THIS CHAPTER, WE (Ryan, a high school English teacher and doctoral student, and Janine, a middle school English teacher), critically reflect on our time together in the classroom during a ninth-grade unit on Shakespeare's *Romeo and Juliet* (1985). Janine was a teacher candidate assigned to Ryan during her student-teaching experience in the spring of 2018. As out educators who value social justice teaching, we formed a personal and professional relationship as we came to acknowledge both our queer presence and practice in subverting the traditional English language arts (ELA) discipline. We are aware of how "queerness and queering pierce or seek to pierce such norms both inside and outside institutional frameworks," emphasizing "breaking habits, rules, and norms to make life survivable and thrivable" (Greteman, 2016, p. 4). In enacting our subversion of the ELA classroom, through challenging students to question and critique traditional gender ideals, we acknowledge that student learning is mobilized by what Medina and Wohlwend (2014) call the "tacit heteronormative school expectations" that "uphold heterosexual nexus" (p. 85) as the privileged norm in secondary English curriculum. Although we believe education ought to be inclusive and supportive of the lived experiences of young adults, the written curriculum still largely remains out of touch with many of our students. Literacy ought to be understood as it exists: already politically and socially situated. However, different ideologies that circulate around curriculum make it difficult to produce systematic improvement in education and limit the possibilities of literacies. Politicians, educators, and administrators "have been unable to settle on a single ideological orientation or a negotiated compromise among ideological orientations" (Shiro, 2013, p. 3). Increasingly in our school and district, growing pressures from state and local accountability measures require the curriculum to be directly linked to increased student achievement on the state standardized assessment for high school students. When such expectations are not met, units of study and even whole courses are identified as problematic, often with administrative intervention in future curriculum development that results in a lack of student choice and teacher autonomy. Despite these curricular contentions combined with our professional vulnerabilities as queer educators, we subverted the traditional curriculum framework and heteronormativity while still meeting school and district requirements.

Ryan and Janine's Collaboration: Subverting the Heteronormative Canon

During the many conversations we shared throughout Janine's student-teaching internship, we found ourselves ruminating on notions of subversion and how our multidimensional identities informed our critically oriented and socially just curriculum ideologies. Despite trends in teaching for social justice and increased attention to equity and diversity, "schools are not often sites of support, affirmation, or safety for LGBTQ students and teachers" (Bloomfield & Fisher, 2016, p. 1). As a result, these oppressive systems "limit people's lives and imaginations so much that they can't see beyond the limitations" (Johnson, 2006, p. 130). This imaginative control serves as a function of heteronormativity and occurs across social systems and settings, including schools. These restrictions are especially solidified within educational spaces that may have remained unchanged over decades and sometimes centuries. Although there are state laws and district policies that protect LGBTQ educators in Rhode Island, we still face challenges and tensions in school. As much as we discussed curriculum and pedagogy during Janine's initial visit, talking about personal and professional safety and vulnerability within the community of queer educators became equally important.

According to DeWitt (2012), high school ELA curricula have inscribed predominantly heterosexual images in text and topic selection. Such exposure to normative sexualities and genders increases forms of "exclusion that limit the scope of how and by whom culture is produced" (Medina & Wohlwend, 2014, p. 14). As we brainstormed possible approaches to a unit on Shakespeare's *Romeo and Juliet* (1985), that we needed to offer our students opportunities to interrogate issues of gender in the play and notions of gender performance in the real world became clear. Again, we believe that in secondary English classrooms, having a curriculum that honors the knowledge, literacy practices, and identities of all our students is paramount.

Subverting the Curriculum, Subverting the Standards

For this unit on Shakespeare's *Romeo and Juliet* (1985), we arranged the following essential question, which helped construct our subversive, critical framework, as well as the following supporting questions:

Essential Question

- In what ways does Shakespeare both reinforce and resist stereotypical gender expectations in *Romeo & Juliet*?

Supporting Questions

- Why and how do people try to determine sex and gender?
- In what ways are girls expected to act differently than boys?
- In what ways do Romeo and Juliet conform to or resist the gender expectations placed on them?

Traditional approaches to scene analysis shift attention to issues of language and imagery in ways that leave students disempowered and disconnected. The curriculum, as it has been historically developed, "is largely designed to keep students from knowing themselves and their environment in any realistic sense . . . it does not allow inquiry into most of the critical problems that comprise the content of the world outside the school" (Postman & Weingartner, 1969, p. 47). To critical educators who question the authority of what Postman and Weingartner call the "Educational Establishment," this moment is layered in complexity as it reveals heteronormative expectations and gender performativity. The selection of texts and topics in the high school English curriculum, then, "signify more profound political, economic, and cultural relations and histories," often functioning as "proxies for wider questions of power relations" (Lankshear & McLaren, 1993, p. 198). The limited scope of texts has created the very canon that is used as a point of reference for what is valued as worth reading and including in the curriculum. When discussions around ELA curriculum development reveal "universal" themes and "timeless" texts, including Shakespeare, educators seemingly redraw the ideological fault lines, carving these boundaries deeper than before. Thus, the decisions made by teachers relating to limited views on curriculum development have real consequences for students. For Freire and Macedo (1987), a high school English curriculum can be radicalized and revolutionized by developing programs "rooted in an emancipatory ideology, where readers become 'subjects' rather than mere 'objects'" (p. 156).

Our Positionalities

I (Ryan) am a 34-year-old White male from a middle-class family, having spent the majority of my life in a small city outside of Providence, Rhode Island. My mother and father never finished high school and never married, and during my early child-hood years, my father was deported from the United States.

Although I was not out in high school, I grew more comfortable in my sexuality as I moved through college and my social justice–oriented teacher education pro-gram. When I first entered the profession after graduation, I was still coming to terms with my own perceptions of my queerness and what this meant for me as a beginning teacher. I needed to be protected, and sometimes that meant hiding behind the mask of assumed heterosexuality. But this performance was exhausting and could not last. Over the past 12 years in education, my place in the culture of queer educators has moved back and forth from fully embracing my queer social identity and commit-ment to social justice to dialing back how I enact more critical literacy practices in the classroom. At these times, my embodiment of queerness was predicated on where I was teaching and my feelings of personal and professional safety.

I (Janine) grew up near the coast of southeastern Connecticut, in an affluent town. I have lived and continue to live a life layered with privileges as a White cisgen-der educator. My happily divorced, heterosexual parents funded my undergraduate degree, and not until finishing my freshman year did I begin feeling undeserving of this advantage. I picked up part-time work during school to compensate for tuition costs. My journey to question everything, including my sexuality, had only just begun as I completed course work in queer and feminist theory.

Before student teaching, I hoped to shatter the bubbles of my students' lives while simultaneously learning about my own privileges and power that I may still be unaware of. In preparing to student teach, I researched basic demographics on the district. In the weeks that followed, I felt a sense of familiarity within the culture of the school, as this town was similar to the community in which I was raised: mostly White, middle class, and politically conservative. From a predominantly homoge-nous area, I found my students to be as sheltered as I was in my youth. However, during my time with Ryan, my positioning as a masculine-presenting woman made my goal more challenging. Without a doubt, there were clear personal and profes-sional disconnects between me and my newfound colleagues.

When I drove to school on my first day of student teaching, I remember think-ing, *I have never felt so gay.* During my teacher education course work, I was in and out of multiple schools, never able to completely integrate into the culture. Feeling a sense of belonging while only spending one to three weeks inside each school was impossible. However, student teaching with Ryan was very different. For four months, my students, and the larger community, would witness my queer-ness. Both sides of my head were shaved. I would be addressed as "Miss" even as I wore men's button-down shirts, slacks, and loafers. Every time I looked down at the tie around my neck, I felt exhilarated. For me, it felt like a symbol of hope, but there was no way of knowing if I would instead get choked for being queer in such a heteronormative space.

Between stoplights during the car ride, I rehearsed my "First Day Spoken Word Poem." I wanted my introduction to be memorable beyond my outfit, so I risked performing in an unfamiliar genre. My lines consisted of quick-witted accounts of my newfound teaching identity mixed with past experiences as a student, describing myself as "the daydream queen on autopilot if I didn't like the teacher." I can still picture Ryan's face, sitting there stunned; this was his first impression of me. What drove me to start my teaching journey this way was a longing to be honest and raw. If I was going to be the real Ms. Boiselle, I needed to unveil my excitement, fears, flaws, and, of course, my colorful taste in men's fashion.

Using My Body to Subvert Gender Roles in Shakespeare

For the purposes of this extended unit on *Romeo and Juliet* (1985), I (Janine) started class with a quick write after students read Act II, Scene ii, the infamous balcony confession between the star-crossed lovers: *Imagine that you are walking down the street and cross paths with a stranger. How do you know if they are a man or a woman?* The responses from students were plentiful, but two categories emerged: clothing and performance (body language/movement, speech). I began scrawling their ideas on the whiteboard while simultaneously playing devil's advocate by using the presentation of my own body as a model. Although I was not fearless in my approach, it allowed students to begin recognizing the complexities that exist within people's presentations of their bodies. Through further questioning, we discussed how my decision to wear men's clothing, as a female-identifying woman, does not necessarily signify a desire to be perceived as male. The conformity and nonconformity of individuals through clothing, and their reasoning behind such selections, are equally as valid. I recall one student's comment that made me happy to teach while dressed as myself. This student perceived the presentation of my body as an inherent part of my identity rather than one that was gay. However, disclosing my decision to leave my sexual orientation unnamed during my student teaching experience, a critical decision I now regret and reflect on later in this chapter, is essential.

What followed was a Think–Pair–Share on the differences between sex and gender before transitioning to an activity related to gender performance. I read a list of gendered and nongendered commands for students to act out, including *stand*, *sit*, and *jog*. I then attached "like a girl or boy" to each. Between performances, I invited students to talk through their movements while encouraging others to answer questions such as *What does it mean to be "ladylike"? Why do men pose for pictures as if they are ready to fight someone? What are the implications for "following the rules" of acting "like a girl" or to "man up"? Who or what communicates these messages to us? What are the implications for us as critical consumers?* With these questions in mind, students returned to *Romeo and Juliet* with a focus on rereading the development of characterization in the scene. By using a reflective exit ticket at the end of class, I was able to document their observations about each character, ranging in subject from power struggles between men and women, overzealous, "first move" flirtation from Romeo, and Juliet's awareness of the female trope "playing hard to get," and her decision to conform by asking Romeo to woo her first. Although the majority of students shared similar learning mementos through their exit tickets, one particular student led me to reflect on the lesson's effectiveness. This student's observation suggested that the activity helped them distinguish men from women. This communicated concern for me as a queer educator because being aware of someone's gender or genitalia should not be a skill one strives to acquire. As critical consumers, we ought to be aware of the role in which the non/conformity of gender stereotypes has an impact on how people are treated in society and to apply this understanding to create a more just world.

A second critical lesson offered students an opportunity to engage with more contemporary and multimodal texts, specifically scenes from Disney's animated film *Mulan* (2017). This media lesson invited students to consider two songs in the film, "I'll Make a Man Out of You" and "Honor to Us All." Students began class with an opportunity to reflect on visual and musical notions of masculinity in *Romeo and Juliet* and *Mulan*, generating ideas ranging from expectations for men and women, including physical and mental strength, limiting exposure of emotions, and equating femininity with weakness. With more explicit instructions on annotation strategies, students reviewed the song lyrics to pair their annotative markers (highlights, underlines, etc.) with active-reading margin notes. Annotations allow students to record what they are thinking in the moment and provides teachers with detailed data samples to identify and assess the depth of student understanding. During this activity, some students expressed displeasure in the oversimplification of men and women in *Mulan* (2017) while others noted that women are only desirable through submission and physical appearance. Students were also able to identify how these dominant discourses on gender were communicated in social settings within the film, particularly through pressure from family members. Even though this annotation activity generated insightful responses, some students were unable to recognize how the heteronormative stereotypes create tension and inequality beyond the lives of characters in an animated film. At the surface, these reflections offer insight into how ninth graders conceive of gender and gender performance. Following the guided viewing of *Mulan* (2017), we transitioned to the play, viewing Franco Zeffirelli's film adaptation of *Romeo & Juliet* (1968). At this point, Juliet has admitted to Lord Capulet, her father, that she has no interest in marrying Paris, throwing her father into a fit of rage. As we viewed the violent altercation, students considered how Juliet's non/conformity to gender exacerbated this fight for power. In addition to sharing personal stories on how adults at home have enacted similar behaviors like Capulet's, students also identified evidence from the text that exemplified how control was established by Capulet and explained how it relates to gender. Unpacking and situating gender, even in the high school classroom, are not possible if there is no conversation that names the tug and pull of patriarchy and heteronormativity.

To Queer or Not to Queer . . .

We use queer theory, which invites endless possibilities that problematize the structuring power of heteronormativity in the classroom (Hall, 2001, p. 234), to frame our curriculum choices and implementation of the required texts. Stemming from early feminist criticism and the gay liberation movement, queer theory "challenges the normative social ordering of identities and subjectivities along the heterosexual/homosexual binary as well as the privileging of heterosexuality as 'natural' and homosexuality as its deviant and abhorrent 'other'" (Browne & Nash, 2016, p. 5). For Sumara and Davis (1999), the theoretical underpinnings of queer theory also function to interrupt heteronormativity in its approach to pedagogy and curriculum in schools as it "does not ask that pedagogy become sexualized, but that it excavate and interpret the way it already is sexualized . . . that it begin to interpret the way that it is explicitly heterosexualized" (p. 192). Sumara and Davis point to the pervasiveness of heteronormativity within K–12 settings: As it maneuvers ideologically, it also separates itself from critical conversations on gender and sexuality. Queer theorists such as Butler (1990) and Foucault (1978) suggest that there is more fluidity within and between sexual identities than the heterosexual/homosexual binary. The literacies around gender and sexuality are themselves "complex literacy event[s], evoking narrations of self, connections with others through complex discourses, and political formations mediated through ideological investments" (Alexander, 2008, p. 1). As power shifts within the dominant culture, stereotypes are created, and the power dynamic is reinforced and built into patriarchy through language. Queer approaches in the classroom, then, are already fraught with the tension between problems and possibilities even before the first lesson begins.

Risks and Rewards to Acts of Resistance in the Classroom

The Act I traditional assessment asked students to identify and define dramatic terminology and character relationships, as well as quote identifications with a surface-level explanation. As this was a common assessment generated with other ninth-grade English teachers, I (Janine) wanted to offer my students the option of a longer, authentic response to analyze a character's embodiment of gender, such as the expectations of "being a man or woman," while also examining how they do or do not follow the societal expectations in Verona. To my surprise, many students chose to write about gender. Alternatively, the "Gender Lens Monologue" assessment, while adhering to the school's formulaic writing framework, PQE (Point, Quote, Explanation), asked students to select and critically analyze a monologue from the play using strong textual evidence to support careful reading through a gender lens. In addition to the written portion of the assessment, students were invited to find an artifact of their choosing, such as an article, advertisement, film or television show clip, or YouTube channel video, that would either reinforce or resist the gender expectations that were under consideration in the selected monologue. The differences between the two assessments were striking, but even more revealing was the student responses to the different assessments. Not only did students express excitement for an assessment that branched away from the standard test or essay, but many were also shocked at how easy it was to find applicable artifacts, which added to its relevance. Students analyzed the *ifs* and *hows* of gender non/conformity in connection to their monologue in everything from sports articles to viral memes.

Critical literacy, then, informs our pedagogical practices as we learn and create with and alongside our students in deconstructing texts and discourses in and out of the classroom. With any type of critical literacy that challenges patterns of power, dehumanization, and inequalities, there is always the possibility of resistance from students, parents, and administrators. My (Janine) positioning as a young, queer educator left me in a vulnerable place, both as a teacher candidate finishing student teaching and, now, as a nontenured faculty member going into my second full year of teaching. I recall a particular incident toward the end of one lesson when I made a comment about the casting of Shakespearean plays and how many female roles were often played by young men. A male student verbalized his disgust. I instantly froze and then repeated what he said back to him in the form of a question. Without giving him a chance to explain, the voices of a dozen students erupted in disbelief. Before I could address his comment, the bell rang, and the student was out the door. Shortly after, he e-mailed an apology to Ryan and me for his comment. Although the student and I later conferenced, I am still unsure what his apology truly stood for. *Was it genuine regret for shaming same-sex intimacy or cross-dressing? The likely age gap between cast members? Or for making a comment of that nature in front of two openly gay teachers?* Then again, I wonder if by naming my identification as a lesbian from the very beginning of my student teaching, would this critical incident have ever happened? Upon reflection, the self-silencing of my identity inadvertently reinforces the notion that discussing sexuality is not acceptable, and this is not a message I am willing to risk sending to my current or future students. As I move forward in my teaching career, I am realizing the inevitable: My body is my pedagogy, and with that comes constant negotiation of what I do and do not share and how it can support my students. Despite these unexpected moments in the lesson, by the end of my student-teaching experience, another student from the same class, assigned female at birth, sent a detailed e-mail thanking me for forming an honest connection with them and for offering opportunities to evaluate gender while reading Shakespeare. At the end of the e-mail, my student felt comfortable to disclose to me that they identified as transgender.

We know there have been shifts and movement in the development of literacy curriculum to reflect certain trends, including an emphasis on multicultural texts. Transformation is possible "because a system happens only as people participate in it—it can't help being a dynamic process of creation and re-creation from one moment to the next" (Johnson, 2006, p. 129). There is a nostalgia, however, from the previous experiences of teachers as students that influences the selection of curriculum materials in ways that privileges some material while disregarding material more relevant to students today. The path to an inclusive literacy curriculum can have a lasting impact on students and teachers alike but only if teachers have the autonomy to collaborate meaningfully and engage in opportunities to question and disrupt the teaching of canonical texts. In our subversion of the traditional Grade 9 English curriculum, students negotiated a critical reading and analysis of Shakespeare's drama and the world beyond the text. The intellectual and pedagogical possibilities for critical perspectives and authentic experiences in the teaching of Shakespeare are endless when we are committed to transformation despite the political and social values of the school or district. Given the conservative ideologies of our community, Ryan and I anticipated pushback to our disruption of the curriculum and explicit critique of gender discourses in and out of the text. Instead, we experienced personal and professional moments of both unity and tension through choosing to queer, prioritizing space for students to critically read, talk back to, and reshape their worlds.

References

Alexander, J. (2008). *Literacy, sexuality, pedagogy: Theory and practice for composition studies*. Utah State University Press.

Bloomfield, V., & Fisher, M. (2016). *LGBTQ voices in education: Changing the culture of schooling*. Routledge.

Boiselle, Janine. (2018). First day of student teaching [Poem]. Retrieved from https://docs.google.com/document/d/1KwOlmgdI5dMfkyudaxMza2lmxvdiZfWoLkgOmlv150/edit.

Brabourne, J., & Havelock-Allan, A. (Producers), & Zeffirelli, F. (Director). (1968). *Romeo and Juliet* [Motion picture]. Paramount Pictures.

Browne, K., & Nash, C. (2016). *Queer methods and methodologies: Intersecting queer theories and social science research*. Routledge.

Butler, J. (1990). *Gender trouble*. Routledge.

Coats, P. (Producer), & Bancroft, T., & Cook, B. (Directors). (2017). *Mulan* [Motion picture]. Walt Disney Animation.

DeWitt, P. (2012). *Dignity for all: Safeguarding LGBT students*. Corwin.

Foucault, M. (1978). *The history of sexuality: Volume 1: An introduction*. Vintage.

Freire, P., & Macedo, D. (1987). *Literacy: Reading the word and the world*. Bergin & Garvey.

Greteman, A. (2016). Contingent labor, Contingently queer. In sj Miller & N. Rodriguez (Eds.), *Educators queering academia: Critical memoirs* (pp. 3–11). Peter Lang.

Hall, D. (2001). *Literary and cultural theory: From basic principles to advanced applications*. Houghton Mifflin.

Johnson, A. (2006). *Privilege, power, and difference*. McGraw-Hill.

Lankshear, C., & McLaren, P. (1993). *Critical literacy: Politics, praxis, and the postmodern.* SUNY Press.

Medina, C., & Wohlwend, K. (2014). *Literacy, play, and globalization: Converging imaginaries in children's critical and cultural performances.* Routledge.

Postman, N., & Weingartner, C. (1969). *Teaching as a subversive activity.* Dell Publishing.

Shakespeare, W. (1985). In A. Durband (Ed.), *Romeo and Juliet*: Modern English version side-by-side with full original text. Barron's Educational Series. (Original work published 1597).

Shiro, M. (2013). *Curriculum theory: Conflicting visions and enduring concerns.* Sage.

Sumara, D. J. & Davis, B. (1999). Interrupting heteronormativity: Toward a queer curriculum theory. *Curriculum Inquiry, 29(2),* 191–208.

CHAPTER FOURTEEN

Interrupting "Single Stories": Using Socially Just Media Texts to Teach Rhetorical Analysis

Lori Garcia and Michael Manderino

In the middle of July, a group of teachers participated in a two-day district workshop on using media texts in the classroom. Michael (Author 2) led the workshop, and Lori (Author 1) was a participant. On the second day, the group discussed possible uses of Childish Gambino's song and video "This Is America" (Glover and Murai, 2018). By the end of the afternoon, a few teachers, including Lori, were still discussing the use of media texts such as "This Is America" and "Apeshit" by Jay-Z and Beyoncé (Carter & Knowles, 2018). Lori stated that she really wanted to rethink some of the texts she was using in her sophomore English course that included a heavy emphasis on rhetorical analysis. Initially, Lori stated she really wanted to redesign the mandated introductory unit. After a few days, Michael e-mailed Lori and inquired if she was interested in conducting a formative design experiment (Reinking & Bradley, 2008) to investigate how her curricular changes would have an impact on her students' engagement with rhetorical analysis. Initially, Lori wanted to shift how she taught rhetorical analysis by simply bringing in more media texts for the first unit. However, after a few meetings, Lori decided she wanted to redesign not only Unit 1 but also the entire first semester to subvert the texts traditionally used for rhetorical analysis.

Theoretical Frame and Research Design

The texts that had predominated the curriculum Lori taught were abstract and disconnected from the lives of her students. Sims-Bishop (1990) argued that texts can serve as windows, mirrors, and doors for students. Lori wanted to confront the fact that the existing sophomore English curriculum diminished students' knowledge and experiences by relying on predominantly Eurocentric printed texts. Instead, we wanted to create opportunities for students to restore their lives and "write themselves into being" in classroom experiences (Thomas & Stornaiuolo, 2016). To meet this pedagogical goal, we used a formative design experiment (Reinking & Bradley, 2008) as a vehicle for disrupting the curriculum and developing theory while investigating the curriculum redesign to do so. Formative design experiments begin with a pedagogical goal that is grounded in theory. Lori's pedagogical goal was to use culturally responsive texts to teach the skills of rhetorical analysis. Her goal was grounded in theories of culturally relevant and responsive teaching (Gay, 2010; Ladson-Billings, 1995). Gay (2010) defined culturally responsive teaching "as using the cultural knowledge, prior experiences, frames of reference, and performance styles of ethnically diverse students to make learning encounters more relevant to and effective for them" (p. 31). The existing curriculum did not reflect any of these tenets. Rather, the curriculum used a narrow set of texts from a Eurocentric authorship and perspective to drill rhetorical analysis skills.

To meet her pedagogical goal, Lori disrupted the texts that marginalized her students by foregrounding the cultural knowledge, experiences, and frames of reference of her students while adhering to the practice of rhetorical analysis. We used formative design as our method so that we could trace the iterative design changes from unit to unit. What consistently emerged in our initial conversations was "Who decides what is worthy of rhetorical analysis?" and "How are the texts in the existing curriculum responsive to the lived experiences of our students?" The remainder of this chapter describes the redesign process of three exemplar units.

Making the Initial Shift

The redesign of the first unit, "Engaging with the Rhetorical Situation," originally served as the unit on which Lori aimed to focus most heavily. The instructional outcomes from the departmental planning guide stated:

> The primary objective of the first mini unit of the semester aims to introduce students to the concept of the rhetorical situation by first understanding how rhetoric they've been exposed to, whether written or spoken is part of a larger rhetorical situation. As sophomore year is predominantly a composition course, students' understanding of how their choices as writers impact the rhetorical situation for their audience requires this foundational understanding and grasp of important associated vocabulary in order to progress through the semester.

Although the planning guide did not specify particular texts, the tradition of the course dictated that decontextualized pieces written predominantly from White men were used. Lori's redesign of this unit started with the texts and how they could be changed to reflect the lived experiences of her students and still meet the stated departmental instructional outcomes.

Although previous iterations of this unit drew mainly from Purdue University's Online Writing Lab's (OWL) resources for rhetorical situation, the various examples provided rarely applied to my (Lori's) "audience" of teens from an urban high school outside of Chicago. I (Lori) still wince recalling the silence I encountered in one instance when I tried to explain how one purpose of writing is "to shock" and used OWL's example of Stephen King's novels as an example and not one of my students registered understanding until I brought up the recent adaptation of *It* (King, 1987) in theaters. That I needed to meet my students where they were was clear: they were not reading Stephen King's *It*, but they were watching it.

After attending the aforementioned summer professional development session on media literacy texts, as well as some important conferences by the Pacific Educational Group, an organization which aims to achieve equity in education, I began reflecting and redesigning the introductory unit. The first important change was to adapt the term of *writer* to that of *creator* as an acknowledgment of how my students' lives rarely revolve around only written text. Additionally, I dismissed our discipline's reliance on "model exemplary texts" traditionally used for rhetorical analysis, such as excerpts from various political speeches, as they not only tended to be predominantly from a White male perspective but also rarely appeared in students' day-to-day experiences. I did not want to continue the narrative that "good rhetoric" comes from White male authors or that what students are encountering outside of my classroom lacks merit simply because that was how I was taught. For me, seeking out other examples of exemplary texts that were not only more racially diverse but whose content also actually connected with students' own experiences with rhetoric within their daily lives, which may or may not include political speeches, was important.

Because one of the unit objectives was for students to gain an awareness of their own powerful role as "creators," bringing in contemporary, relevant examples from their current everyday lives as exemplary "media texts" for them to observe how previous creators have impacted them as teens before they could truly demonstrate their understanding and eventually apply it to their own writing was important for me.

Shifting the Instruction in the First Unit

Although I still relied heavily on Purdue University's OWL's resources on rhetorical situation, I made significant changes to my instruction. The first change was to include more relevant, contemporary exemplary models, such as social media posts, when introducing students to the foundational vocabulary via a simple slides delivery. Students were responsible for completing an accompanying handout, which concluded by asking them to reflect on one of their recent social media posts and contextualize the six primary elements of the rhetorical situation (the author, the audience, the topic, the purpose, the context, and the culture) within their own posts. Subversion of the curriculum was not only to shift the texts used but to also better affirm students' existing rhetorical skills and provide the rhetorical labels by which to describe their own rhetorical moves.

By asking the students to reflect on their own "writing/creation," my goal was to show them how they already engaged in rhetorical situations every day while also refraining from simply drawing on more traditional models of exemplary texts. In previous years, students had shown strained attempts at contextualizing with little significance once they left my English classroom. My instructional shift was to then make the tacit rhetorical practices students use in their everyday lives more explicit.

The second change was my decision to include the Black Eyed Peas' "Where Is the Love?" (Black Eyed Peas, 2004) as another exemplary text, albeit a media text. This choice was more calculated given that so many of my students would prefer to remain plugged in with their earbuds listening to their favorite artist as opposed to their sophomore English teacher. In an earnest attempt to meet my students halfway, I decided to use two versions of "Where is the Love?": the original version from 2004 and the recent remake from 2016 that includes the appearance of several social media influencers, which I hoped students would find more engaging.

Adapting an approach I observed within the media literacy texts professional development, I first showed my students the lyrics and using the Gradual Release Method (Pearson & Gallagher, 1983), we all attempted to contextualize the six elements of the rhetorical situation based solely on the lyrics through a think-aloud. After we had exhausted that method, I then showed them the 2004 music video but with the audio muted. I paused on various segments of the video and guided the students in think-alouds on various frames asking them to consider the audience, the purpose, the context, the culture that the Black Eyed Peas (author/creator) wanted us (the audience) to think about when it came to war, race, and police-community relations (the topic). Finally, we merged them and viewed the video with the audio and the lyrics handout without interruptions. Students were allowed to amend their accompanying document throughout this lesson as we progressed through the various iterations. Although song lyrics have been used in various forms within English language arts (ELA) classrooms, the use of accompanying videos as a comparison of the two and analysis of the rhetorical situation in each was something new in that I purposely placed a contemporary medium, music video, as a mentor text because of the relevance to my students' everyday life experiences.

Guiding the students through the context of the exemplary text provided me with several points of consideration as we moved forward with the formative design process. Given that so many of my students were not yet born in 2001, they had little to no real grasp of the context of America post-9/11 in which a Black artist, will.i.am, was reacting to the group's 2004 version of the song. This gap in contextual understanding became all the more apparent when reflecting on how we (educators) oftentimes ask students to analyze texts to contextualize and reflect on experiences which they have little to no connection to nor understanding, particularly as a result of our reliance on arguably antiquated exemplary texts from traditionally White male authors/creators. So, although I succeeded in disrupting the traditional texts used in my ELA classroom through the use of a socially just media text from a group with which some students were familiar, I knew I needed to do more because this song and the context surrounding its production were still largely removed from my students' lived experiences.

The final change in instruction was an inclusion of student choice as students selected a song of their choosing and applied their understanding of the six elements of the rhetorical situation via the same handout we had completed as a whole class with "Where Is the Love?" The variety of lyrical selections made by students was intriguing, from Drake's "Back to Back" (Drake, 2015) to Childish Gambino's "This Is America" (Glover & Murai, 2018) which I had contemplated using before settling on "Where Is the Love?" (Black Eyed Peas, 2004). These observations further supported our estimation that students were yearning for something more relevant, contemporary, and real to their lived experiences.

My students' reactions to this mini unit cemented my continued disruption of the traditional sophomore English curriculum texts for the remainder of the semester to include marginalized voices (creators) that address issues (topics) that students were faced with and interested in exploring and discussing while also aiming to have my students consider their audience when crafting their own rhetoric as we progressed through the semester. Although arguments for the preservation of the canon may exist, this experience led me to subvert the curricular texts if the curriculum was not going to shift in the foreseeable future.

Thus, my reconfiguration of one mini unit resulted in reassessing my entire first semester. Given our observations from the first mini unit, I continued to meet with Michael and eventually settled on the tentative plan of continuing to disrupt the traditional texts used in each of the subsequent units of the semester (see Figure 14.1). I continually revisited and reconfigured the semester plan based on my observations of what appeared to be going well and what would require modifications for next year's rollout. Regrettably, some of my loftier goals had to be tabled because of the lack of time: time to devote to each units' objectives when also competing with the time needed to meet our perennial reading, grammar, and state testing objectives, along with the various other pulls we feel as classroom teachers.

The rest of this chapter describes two units to highlight my successes yet challenges with the redesign in disrupting previous years' implementation of the unit

Figure 14.1.

Working document for planning to subvert the curriculum across the semester

	Unit 1 Introductory Mini-Unit 1.5 weeks	Unit 2 Development by Description 2.5–3.5 weeks	Unit 3 Developing by Example 2.5–3.5 weeks
Texts	OWL Purdue Social media posts Black Eyed Peas – "Where Is The Love" (reinforce the 6 elements of the rhetorical situation)	Past student work Rwandan Genocide Photos by James Nachtwey Ieshia Evans protest photo by Jonathan Bachman "Stereo Hearts" by Gym Class Heroes	Disney's *Peter Pan* excerpts "The Danger of the Single Story" by Chimamanda Ngozi Adichie

Skills	Develop foundational rhetorical vocabulary and concepts
	Author
	Audience
	Purpose
	Topic
	Context
	Culture
		Figurative language –
		    Metaphor
		    Simile
		    Personification
		Sensory details
		Dominant impression
		Vantage point
		Connotation vs. denotation
		Varied sentences
		Active verbs
			Analogy
			Examples
			Transitions
			Textual evidence –
			    ICE [Introduce, Cite, Elaborate]

objectives—from relying on White male–dominated voices via print mentor texts to instead using a variety of socially just media texts. I conclude with important reflections on what I need to change for next year based on my shortcomings this first time around.

Continuing the Shift

Now determined to redesign the entire semester, we decided to meet to map out our own curriculum planning guide. The stated learning outcome(s) for the second unit, "Developing by Description," in the departmental planning guide was to introduce students to a variety of descriptive writing techniques in order for students to understand and develop their own abilities to craft writing that is demonstrative of showing versus telling and thus differs from narration. Students would be introduced to these various descriptive writing techniques through various excerpts from memoirs, essays, and informational texts, such as a composition textbook, that would serve as mentor texts. The unit culminates with students crafting their own descriptive piece demonstrating their use of the various techniques from the unit as well as a reflective meta-text evaluating their writing choices and potential revisions for future writing projects.

The sophomore team had already attempted to bring in more relevant, contemporary pieces as mentor texts for the unit. As there were no required texts, we would oftentimes share the texts we were using in our instruction in order to help with the burden of having to find the texts for ourselves. But I realized that most of our resources showcased the voices of White male authors, including examples provided in our composition textbook, excerpts from well-known contemporary writers such as David Sedaris or Anthony Bourdain, and my own student models. I realized that the student models I had been using were both from White students, with only one of those two being from a female student. One of our team members did share excerpts from Sandra Cisneros's *House on Mango Street* (Cisneros, 1984) as possible mentor texts. Regrettably, these excerpts served as the only representative of a female, person-of-color point of view within my classroom instruction in previous years' rollout of the unit.

Keeping with my commitment to subvert the agreed-on texts and showcase more socially just media texts this time around, I began to supplement my mini lessons of each descriptive writing technique accordingly. Although I still incorporated some of the mentor texts from previous years, including excerpts from Sandra Cisneros's *House on Mango Street* (Cisneros, 1984) and our composition textbook, I made conscious efforts to provide students with more media texts that were representative of diverse voices while still fitting into the theme of socially just works.

One such change occurred during the mini lesson on dominant impression or the mood within one's story. I reached out to a couple of my colleagues in the art department for inspiration on how dominant impression is explored through their art mediums. They were extremely helpful and open with sharing their resources, which I feel ultimately helped in my instruction as I attempted to bridge this writing technique to media that they interact with outside of my classroom every day. I eventually settled on using the photography medium as opposed to the more traditional art medium of painting, as I felt the photography medium was more prevalent and thus relevant to my students.

As part of the mini lesson, I included an interview from *Time* magazine with James Nachtwey (www.jamesnatchwey.com) in which he discussed his experiences capturing the devastating famine in Somalia in 1992. The interview helped provide students with important background information on the author, the topic, his purpose, and such before we moved on to the chosen image.

The untitled image is simply captioned "Somalia, 1992 – Child starved by famine, a man-made weapon of mass extermination" on Nachtwey's website and depicts an emaciated young child. The unclothed child is completely hunched over, with his feet and palms on the ground and his head resting on top of his hands. Two other figures, presumably a soldier and the lower half of another apparently starved figure, are also present.

Walking students through a class discussion of the various elements and details of the image was one of the most humbling moments in my classroom as we tried to use our observations and newly acquired background knowledge to then make inferences about what we felt was the creator's dominant impression. Using a simple graphic organizer engineered by an art colleague, students first noted observations, then background knowledge, some questions, and finally inferences before noting their conclusions on the dominant impression of this particular media text. Our discussions eventually evolved to include commentary on how everything, from the angle at which the shot was taken to the development of the image in black-and-white, consisted of choices the creator made to further support a specific dominant impression.

By including media texts that documented a devastating event in our history in conjunction with more traditional model texts from the composition textbook and student models, I felt that students not only were more engaged but also began to see the relevance of this descriptive technique in rhetorical situations and mediums outside of writing. It was my hope that Nachtwey's opening website message "I have been a witness, and these pictures are my testimony. The events I have recorded should not be forgotten and must not be repeated" (www.jamesnatchtwey.com) in conjunction with the video interview and chosen image would resonate with my students. They examined the unjust circumstances that people are faced with in regions of the world that we are rarely exposed to within our American classrooms, thus subverting the tradition of using and focusing on only American voices and thus American issues to be rhetorically analyzed.

Iterative Designing for More Inclusive Texts

By the third unit, "Developing by Example," I felt very confident in my design choices from the first two units. The instructional outcome in the course curriculum states that students should

> understand the importance of using examples to illustrate. Whether the purpose is to exemplify an idea, a belief, or a generalization, students would need to aid readers' understanding by using various examples to help clarify what they mean while also connecting them altogether for readers to arrive at the same conclusion.

To subvert this instructional outcome, I chose to not only continue to diversify the exemplary texts analyzed but, more important, also disrupt the unit's core texts so that the diverse texts I added did not live on the periphery of the traditional Eurocentric texts that populated the curriculum.

Several fellow team members and I had used "This I Believe" (Allison et al, 2006) as it serves as a natural fit based on its instructional framework and the unit's three objectives. However, reflecting on previous year's experiences with this approach left me dissatisfied as most of my students struggled to identify a "good" belief that was based on concrete examples. Their disengagement with this unit combined with my apprehensions in attempting it yet again prompted my leaving behind "This I Believe" (Allison, et al., 2006). I chose to use Chimamanda Ngozi Adichie's 2009 TED Talk as the anchor text as we felt it was an effective, culminating piece that also met our goals of a socially just media text.

One of the activities I included for this redesigned unit was in direct response to some of the class discussions that resulted from our analysis of Adichie's (2009) speech. Some of my students did not yet seem ready to acknowledge that her message was significant enough in their own lives or that single stories, positively or negatively, had had an impact on their lives. So I disrupted their Disney-memoried childhoods by leading them in a discussion about various Disney classics and what single stories were often portrayed about various groups of people as well as just male and female gender roles. This mini lesson culminated with an analysis of Disney's *Peter Pan*'s (Disney & Geronimi, 1953) portrayal of Native Americans. I included the musical scene "What Makes the Red Man Red?" ((Disney & Geronimi, 1953) as one of the media texts. Students were quite humbled in their acknowledgment of how such scenes and other early films from the franchise had indeed had an impact on their lives and warped their perception of men's roles, women's roles, and stereotypes of various groups of people.

Building off these newly discovered realizations, I transitioned to students identifying single stories that we are often limited to by asking them to reflect on the various stories, whether whole novels or short stories, that they had read whether in or out of school. For those students who claimed that they did not remember any, I had them focus on their current silent sustained reading book, and through a variety of questions, we were able to isolate several examples of single stories within these texts: Male narrators were often young and troubled; they rarely were portrayed as the "good student" and instead were usually trying to overcome some troubling obstacle. In stark contrast, the texts they had read that included female narrators, while also revolving around young characters, oftentimes their conflicts revolved around relationships, usually the female character's need or want of having one with their love interest. We were then able to critically analyze how many stories are left out as a result of the preponderance of such gendered characterizations along with the impact that constantly reading such similarly structured stories could have on impressionable young readers.

Before moving to the final summative assessment of the unit, we used Adichie's (2009) assertion that

> all of these stories make me who I am. But to insist on only these negative stories is to flatten my experience and to overlook the many other stories that formed me. The single story creates stereotypes, and the problem with stereotypes is not that they are untrue, but that they are incomplete

as inspiration for a follow-up activity. Students were asked to complete a "flattened" paper cube cut out with single stories, stereotypes that people had made of them. Afterward, they briefly noted how little of their whole story was reflected via these assumptions that others had made of them. We then "unflattened" these single stories and their rebuttals by assembling them and hanging them in our classroom.

The unit culminated with students crafting an essay in which they defended Adichie's (2009) argument with examples from her speech in conjunction with examples from their own lives using our various class activities as inspiration. Seeing several instances of students sharing a newfound awareness of the dangers of a single story in print and media they had been exposed to throughout their lives heartened me. Several students also shared some more personal anecdotes of how people had made assumptions about them in various situations. I was most struck by students who not only connected with the subversive text but also welcomed the opportunity to have their marginalized voices, as Lesbian, Gay, Bisexual, Transgender, Queer (LGTBQ) or Latinx individuals, shared through their writing. I recognized the need in the future to question my own assumptions and blind spots when selecting texts for units to provide more opportunities for an audience beyond myself as the teacher and to be more inclusive of my students' lived experiences.

Subverting the Curriculum Through Research and Texts

My collaboration with Michael using formative design experiment methodology helped me focus on key areas of my instructional design. In the future, I plan to incorporate a more concerted effort to present students with a variety of mediums in which they are allowed spaces to create as opposed to simply continuing with writing workshop spaces. In addition, I plan to find opportunities for them to share their self-selected media texts as their current audience defaulted to me as their class-room teacher. By conducting a classroom study, I was able to subvert many of the texts that are typically used for rhetorical analysis, but this alerted me to the reality that I should strive to be more inclusive rather than simply aiming to be culturally relevant. The use of a research study allowed me to not only interrogate my own practice but gave me the language and evidence to support the changes I made in my text selection and instruction.

Outside of the classroom, that larger systematic changes are needed is clear. Although I was allowed the freedom to disrupt the traditional sophomore curriculum, it was individual work that was not only taxing at times but also quite isolating. There were fewer opportunities to seek input from the rest of the sophomore team as I had chosen this on my own because of the importance I felt it warranted for my students and their experiences within my classroom. If the belief that such disruptive work is not only important but also necessary, then we need to be more committed to moving from individual acts of resistance to collective action toward equity and justice in our classrooms.

References

Adichie, C. (2009). *The danger of a single story* [Video file]. Retrieved from http://www.ted.com/talks/chimamanda_adichie_the_danger_of_a_single_story.html

Allison, J., Gediman, D., Gregory, J., & Merrick, V. (Eds.). (2006). *This I believe: The personal philosophies of remarkable men and women*. Macmillan.

Bishop, R. S. (1990). Mirrors, windows, and sliding glass doors. *Perspectives: Choosing and Using Books for the Classroom*, 6(3), ix–xi.

Black Eyed Peas. (2004). Where is the love? In *Elephunk* [CD]. A&M Records, Inc.

Carter, S. & Knowles, B. (2018). *Apeshit*. Retrieved July 9, 2018, from https://www.youtube.com/watch?v=kbMqWXnpXcA.

Cisneros, Sandra (1984). *The House on Mango Street*. Vintage Books.

Drake (2015). *Back to Back*. Cash Money Records, Inc.

Gay, G. (2010). *Culturally responsive teaching: Theory, research, and practice*. Teachers College Press.

Gambino, Childish. "This Is America." YouTube, uploaded by Donald Glover, directed by Hiro Murai, 5 May 2018, www.youtube.com/watch?v=VYOjWnS4cMY.

Geronimi, C., Jackson, W., Luske, H., & Kinney, J. (1953). *Peter Pan*. RKO Radio Pictures.

James Nachtwey. (n.d.). Retrieved October, 2018, from http://www.jamesnachtwey.com/.

King, S. (1986). *It*. Viking.

Ladson-Billings, G. (1995). Toward a theory of culturally relevant pedagogy. *American Educational Research Journal, 32*, 465–491.

Pearson, P. D., & Gallagher, M. C. (1983). The instruction of reading comprehension. *Contemporary educational psychology, 8*(3), 317–344.

Reinking, D., & Bradley, B. A. (2008). *On formative and design experiments: Approaches to language and literacy research* (Vol. 3). Teachers College Press.

Thomas, E. E., & Stornaiuolo, A. (2016). Restorying the self: Bending toward textual justice. *Harvard Educational Review, 86*(3), 313–338.

CHAPTER FIFTEEN

Can We Talk?: Promoting Anti-Oppressive Futures for Girls of Color Through a Social Justice Enrichment Program

Dorothy E. Hines, Jemimah Young,
Rossina Zamora Liu, and Diana Wandix-White

In Beverly Tatum's book *Can We Talk About Race?: And Other Conversations in an Era of School Resegregation* (2008), she discusses how race has an impact on education and how the curriculum can be more inclusive for African American children. Consequently, her poignant question, "Can we talk about race?" is a question that many educators have yet to ask themselves or answer when it comes to teaching Black girls and girls of color who are often overlooked and intellectually underestimated in the classroom (Carter Andrews et al, 2019). Although Tatum's book focuses on African American students belonging to multiple marginalized communities, including Black girls and girls of color, we use the term *Black* to be inclusive of girls from, within, and across the African Diaspora. Research has shown that Black girls and girls of color within suburban and predominantly White schools have higher rates of disciplinary punishments and are more likely to be suspended, expelled, an arrested at school than their White female counterparts

(Hines-Datiri & Carter Andrews, 2017; Morris, 2016). Young women of color in secondary schools (9th–12th grade) are made to be invisible in the curriculum to maintain mainstream educational practices and hegemonic policies that have rendered them erasable. For example, curricular standards, textbooks, and classroom décor (bulletin boards, wall art, or classroom murals) rarely have any images of girls of color depicted in ways that are not stereotypical—if they are even pictured at all.

Consequently, their herstories (Lindsay-Dennis, 2015) and narratives are often misrepresented (Patton et al, 2016), and such misrepresentations extend throughout English language arts (ELA) curricula, classrooms, and pedagogical stances that teachers employ. There is a lack of what we call a social justice-oriented school-based ELA curriculum that bridges social justice work with ELA. The effects of these challenges are evident in national assessments of ELA proficiency. For instance, data from *The Condition of Education 2018* report (McFarland et al., 2018) suggest that African American students did not make a substantial increase in performance in Grades 4 or 8 between the 2015 and 2018 administrations. The term *African American* is used to describe persons who are of African descent and born within the United States. In some cases, statistical data from federal databases disaggregates African American from the term *Black* and does not include Africans or those who are biracial (African American and another race). Unfortunately, similar trends exist for African American girls specifically in both writing and reading (Young, 2017; Young & Scott, 2016). Therefore, schools must develop innovative programs and (re)story the curriculum in ways that offer a means for recapturing the intellectual curiosity and brilliance of young women of color while intentionally incorporating social justice–oriented practices.

In this chapter, we examine how the cofounders of the program *Can We Talk: Young Women of Color* instituted a social justice-oriented school-based ELA curriculum. We address, in general, the presumptions of current standards-based curricula and practices in the ELA classroom and, in particular, in the reading and writing of nonfiction texts. We highlight how a curriculum for young women of color that centers social justice-oriented learning is an example of subversive teaching, and we discuss strategies for how educators can integrate subversive pedagogies from the *Can We Talk?* program. We conclude with recommendations for how educators can utilize social justice-oriented learning to circumvent hegemonic curricula in ELA classrooms. As Black female educators and educators of Black female students, we draw on our experiential, as well as professional, knowledge throughout this chapter.

Positionality

In writing this chapter, we wanted to disclose our social location and positionality as women of color who have received PhDs. However, as women of color, we are not exempt from experiencing racism, sexism, and other "isms" due to who we are and what we represent when we enter into a classroom. Educators do not immediately see our doctoral degrees, but society will be hyper-aware of its perceived racial classification of us. Some of us are mothers, former public school teachers, and sisters, but we are all birthed from a historical legacy that has disenfranchised, in general, the lives of women and, in particular, women of color. When we enter into classrooms in predominantly White schools, our bodies mean something. Our bodies are perceived as something (good or bad). Our experiences as women of color who grew up in small towns, the suburbs, and urban core are not only indicative of who we are and who we have become but also demand that we utilize subversive teaching practices in our own classrooms and spaces as we educate students at predominantly White institutions.

We all have different experiences and perspectives that inform this chapter. As social justice scholars, we all seek to leverage the cultural funds of knowledge (Risko & Walker-Dalhouse, 2007) that Black girls bring to their ELA experiences as important pedagogical tools to help Black girls construct and (re)construct their truths within the classroom. Race and gender intersect to shape the schooling experiences and muted voices of young women of color. Despite the urgent need for social justice education that intentionally subverts mainstream curricula in predominantly White schools, there is limited understanding of how educators (defined as including teachers, social workers, school personnel) can actively and explicitly circumvent institutionalized color-blind curricula to develop more anti-oppressive futures, socially inclusive practices, and justice in schools for girls of color. As suggested, part of this can be pointed to current standards-based curricula and practices in the ELA classroom. In the sections that follow, we call on our combined knowledge and experiences working with Black girls in urban, suburban, and rural classrooms to present a unique perspective on what matters for teaching and learning for social justice in ELA classrooms.

Why Black Girls?

Students are expected to master competencies in the reading and writing of nonfiction texts. For instance, the insistence on privileging rhetorical conventions and techniques as well as "standard English" continue to confine the curriculum to the status quo, wherein Black girls and girls of color remain perpetually unseen and unheard (Muhammad & Gonzalez, 2016; Paris & Alim, 2017). Indeed, writing instruction predominantly stresses formulaic paradigms and code-switching rather than honoring students' multiliteracies and multilingualism as strengths and assets. Often regarded as secondary to reading, writing is generally taught as a set of discrete skills for responding to published texts rather than for expressing and creating knowledge and self. To this end, White cultural and linguistic values continue to pervade pedagogical practices, and even when teachers may understand the need to engage students in racial discourse, most remain underprepared and/or uncomfortable to do so (DiAngelo, 2018; Greene & Abt-Perkins, 2003). Similarly, canonical texts (including nonfiction biographies) taught in ELA classrooms overwhelmingly center Whiteness and Western traditions and identities (Carter, 2007). Rare are the opportunities for students to read and respond to writing by writers of color and/or about historic figures and characters of color. Rare are the chances for them to speak truth about race and racism in overt and explicit ways. These practices contribute to the cultural discontinuity that exists between traditional modes of expression in ELA and the cultural funds of knowledge of Black girls.

Cultural discontinuity is defined as "a school-based behavioral process where the cultural value-based learning preferences and practices of many ethnic minority students—those typically originating from home or parental socialization activities—are discontinued at school" (Tyler et al., 2008, p. 281). This cultural disconnect between classroom practices and student cultural funds of knowledge fosters gaps in educational opportunities for African American girls. Thus, cultural discontinuity explains some of the negative impact of traditional curricula on the learning outcomes of students of color (Rouland et al, 2014). To address this phenomenon, numerous pedagogical approaches have been implemented in ELA classrooms (e.g., culturally responsive pedagogy, culturally relevant pedagogy, and, more recently, culturally sustaining pedagogy), all designed to minimize cultural discontinuity by leveraging the cultural and experiential knowledge of students of color through culturally informed instructional approaches. The curriculum that we used centered a more nuanced approach to ELA by trying nontraditional approaches that are rooted in hegemonic practices.

(Re)Imagining ELA Curricula

Fortunately, these important issues can be effectively discussed through the experiences of book characters (Bennett, 2018), putting a level of personal distance in the discussion that allows teachers and students to address such truths as race and racism from a third-person perspective. If White teachers are reading experiences through their own eyes, they will not be able, hear, or understand the Black girl that they are reading about in the text. They must distance themselves, and their lens, to adequately "see" Black girls or girls of color. Carefully selected literature for the classroom not only helps teachers develop into and grow as culturally sustaining pedagogues (Paris & Alim, 2017); they can also cultivate students' literacy development, increase their capacity for compassion, and encourage their acceptance of themselves and of others. Their voices and stories, thus, must be centered as nonfiction texts about the world in which they live (Muhammad & Gonzalez, 2016). Such works, including some biopics and living books, can provide a human library that serves to enrich student experiences and offer them authentic cultural knowledge. Importantly, by acknowledging, valuing, and including students' funds of knowledge as welcomed assets to school curriculum (González et al, 2005; Paris, & Alim, 2017), we not only validate students' existence and ways of being; we also embolden them to contest the literacy values, practices, and identities that dominate ELA classrooms.

In ELA classrooms, teachers can often be a source for preparing and encouraging students to participate in a democratic society. As such, they must recognize that teaching, as well as learning, are not separate from issues of democracy and social justice. Finding "the most inclusive ways to develop sustainable leadership, reflexivity, and critical thinking" (Cruz, 2012, p. 460) in students will aid them in analyzing their own, as well as others', lived experiences. One of the simplest ways to accomplish this task is by providing students with literacy-rich environments, including both traditional and living books, that include not only the traditional Western canon but also works by authors who look like the students and present them in the gamut of diverse ways in which they live. In this way, students can gain knowledge that allows them to see themselves and the world more objectively, leading to critical thinking that helps them make sense of what they see. Reading and expanding one's knowledge about relevant topics can lead to critical thinking, and this is an essential traditional element of ELA (Alverman, 2002; Graham & Perin, 2007). Providing this experience for young girls of color is paramount as they attempt to navigate the world. So, we ask: Can We Talk?

Bridging Social Justice Enrichment With a Girl-Centered Curriculum

The *Can We Talk: Young Women of Color* program was cofounded in 2018 at a high school in Kansas to serve the academic and socio-emotional needs of girls of color who are suspended and/or expelled from school and who are at-risk for disciplinary punishments. Research indicates that girls of color and, in particular, Black girls have higher rates of in-school and out-of-school suspension than White female students, and their cultural norms, racial heritage, and traditions are more likely to be excluded from mainstream curricula (Young & Butler, 2018). The *Can We Talk?* program is a co-collaborative and community-based effort between local educational advocates and stakeholders. The *Can We Talk?* program is offered twice a month during the school day. During the program, we invite community members who are professional women of color to discuss different topics that have an impact on their world. Our program mission is not only to serve the academic needs of girls of color but also to teach to the "whole child" and their holistic needs as young women. The young women are able to freely discuss what it means to be female students of color within this sociopolitical climate while also having the liberation to speak their truths, their voices, and their narratives unscripted. Although this intervention began as a research-oriented project, after reviewing the data we collected and talking with the girls individually and in groups, we discovered that simply meeting with them was not enough. The young women's futures necessitated that we provide a structure that was built into the school day that fostered anti-oppressive and liberatory futures for them within school. Such programmatic and systemic efforts required a more nuanced curriculum that centered the historical and contemporary experiences of women and girls who looked like them.

Spoken Word as Curricular Subversion

In the development and implementation process of our curriculum for girls of color in a predominantly White school, we decided to foreground spoken word as a tool for eradicating hegemonic practices that were actively erasing their communal experiences (Muhammad & Gonzales, 2016). Spoken word allows young people to blend the arts, poetry, creative expression, and literature to (re)configure their stories of success in spaces that have once determined that they could not be successful. Because spoken word can promote girls of color "herstories to privilege their cultural knowledge and brilliance in school" (Hines, 2019), we wanted to ensure that our curriculum showed all aspects of their lives and literacies as young women of color. This includes their successes, struggles, pain, and triumphs in ways that honored their girlhood. We wanted to speak to their trauma-informed narratives while not subjugating them to only trauma-informed beliefs about their lives. Using spoken word as a foundation, we created six pillars that our curriculum would focus on (1) girlhood, (2) women's health, (3) self-affirmation, (4) creative expression, (5) financial literacy, and (6) careers and futures. We realized that spoken word and social justice-oriented learning would be foundational to what the young women who participated in the program needed but that it is also integral to the curriculum being sustainable and impactful. The girls read the literary works of authors such as bell hooks and Maya Angelou, wrote their own poetry, and discussed how their poems and life narratives transcended their own. Moreover, we focused on social justice-oriented learning and not just a social justice-oriented curriculum because we knew that simply having a curriculum or lesson plan without having intentional learning taking place would do more harm than good. In the rest of this chapter, we use the concept of subversive pedagogy to describe how our curriculum was used to teach for social justice learning in the context of ELA.

Teacher and Curriculum Illustration

While thinking about how to construct a curriculum that is focused on the needs of girls of color, we discussed how we could highlight their experiences through social justice-oriented learning that transcended who they are and who we thought they would become. We used readings from women of color authors to capture the racial and gendered nuances that they would have to narrate about their own lives in the classroom. This meant that we had to give the girls space to dissect what they were reading while collaborating with them as they read through the text and see themselves within the text. This step helps to meet an ELA marker—comprehending/

performing a close reading of a text. For example, when we read a poem by women of color authors—take Maya Angelou—we were not just trying to understand the lyrical rhythm and heartbeat of the words that we were reading; we were also inviting the girls to craft their own herstories of regret, of pain, of triumph, of life in and outside of school.

One critical component of our *Can We Talk: Young Women of Color* program has been the explicit centering of nontraditional teachers who work in school buildings but who do not have ownership of the classroom (e.g., social workers, support staff, counselors). These nontraditional teachers engage with students on a daily basis, and they provide support to teachers in a variety of classrooms, including in ELA. We introduce Janice the social worker, and Rhianna the educator who collaboratively work together to support the *Can We Talk?: Young Women of Color* program.

Janice is an African American in her 40s. She is from California but has been working at this high school in Kansas for more than seven years. She holds a bachelor's and a master's degree from a university across the street from a local high school where she works. Janice is not only committed to her students, but she also organizes her office to be "kid-friendly" and as welcoming as possible. When you enter her office, you are greeted with a comfy futon and with a mid-sized refrigerator. Many students will go to her office to talk and to embrace her loving yet stern spirit. Janice is no stranger to suffering, but she uses her past experience to gauge the hearts and minds of young people marginalized and overlooked in school.

Janice's collaborator, Rhianna, is a teacher who has instructed a workshop with the program. She is Afro-Latina from Chicago. She is in her early 30s, and her father is currently incarcerated.

In many cases, she not only understands the girls' narratives, but she also has experienced many incidences in which she did not know if she would graduate high school. Rhianna is a spoken word artist, and she draws from literature written by women of color, in general, and Afro-Latinas, in particular. This includes drawing from Dominican women's narratives of resistance and humanization. Both Janice and Rhianna use their cultural, racial, and gendered backgrounds to foster a classroom space that is inclusive and humanizing for young women of color.

Social Justice-Oriented Learning in Motion

At the start of every workshop, Rhianna has the students do a "PRAISE." PRAISE is an activity during which the girls give praise to things for that day. Using a sheet of paper or their cell phone, they compose about the following: four items that are good, four items that are negative, and four items that are random. When the students give praise, they are tapping into their socio-emotional health prior to starting the lesson for that day. Students have 10 minutes to think of four items for each category. After the 10 minutes, students are able to freely share what they wrote with one another, and all comments are greeted with "snaps" (a normal practice after someone says poetry or something using a poet's tongue that resonates with them). The snaps communicate such sentiments as "I see you, and I acknowledge your existence." After students share their praise, they ask each other questions about the praise. During one of the PRAISE sessions, one student shared that she was not having a great day and felt alone. She was overwhelmed with her life outside of school. In her praise, she said, "PRAISE that I didn't die last night. PRAISE that I had a place to sleep. PRAISE that I woke up today." Social justice learning is not just about students reading literature in the classroom, but it is also recognizing that they themselves are books waiting to be written. They themselves have songs within them waiting to be sung.

After our PRAISE activity, we then transition into reading short poems written by women of color examining some aspect of their lives, ranging from loneliness to self-love. The girls choose one poem that resonates with them and then write their own poem by inserting segments of the chosen poem into their version. The girls have about 15 minutes to rewrite the poem, and then they share their reimagined poem with the group using spoken word. This part of the lesson can be challenging for the young women because in these poems, they authentically expose themselves. They have to uncover their true feelings about their own self-worth, value, and regrets. Through this activity, ELA is presented in a way that many of the girls rarely get to experience. They are able to assist in crafting the lesson through the creation of their own poem and spoken word. They are able to address their own issues—whether school- or community-based—without judgment. As the girls shared their spoken word, we were met with anger, pain, and tears—and love: love for them being authors who could voice their voices and love for young women of color who are brilliant and to be able to see their creative curiosity come to life.

An Example of Spoken Word in Practice

Despite the call for students' right to their own language and, thus, identities, current standards in ELA writing instruction continues to center paradigmatic conventions of rhetoric and standard English. Yet through activities such as PRAISE, students push back at these rhetorical and linguistic traditions, using spoken word (poetry) as form and their own language. In so doing, they re-center themselves and their embodied narratives. Similarly, nonfiction, as currently taught, focuses on the reading of Western texts that forefronts Whiteness and White perspectives. When students are asked to compose their response to these texts, they are also expected to abide by formulaic structures rather than afforded the chance to create meaning and become the text in and of itself. Through activities such as PRAISE, however, students are able to reimagine what constitutes a readable text.

Similarly, students rarely have the chance to see writing by women of color. To this end, as we developed and implemented our curriculum that is focused on girls of color, we had to redefine what is "traditional literature" or "seminal pieces." Given that much of the literature written by women of color is not given credence as much as authors of color, we wanted to ensure that the girls understand that women of color have seminal and premier pieces of literature while allowing them to practice social justice learning through nonhegemonic lenses. Students developed their analytical abilities when they read the poems and interacted with the stories plot, main characters, and story lines. We encouraged them to critically analyze the overall message presented in the texts and to consider what is missing from the text by drawing on their own lives. We also had the students consider how the women of color authors were being comedically inclined in the text and using figurative meaning to illustrate a point. Last, we collaborated with the students to integrate meaning with the text. This was a major component of our curriculum because without meaning, there is no purpose. We welcomed the girls' "meaning-making" of the texts with their own lives. In particular, we focused on women of color authors who wrote about the 18th, 19th, and 20th centuries, and we redefined "American literature" to include narratives of enslaved people and the herstories written about and for women of color.

Closing

Expression, whether written or through spoken word, remains an important tool for Black women and girls to escape the challenges they face as a dually marginalized population of learners. The *Can We Talk* program provides a platform for this type of expression that also supports the development of invaluable literacy skills that can be leveraged to increase achievement and their future academic outcomes.

References

Alvermann, D. E. (2002). Effective literacy instruction for adolescents. *Journal of Literacy Research*, *34*, 189–208.

Bennett, L. (2018). *Before the* Mayflower: *A history of the Negro in America, 1619–1962*. Colchis Books.

Carter, S. P. (2007). "Reading all that White crazy stuff": Black young women unpacking Whiteness in a high school British literature classroom. *The Journal of Classroom Interaction*, *41*(2). 42–54.

Carter Andrews, D. J., Brown, T., Castro, E., & Id-Deen, E. (2019). The impossibility of being "perfect and White": Black girls' racialized and gendered schooling experiences. *American Educational Research Journal*. Advanced online publication. doi:0002831219849392.

Cruz, C. (2012). Making curriculum from scratch: Testimonio in an urban classroom. *Equity & Excellence in Education*, *45*, 460–471.

DiAngelo, R. (2018). *White fragility: Why it's so hard for White people to talk about racism*. Beacon Press.

González, N., Moll, L. C., & Amanti, C. (Eds.). (2006). *Funds of knowledge: Theorizing practices in households, communities, and classrooms*. Routledge.

Graham, S., & Perin, D. (2007). A meta-analysis of writing instruction for adolescent students. *Journal of Educational Psychology*, *99*, 445–476.

Greene, S., & Abt-Perkins, D. (Eds.). (2003). *Making race visible: Literacy research for cultural understanding*. Teachers College Press.

Hines-Datiri, D., & Carter Andrews, D. J. (2017). The effects of zero tolerance policies on Black girls: Using critical race feminism and figured worlds to examine school discipline. *Urban Education*. Advanced online publication. doi: 0042085917690204.

Hines, D. (2019). When girls spit: The power of spoken word. Retrieved from https://www.edutopia.org/article/when-girls-spit-power-spoken-word.

Lindsay-Dennis, L. (2015). Black feminist-womanist research paradigm: Toward a culturally relevant research model focused on African American girls. *Journal of Black Studies*, *46*, 506–520.

McFarland, J., Hussar, B., Wang, X., Zhang, J., Wang, K., Rathbun, A., Barmer, A., Forrest Cataldi, E., Bullock Mann, F. (2018). *The condition of education 2018* (NCES 2018–144). National Center for Education Statistics, U.S. Department of Education. Retrieved from https://nces.ed.gov/pubsearch/pubsinfo.asp?pubid=2018144.

Morris, M. W. (2016). Protecting Black girls. *Educational Leadership*, *74*(3), 49–53.

Muhammad, G. G., & Gonzalez, L. (2016). Slam poetry: An artistic resistance toward identity, agency, and activism. *Equity & Excellence in Education*, *49*, 440–453.

Paris, D., & Alim, H. S. (Eds.). (2017). *Culturally sustaining pedagogies: Teaching and learning for justice in a changing world*. Teachers College Press.

Patton, L. D., Crenshaw, K., Haynes, C., & Watson, T. N. (2016). Why we can't wait: (Re)examining the opportunities and challenges for Black women and girls in education [Guest Editorial]. *The Journal of Negro Education*, *85*, 194–198.

Risko, V. J., & Walker-Dalhouse, D. (2007). Tapping students' cultural funds of knowledge to address the achievement gap. *The Reading Teacher*, *61*, 98–100.

Rouland, K., Matthews, J. S., Byrd, C. M., Meyer, R. M., & Rowley, S. J. (2014). Culture clash: Interactions between Afrocultural and mainstream cultural styles in classrooms serving African American students. *Interdisciplinary Journal of Teaching and Learning*, *4*, 186–202.

Tatum, B. D. (2007). *Can we talk about race?: And other conversations in an era of school resegregation*. Beacon Press.

Tyler, K. M., Uqdah, A. L., Dillihunt, M. L., Beatty-Hazelbaker, R., Conner, T., Gadson, N., & Stevens, R. (2008). Cultural discontinuity: Toward a quantitative investigation of a major hypothesis in education. *Educational Researcher, 37*, 280–297. doi.org/10.3102/0013189X08321459

Young, J. L. (2017). One book and one girl at a time: Analyzing and explaining Black girl's reading achievement in elementary school. *Literacy & Social Responsibility*, *9*(1), 3–10. Retrieved from http://web.csulb.edu/misc/l-sr/ejournal/issues/issues-index.html

Young, J. L., & Butler, B. R. (2018). A student saved is NOT a dollar earned: A meta-analysis of school disparities in discipline practice toward Black children. *Taboo: The Journal of Culture and Education*, *17*(4), 95–112.

Young, J. L., & Scott, C. (2016). Writing outside the margins: An exploratory analysis of Black girls' achievement in middle grades writing. *The National Journal of Urban Education & Practice*, *9*, 506–523.

CHAPTER SIXTEEN

"Why Can't They Test Us on This?" A Framework for Transforming Intensive Reading Instruction

AMANDA LACY AND ANGELA M. KOHNEN

Thursday, May 10th
The last two weeks we took time off [from reading Othello] to discuss/reflect/
analyze the new Childish Gambino video "This is America." Students were
interested and engaged. After watching the video in 4th [period], students in-
troduced me to Joyner Lucas' "I'm Not Racist," a shocking and compelling
music video/drama that acts almost like a double text. Tuesday, I shared the
video story with my other classes and students were absolutely riveted—no
one glancing down at their phones, no heads down, no asking to go to the
bathroom. One student said, "This is real shit, right here. Why can't they
test us on this?"

Always back to the test.

—excerpt, Amanda's teaching journal

FOR 9 OF THE 15 years that Amanda (Author 1) has taught at a large public high school, her teaching assignment has included Intensive Reading, a course for juniors and seniors who have not passed the high school standardized English language arts (ELA) exam required for graduation. The exam, initially given in 10th grade, consists of approximately 60 multiple-choice questions and is purported to assess the state's reading standards. Test items address identifying key ideas and details, craft and structure, the integration of knowledge and ideas, and language and editing. Reading passages vary according to test version, but all readings on the publicly available practice tests were published before 1895.

In many schools where students are struggling to achieve on such tests, the answer is to add more test preparation. Alternately (or additionally), schools may purchase curriculum that is advertised to align with the tests. In other words, remediation for students with reading challenges often focuses exclusively on test performance, while de-emphasizing or even ignoring aspects of literacy that are not tested. In this chapter, we describe a different approach to reading intervention curricula, one that centers student engagement, multimodal texts, student inquiry, and critical literacy. The approach we advocate repositions the teacher as a creative expert in her own classroom, able to draw on the knowledge of her students and community to teach an expanded version of literacy. Our goal is to disrupt exigent notions of what a remedial reading course at the secondary level can be.

Subversive Approaches to Meeting Rigorous Standards

The Limits of Traditional Approaches

The state's reading standards are rigorous, asking students to read closely, cite textual evidence, determine themes, evaluate arguments, and compare passages. Traditional approaches to reading intervention often treat these standards as if they are comprehensive, representing all that a reading curricula must accomplish and, by extension, all that is necessary to be considered "literate." Test preparation is essential to such curricula, and students are generally asked to practice taking tests in circumstances similar to the testing situation—in isolation, reading decontextualized passages about which they have little interest or background knowledge.

Yet a great deal of research in the field of literacy and ELA education challenges this view of literacy and reading. Although the tested skills—close reading, citing evidence, and the like—are required to achieve expertise in ELA, they are only one piece of the complex work that expert readers and writers do. For example, scholars working in the area of disciplinary literacy have noted that literature professors read in order to engage with problems or puzzles raised in the text; these problems or puzzles never have a single correct answer (Rainey, 2017). Making claims and arguments about literature is a social practice; claims are defended to other scholars within a community of practice, with norms regarding what counts as evidence, the role of theory, and drawing on information external to the text (Rainey, 2017; Spires et al, 2018). Apprenticing students to such ways of reading and writing requires far more than multiple-choice tests or timed-writing assessments.

Even if we (temporarily) concede the point that reading intervention curricula are not designed to apprentice students to the practices of experts, decades of scholarship has found that *all* readers construct meaning by drawing on background knowledge and that a reader's level of engagement has an impact on understanding (e.g., Baldwin et al, 1985; Neuman & Celano, 2012; Recht & Leslie, 1988; Willingham, 2006). Reading intervention curricula that do not work to build students' background knowledge or support students to engage deeply with texts are unlikely to lead to lasting improvements in literacy. Furthermore, sociocultural literacy research has illuminated the impact of reader agency, identity, and power, along with the importance of context, on reading practices and comprehension (e.g., Lewis et al, 2007). As Moje et al (2008) argued,

> Youth read and write for social, emotional, intellectual and spiritual purposes. Their reading and writing practices foster communication, relationships, and self-expression among peers and family members; support their economic and psychological health; and allow them to construct subjectivities and enact identities that offer them power in their everyday lives. These consequences of literate practice in the everyday world should not be diminished by the quest to improve school achievement for all young people. (p. 140)

Despite this warning, frequently literacy instruction has been diminished by testing mandates. Although the standards themselves do not explicitly prohibit the teaching of ELA as a sociocultural endeavor, the tests advance a very different definition of *reading* (see also Graves, 2017, for a critique of the importance of "challenging text" to the Common Core State Standards).

A Subversive Approach to Reading Intervention

With the support of her administrators, Amanda has spent the last nine years creating and re-creating Intensive Reading instruction (see also Lacy, 2019) to challenge narrow views of what such a course can be. Over time, Amanda has developed a theoretically grounded framework for Intensive Reading, one that has led to student success on standardized tests while also supporting students' growth as literate learners in and out of school. Her curriculum is always in development as students enter and leave the course, current events arise that demand student discussion, and school mandates come and go. Officially, Amanda's curricular goals are tied to test requirements; although the course was not created to support students as writers, Amanda also added curricular goals related to writing, thus subverting the reading/writing divide in many reading intervention curricula.

Beyond these school- and standards-mandated goals, Amanda has developed her own set of course principles. Her curricular framework (explicated in the following section) is informed by Freire's (2018) model of dialogic education, along with Ladson-Billings's (1995) culturally relevant pedagogy and Delpit's (1988) ideas about the culture of power. Furthermore, Amanda engages students in critical literacy activities, influenced by Luke's (2012) "classical questions of critical literacy": "What is 'truth'? How is it presented and represented, by whom, and in whose interests? Who should have access to which images and words, texts, and discourses? For what purposes?" (p. 4). These questions invite the exploration of multimodal and mass media texts; therefore, Amanda draws on critical media literacy studies (Hobbs, 1998; Scheibe & Rogow, 2012) and multiliteracies frameworks (New London Group, 1996), all of which subvert the privileging of print texts.

Corporate, packaged reading intervention curricula can never take into account context, student interests, or rapidly changing current events. Far from being neutral or objective, prepackaged reading intervention curricula may, in fact, rely on reading passages that include problematic representations of race and, thus, perpetuate oppression (see Thomas & Dyches, 2019). In contrast, Amanda's curriculum incorporates student choice, inquiry, culture, and experiences while also providing background and instruction in traditional academic discourses.

Context and Teacher Positionality

Amanda works in a school known locally for its International Baccalaureate (IB) program, an academically prestigious magnet program housed within the school. The overall student population is Black or African American (50%), White (27%), and Asian (12%), with Black or African American students making up the majority of the students in the regular (i.e., not IB) program (75%) and composing a very small percentage of the IB program (9%). Students enrolled in Intensive Reading are among the lowest performing students in the school and thus are further marginalized; this population is typically 98% Black or African American, with 100% qualifying for free or reduced-price lunch. Amanda also receives new students throughout the year, while other students are transferred out of the class to another elective after they have met their reading requirement as part of an effort to keep class sizes low.

As a White teacher, Amanda continues to research and reflect on the connections among race, power, privilege, and literacy teaching and learning. Specifically, she considers how her positionality as a middle-class, college-educated White woman has informed her teaching, classroom processes, expectations, strategies, and assumptions. She attempts to integrate her reflexive racial awareness with humility and care for her students, while also working within a macrosystem that privileges high school graduation (and the requisite test scores) above all.

A Framework for Successful (Subversive) Curriculum

In order to meet the myriad of goals of Intensive Reading, Amanda develops curriculum through a regular set of steps. Amanda's framework relies on a predictable weekly structure, yet the content of her lessons is ever-changing. Students learn the skills needed to pass standardized assessments while being exposed to highly relevant content that builds background knowledge and sparks engagement in the community and the world.

Instructional plans are developed through the following process:

1. Use students' interests or background knowledge as a starting point. Alternately, use current events (especially local news) that may be relevant to students, even if students have not voiced knowledge of the event.

2. Identify multimodal sources (including primary sources) to explore the issue. For example, she paired Childish Gambino's music video "This Is America" with articles critiquing the work. Often students will bring in additional sources, as when students suggested the class examine Joyner Lucas's "I'm Not Racist" alongside "This is America."

3. Facilitate student discussion of the issue. During this time, encourage multiple perspectives and readings of the texts. Model respectful dialogue even when disagreement arises. Encourage students to refer to specific aspects of the texts during discussion.

4. Model and scaffold reading and writing processes. Composing thesis statements and including specific text support are regularly practiced.

5. Invite students to synthesize information and articulate their ideas through speaking and writing or graphic representations. Examples include Venn diagrams, memes, and "Snapchats" representing the main idea of a text. Amanda encourages critical perspectives by inviting students to examine issues of power, ideology, and oppression embedded in the texts examined.

Students also complete a standardized practice test, usually once a week. The curricular framework informs the other days of class instruction.

An Example: The Obama Portraits

When the National Portrait Gallery unveiled portraits of Barack and Michelle Obama in 2018, Amanda knew she wanted her students to view and discuss the artwork. Understanding the portraits as visual texts, she decided to pair them with news stories about the paintings. She was especially interested in finding a story with biographical information about the artists, both of whom were African American and relatively young, with a history of creating art that provoked conversations about race. Because the lessons were slated for April, a challenging time of year in the school, she decided to include poetry writing, an activity students found engaging. The preceding framework was used to create a week of lessons that unfolded as follows:

- **Monday:** Students read the Februray 12, 2018 *New York Times* article "Obama Portrait Artists Merged the Everyday and the Extraordinary" by Robin Pogrebin. (Framework Elements 1–2)

- **Tuesday:** Students discussed the article, raising questions and connecting to the art. They noticed that Kehinde Wiley, Barack Obama's portrait artist, is from South Central Los Angeles, and one commented that he was from the "ghetto" because "that's where Grand Theft Auto takes place." They also questioned whether Michelle Obama deserved to have her portrait in the gallery and wondered if Barack wore the same suit every time he sat for the portrait. The conversation was relaxed, although Amanda nudged students to refer to the text as they thought through their reactions to support their ability to use textual evidence. (Framework Element 3)

- **Wednesday:** Students viewed and discussed the portraits. Once again, students engaged in discussion, this time around visual images. Students were encouraged to look for evidence in the images to support their ideas; multiple perspectives on the paintings naturally emerged, and students practiced listening respectfully. (Framework Element 3)

- **Thursday–Friday:** Students constructed original poems inspired by the portraits. At this point in the year, students had discussed and written poetry several times, so little overt instruction on poetry writing was required, although students were encouraged to brainstorm ideas, draft, share their emerging thinking with one another, and revise. Some students volunteered to share their work at the end of the week. (Framework Elements 4–5)

The writing that emerged from these lessons showcased students' facility with language. Students also took the opportunity to address issues of race, gender, and power, as in this student example (used with permission):

Dear Young Black Man

Dear Young Black Man,
Those with pants low and egos high
Those who keep their right hands on thighs
Sit up, ears listening and eyes open.
Pay attention to the words that are spoken.
The system puts forth requirements and laws
Despite your progressive and unforgiven flaws.

Dear Young Black Man,
Society hampers you from being dominant.
Society deprives you of opportunity and enlightenment,
Telling you to acknowledge violence.
Keeping the Young Black Man envious of
Another Young Black Man's significance.
American society pushes you to be ignorant and flashy
That you are lame if you are different and classy

Dear Young Black Man,
Be Tall, Grand and Assertive
Never fall; stand and be supportive.
You are descended from royalty to which you shall return.
Your morality, your dignity and your prominence you earn,

Dear Young Black Man,
Honor your Dear Young Black Woman,
For she is the strong backbone of
Our Dear Young Black Man

Through the subversive teaching framework, students are also given permission to be subversive, and this author challenges the way society positions young Black men while simultaneously challenging the way Black women are treated by Black men. Poetry, a form of writing notably absent from many state writing curricula, allows for a more nuanced response than answering multiple-choice comprehension questions or writing a paragraph with textual evidence.

Beyond Traditional Markers of Success

Amanda's course has been deemed "successful" by the school administration based on student test scores. Students enrolled in Amanda's class overwhelmingly achieve the required score on their state assessment or the accepted concordant score on the ACT or the SAT. Amanda has collected surveys and conducted focus groups with her students, and many claim that their success on the standardized test is because they take practice tests as part of the class. This may be the case; these tests give students additional practice with the test format, question types, and language found in the typical reading passages, all of which allow the course to meet its traditional goals.

More important, however, are the other ways success can be measured. For Amanda's students, success may look like increased civic engagement, deep critical thinking, confident classroom participation, or authentic integration of course concepts into their daily lives. Students in Amanda's class have published letters to the editor of their local paper, advocating for a change in the way the school is covered in local media; written letters to their local congressman both in support of and in opposition to gun control; started home gardens; and changed their eating habits as a result of class readings and research. As she works alongside her students, Amanda models critical engagement, frequently writing essays for the Sunday opinion section of the paper on standardized tests and scripted curricula, and becoming active in efforts to revise the school's curricula to address racial disparities in achievement. Although the class leads to success according to traditional markers, the class has also led to the students and Amanda herself challenging these very markers.

Engagement, Expectations, Exhaustion

Despite these successes, transforming intensive reading has led to personal and professional challenges as well as existential questions about the purpose and nature of public education. Although intensive remedial reading programs can lead to success on academic benchmarks and graduation rates, students' lives are rarely improved through these initiatives alone. Amanda's work with her students and her understanding of how intensive reading interventions fail to improve their lives beyond school has pushed her to continue to reimagine the role of intensive reading.

"Rein Them In": What Should Engagement Look Like?

For Amanda, student engagement, in the form of lively discussions and impassioned debate, is essential. However, high levels of student engagement can lead to two different kinds of challenges. First, students come to expect all classes to include highly relevant readings. For example, upon arriving to class and seeing that they were returning to *Othello* after several class periods of looking at more contemporary texts, one student sighed and said, "Man, I knew today was gonna be a boring day." His reaction was not uncommon. But Amanda continues to teach Shakespeare alongside contemporary texts because of the power of the plays themselves—and, like many other teachers before her, has found that most students grow to appreciate and enjoy Shakespeare, to feel empowered once they made their way through the text. Even the student who thought of *Othello* as "boring" became a class favorite for reading the role of Othello and, upon the play's conclusion, claimed it was one of the first pieces of literature he "really understood." Yet when students come to expect immediately engaging texts, motivating students to work with more difficult texts can be a challenge. Here, noting that subversive teaching does not mean throwing out traditional texts is important; subversive teaching methods can be used as a means to provide and promote access to traditional literary texts.

A second issue with engagement can be administrative response. An administrator formally observed Amanda's lesson using the Obama portraits and, at the lesson's conclusion, commented, "You need to do a better job reining them in." In her teaching journal that evening, Amanda wrote, "I probably could do a better job at containing the conversation, but I'm not sure I want to. What for?" In a classroom that invites students to co-construct the curriculum and to consider themselves as worthy intellects in their own right, students are not something to be managed or controlled. They are not animals who need to be "reined in." Yet the administration's fear of student voices, student interests, and student bodies is an undercurrent in many schools, particularly those that serve students of color, and may lead to the well-documented racial disparities in school punishment (e.g., Scott et al, 2017).

Is It Too Late? Managing Expectations

For the first few years that she taught Intensive Reading, Amanda was consumed with developing curriculum and connecting with students. Her expectations centered on the administration's expectations (help students pass the test) and on her own immediate goals (create authentic opportunities for literacy). However, now that she has an established identity within the school and a track record of success, she finds herself questioning the system even more than ever. After the students walk across the stage and receive their diploma, then what? What has all this schooling really prepared them for?

The effort many students in Amanda's classes expend to achieve their graduation requirements is admirable—and the sense of pride in achieving a hard-fought goal is an invaluable life experience. However, despite students' success, she observes many graduating students living lives that look nearly identical to those of a high school dropout (living in poverty, working at minimum wage jobs, a college education nearly unobtainable), and she wonders if all the effort to support students in 11th and 12th grade is too late. After graduation, it seems as if students are abruptly pushed off a precipice to adulthood, where many struggle. Although Amanda sees students internalize the narrative that a high school diploma will improve their opportunities after graduation, the reality is that many students have the same limited career options with or without a diploma. Keeping in contact with many students after graduation, Amanda observed former students struggling in oppressive social paradigms. Although a number of students continue to colleges after graduation, many drop out in the first years due to financial hardship or lack of educational support. Subverting Reading Intervention curricula may improve school experiences but does little to disrupt the power structure beyond high school.

Even as Amanda grapples with her students' expectations—and wonders how schooling can be more equitable earlier so that students are not scrambling at the end just to graduate—her administration expects that she will continue to shepherd all Intensive Reading students to graduation, regardless of how many are enrolled in her class. Amanda is the only teacher to stay in Intensive Reading for more than a few years; her classes are filled with anywhere from 10 to 28 students, and students whom other teachers find challenging are frequently moved in without notice because of her reputation of "success."

"So Much Hinges on the Teacher": Battling Exhaustion

The curricular framework outlined in this chapter, like many subversive teaching methods, also requires a great deal of energy, effort, and creativity on the part of the teacher. We believe this curriculum respects the teacher's professional expertise and pedagogical knowledge and, therefore, is a more fulfilling to enact than a scripted curriculum, but like most acts of subversion, this curriculum requires more preparation time than following a textbook. It probably goes without saying that this time is not built into her teaching assignment (in the form of additional planning periods). In addition, because Amanda's students are writing much more frequently than a prepared reading curriculum would ask, her grading/assessment/response workload increased.

The personalization of the curriculum is what makes it meaningful for both Amanda and her students, but it does not come without cost. One school administrator noted,

> The course would be difficult to replicate because so much hinges on the teacher in the classroom. Any teacher who followed this model would have to be willing to spend a significant amount of time researching and gathering material and developing challenging and timely lessons.

This, we argue, is the actual *work of teaching*, and the administrator's response is telling. If "researching and gathering material and developing challenging and timely lessons" are framed as "extra" work for a teacher, and the teacher herself a potentially uncertain variable in the equation of instruction, then the vision of a transformed intensive reading curriculum presented here is even more disruptive than we thought.

Conclusion

February 2017

> *Days like today, I want to run for the parking lot. I, like my students, feel like a powerless pawn in the system. One student who was particularly squirrely slides a pink Starburst on my desk apologizing for his behavior before running to catch up with his friends. He knows pink is my favorite flavor.*
>
> *—excerpt, Amanda's teaching journal*

Teachers who wish to disrupt notions of remedial or intensive reading face a myriad of challenges: class sizes, testing systems, spotty student attendance, curricular mandates and materials, and student behavior. As we noted, Amanda is the only teacher in her school to remain an Intensive Reading instructor for more than a year or two; it is often seen as a temporary assignment handed off from teacher to teacher. The humanity of the children enrolled in these courses is often lost in the process.

Yet moments of humanity and kindness still bloom amid this often oppressive system. We argue that for courses such as Amanda's to be truly subversive, we must find even more ways to prioritize the real lives—present and future—of the children they serve. Testing metrics that do not lead to the material improvement of the lives of children, especially children of color and those living in poverty, should be rejected. Teachers should be supported in terms of small class sizes, support staff, and extra planning time so that they can enact a curriculum that is culturally relevant and responsive to student needs. Otherwise, we will continue to see students reduced to test scores and teachers suffering from emotional burnout. A single teacher can only subvert an entire system for so long.

References

Baldwin, R. S., Peleg-Bruckner, Z., & McClintock, A. H. (1985). Effects of topic interest and prior knowledge on reading comprehension. *Reading Research Quarterly, 20,* 497–504.

Delpit, L. (1988). The silenced dialogue: Power and pedagogy in educating other people's children. *Harvard Educational Review, 58,* 280–299.

Freire, P. (2018). *Pedagogy of the oppressed: 50th anniversary edition* (M. B. Ramos, Trans.). Bloomsbury Publishing. (Originally published 1968).

Glover, D. [Childish Gambino]. (2018, May 5). *This is America* [Video file]. Retrieved from https://www.youtube.com/watch?v=VYOjWnS4cMY

Graves, M. F. (2017). Scaffolding adolescents' reading of challenging text: In search of balance. In K. A. Hinchman & D. A. Appleman (Eds.), *Adolescent literacies: A handbook of practice-based research* (pp. 421–442). Guilford Press.

Hobbs, R. (1998). The seven great debates in the media literacy movement. *Journal of Communication, 48,* 16–32.

Lacy, A. (2019). Starting with students: A framework for high school reading. *English Journal, 108*(4), 17–20.

Ladson-Billings, G. (1995). Toward a theory of culturally relevant pedagogy. *American Educational Research Journal, 32,* 465–491.

Lewis, C., Enciso, P., & Moje, E.B. (2007). *Reframing sociocultural research on literacy: Identity, agency, and power.* Erlbaum.

Lucas, J. (2017, November 28). *I'm not racist* [Video file]. Retrieved from https://www.youtube.com/watch?v=43gm3CJePn0

Luke, A. (2012). Critical literacy: Foundational notes. *Theory into Practice, 51,* 4–11.

Moje, E. B., Overby, M., Tysvaer, N., & Morris, K. (2008). The complex world of adolescent literacy: Myths, motivations, and mysteries. *Harvard Educational Review, 78,* 107–154.

Neuman, S. B., & Celano, D. C. (2012). *Giving our children a fighting change: Poverty, literacy, and the development of information capital.* Teachers College Press.

New London Group. (1996). A pedagogy of multiliteracies: Designing social futures. *Harvard Educational Review, 66,* 60–92.

Pogrebin, R. (2018, February 12). Obama portrait artists merged the everyday and the extraordinary. *The New York Times.* Retrieved from https://www.nytimes.com/

Rainey, E. C. (2017). Disciplinary literacy in English language arts: Exploring the social and problem-based nature of literacy reading and reasoning. *Reading Research Quarterly*, *52*, 53–71. doi:10.1002/rrq.154

Recht, D. R., & Leslie, L. (1988). Effect of prior knowledge on good and poor readers' memory of text. *Journal of Educational Psychology*, *80*, 16–20.

Scheibe, C., & Rogow, F. (2012). *The teacher's guide to media literacy: Critical thinking in a multimedia world.* Corwin.

Scott, J., Moses, M. S., Finnigan, K. S., Trujillo, T., & Jackson, D. D. (2017). *Law and order in school and society: How discipline and policing policies harm students of color and what we can do about it.* National Education Policy Center.

Shakespeare, W. (1993). *The tragedy of Othello, the Moor of Venice* (B.A. Mowat and P. Werstine, Eds.). Simon and Schuster. (Originally published 1604).

Spires, H. A., Kerkhoff, S. N., Graham, A. C. K., Thompson, I., & Lee, J. K. (2018). Operationalizing and validating disciplinary literacy in secondary education. *Reading and Writing*, *31*, 1401–1434. https://doi.org/10.1007/s11145-018-9839-4

Thomas, D., & Dyches, J. (2019). The hidden curriculum of reading intervention: A critical content analysis of Fountas & Pinnell's leveled literacy intervention. *Journal of Curriculum Studies*, *59*, 601–618.

Willingham, D. T. (2006). How knowledge helps. *American Educator*, *30*(1), 42–46.

CHAPTER SEVENTEEN

The Case of Courtenay: Subversive Resistance in English Teacher Evaluation

Meghan A. Kessler and Angela L. Masters

Over the last several decades, the daily practices of teachers have come under greater scrutiny from a progressively more unified gaze. As a multitude of stakeholders—from policy advocates to federal- and state-level policy makers to local school officials—has become increasingly swayed by neoliberal ideologies within education, they have formed unexpected policy alliances (Lipman, 2004; Ravitch, 2013). Reaching across the political aisle, these groups have united to affect teaching through supporting an outputs-based reform agenda of standards, testing, and high-stakes accountability as well as, to varying degrees, public education's marketization (Lipman, 2011; Ravitch, 2010, 2013). More recently, and partially in response to the failures of these earlier policies, they have coalesced their efforts around the role that teachers play as inputs into the educational process and extended their reach into teacher evaluation (Ravitch, 2013). In this chapter, we highlight the experiences of Courtenay, a high school English teacher with the performance-based evaluation component of these reforms.

In particular, we draw on Courtenay's "enactment" of evaluation policy to consider how she worked to navigate this new neoliberal influence on her practice (Ball et al, 2012). We chose Courtenay for several reasons. First, research shows that often teachers in tested subject areas, such as English language arts (ELA), most sharply feel the pressures of neoliberal policies (Nichols & Berliner, 2008). Thus, we see Courtenay's case as a useful entry point into discussions about the implications of such forces, particularly with respect to the intersection of evaluation and teaching practices. Second, we know that teachers push back against restrictive authorities (e.g., Mills, 1997; Portelli & Konecny, 2013; Postman & Weingartener, 1969; Zembylas, 2003). Such pushback is often characterized as problematic; however, our analysis finds that by relying on reform's interpretive spaces, Courtenay was able to push back in ways that were both principled and productive (Ball, 2003; Ball et al., 2012). By foregrounding one example of this—how she mindfully selected critically framed readings her students—we hope to give ELA teachers food for thought about how they might negotiate reform pressures within their own schools.

Positionality and Context

Courtenay was a White, female-identifying high school ELA teacher at Parsons High School. Parsons High School was in a consolidated school district located within a semirural community several miles away from a small city that is home to a large research university. Compared to the nearby university city, the demographic makeup of Parsons was noticeably Whiter and white collar. In recent reports, approximately 4% of students identified as having mixed ethnic heritage, 3% identify as Latinx, 2% Asian, 1% African American, and 90% White. Approximately 16% of the students in Parsons were from households labeled as low income.

Courtenay had actually been employed with the district some years prior to data collection but had left to pursue doctoral education. When she returned to Parsons five years later, her most recent teaching experiences had been in college classrooms. This experience reshaped Courtenay's perspective on education to be much more critical and justice-oriented. However, this perspective sometimes ran at odds with other initiatives being pursued at Parsons.

As the authors of this chapter, we (Meghan and Angie) were positioned as researchers of and colleagues with Courtenay who were also engaged in doctoral studies and identify as White women. We therefore share several subjectivities with Courtenay (Peshkin, 1988) and have ourselves been under the gaze of accountability. Angie taught in the school where Courtenay worked, and Meghan held appointments at Courtenay's school supporting teacher candidates during field placements. Our experiences as teachers and teacher educators informed our curiosities, stances, and lenses toward our inquiry into Courtenay's practice (DeVault, 1999).

Parsons prided itself on its reputation as a "good school" that was responsive to its parents and families. To this end, the administration at Parsons invested significant resources in many of the external markers of a good school. In recent years, this included several new renovations and building projects and the purchase of new technology.

However, the community surrounding Parsons was beginning to change. The percentage of families receiving financial support for school meals was on the rise as was the number of students of color. Furthermore, the school began to stop making "AYP," or adequate yearly progress, on standardized assessments. The shifting demographics slowly started calling into question some of the long-held assumptions of the traditionally White community and school district, and Parsons' administrators became increasingly focused on the image being presented. This manifested as pressure on teachers to enact teaching that, in Courtenay's perspective, did not embrace or appropriately leverage the district's growing diversity for justice-oriented teaching and learning.

The students in Courtenay's class were considered "lower" division students—those who were often from homes with limited resources who were traditionally held to lower standards or engaged in less critical thinking due to relatively tracked course offerings. Although these students were primarily White and native English speakers, their lived experiences were ones in which the manifestations of power and privilege were more clearly seen. They were thus in an ideal position to question the world around them.

High-Stakes Evaluation, the Danielson Framework, and Local Evaluation Reform

To set the stage for these conversations, we begin with some context. More specifically, we place the deliberate decisions that Courtenay made with respect to her professional evaluation within, what was for her, an exceptionally tense cacophony of reform. During the time that she shared with us, both her state and school were engaged in major overhauls of their evaluation protocols. Although Courtenay did not find these efforts to be entirely unwelcome, she did see them as problematic. As she explained, these measures not only embraced discordant visions of teaching themselves but also promoted practices that were incompatible with her own understandings of good ELA instruction. In what follows, we detail these changes along with the professional practices they privileged. We then lay the groundwork for assessment of Courtenay's policy activity (i.e., subversive teaching in an evaluation context) by considering the compatibility of these markers of success with Courtenay's more justice-oriented values.

Although the policy changes that Courtenay struggled with were localized by the time we worked with her, they actually began in earnest nationally in 2009. It was then that the Obama administration, as part of its Great Recession stimulus, announced a $4.35 billion competitive grant called Race to the Top (RttT). Courtenay's state was one of the first to apply to the program, and its successful application had major implications. Because adopting a qualifying performance-based evaluation was worth just over 10% of the points on RttT's scoring guidelines, her state passed statutes obliging schools to combine student growth with a rubric-based tool to create a purportedly more objective multimeasure evaluation. In an attempt to meet these requirements efficiently and efficaciously, Courtenay's district opted to "borrow" heavily from other schools' plans and chose to implement a simple growth model along with the Danielson Framework for Teaching (Danielson, 2014).

In so doing, Courtenay's administrators made it clear that they wanted their teachers to privilege very particular professional practices. With respect to the growth component, Courtenay's school, like most, lacked the technology and funding for anything statistically sophisticated. Instead, it required teachers to use whatever was available, which meant that growth was often assessed narrowly and/or in ways that had a questionable bearing on practice. As implementation progressed, the district became more technocratic and prescriptive in its directives. Eventually, Courtenay's evaluation growth score would be determined by a singular standardized test that reported out only whole numbers. Although no one could explain what students were being tested on—and the English department chair had provided proof from the test maker that students' expected gain was less than a point—the district continued to insist on its use. The implication was that a truly high-quality teacher could consistently improve test scores, regardless of the quality of the test itself.

The other measures included within the Danielson Framework (Danielson, 2014) put the onus on teachers to demonstrate quality teaching through observations and artifacts. Although the Danielson Framework did not require any particular curriculum or pedagogy, it did contain leveled rubrics with specific descriptors of practice in 22 areas categorized under the headings, "Planning and Preparation, Classroom Environment, Instruction, and Professional Responsibilities" (Danielson, 2013). These rubrics and descriptors were used by Courtenay's administrators to score her practice during classroom observations, a cumulative portfolio of teaching artifacts, and longitudinal student assessment data. As the pressures to conform mounted, that Courtenay was situated within a particularly tested and *con*tested content area became apparent, and she began to push back.

Courtenay's Subversive Stance Toward ELA Teaching in Evaluative Contexts

Courtenay's subversion of narrowed teacher evaluation manifested through her commitment to challenging and critically engaging ELA teaching. Zeros were unacceptable, complex texts were key, and students would work through their thinking with lots of writing and feedback. This earned her the reputation as the "hard English teacher" at her high school, but Courtenay was proud of the designation. This stance was not in opposition to the Danielson Framework itself but to her administrators' standardized, technocratic interpretations of the Framework. These interpretations seemed inhibitive of critical questioning or challenging normative structures and power dynamics. Put simply, Courtenay's subversion most often meant doing what was required of her but creatively and in a way that aligned with her commitment to justice.

When asked to describe these motivations, she expressed how nurturing students' "academic lives" was important so that writing was a tool for exploring "how we think and what we know . . . to talk about purpose, audience, and arrangement [in order to] transfer to other settings and other products." As explicated in the following section, this writing often went hand in hand with reading challenging texts such as excerpts of Foucault. Although such engagement may not have been expediently measured by the tests included in her district's teacher evaluation system, she was able to explain her choices this way:

> Writing about developing understandings of complex texts allows students to use writing both as a way of thinking and as a way of entering into a conversation; specifically *not* to show that they are an "expert" on a topic or to show that they have "*the* answer," which is what academic writing so often asks student writers to pretend they are/have. In this way, [we create] space for students to practice critical thinking processes that are often either considered inherent (which they are not) or unimportant (which is terrifying to think).

This quote illustrates the contrast between narrowed, neoliberal ELA expectations and Courtenay's commitment to equipping them to "enter into a conversation." This was of particular importance for her students, most of whom had long been tracked in "lower" division English courses.

Courtenay's perspective echoes Lisa Delpit's (2006) call for teachers to explicate cultures of power within schools and classrooms through academic rigor. In particular, as Courtenay's students struggled with difficult texts, they gained not only skills for literacy but also social agency and critique. Because her senior seminar class was largely populated with students receiving special education services, pushing the same level of critical engagement as the honors-track students was crucial—and just. Without this, she would be guilty of enabling the trend of low expectations for underserved students perpetuated by tracking and test prep (Picower & Mayorga, 2015). She was subverting the convenient metrics of neoliberal policy enforcement and pushing back against a culture of compliance that would have encouraged more narrow content coverage. To help make these challenges accessible, Courtenay bolstered her students by helping them recognize the assets they brought to the table: "I convinced my students that they really were smarter than the honors students. They know how to think better, and I wish there were a way we could assess that." Like many teachers, she neither outright accepted nor rejected neoliberalism nor wholly adopted or resisted her school's evaluation changes. Instead, she struggled with how to respond to a policy that she found somewhat logical in theory but egregious in translation.

Subversive Resistance in English Teacher Evaluation and Practice

In this section, we show how Courtenay's ambitious teaching subverted the traditional expectations of "quality" teaching asserted by her administrators' interpretation of the Danielson Framework (Danielson, 2014). Courtenay's instructional philosophy and style were key to her creative subversion of narrow ELA evaluation criteria. She quickly developed a reputation for being a teacher who challenged the status quo. As her administrators were pushing for test compliance and similarly traditional measures of success, Courtenay was asking the hard questions:

> Even just last week we had a meeting with the English I teachers and this is an assignment that we've done for probably two or three years that we're about to start—a new unit—and I said, "Wait! *Why* are we doing this? What do we *want* from this?" I don't think we're asking that question enough. . . . I understand that we need to do x, y, and z, but we're going to have to figure out how to do [those things] at the same time that we are doing this thing that we fundamentally *believe* in.

This critical perspective directly paralleled her instructional stance. The "thing" she most believed in was developing her students' deep literacy and critical thinking skills, helping them identify when and how power is culturally enacted inside schools, classrooms, and society (Delpit, 2006). To her, that her students be given time and space to truly reflect on or "ponder" what they were learning, instead of giving in to the "flashing lights" of new technologies or trendy best practices, was important. Furthermore, Courtenay felt that true analysis of student work (required in Domains 3 and 4 of the Danielson Framework) should go beyond "just seeing students as just data points." Rather, the Danielson Framework and related teacher evaluation procedures should be used to engage teachers in a deeper exploration of their practice.

While she voiced these concerns, Courtenay took action in her own classroom; she took her administrators' calls for increased rigor and high standards as permission to dig deep with complex texts and writing. She did this intentionally with students who were otherwise overlooked and underappreciated as scholars. Where others may have overlooked the critical capacity of her students, Courtenay saw great strength. And so, she chose to engage them in conversations about power through reading excerpts from Foucault's (1977) *Discipline and Punish*:

> I selected the Foucault passage from *Discipline and Punish* for two reasons: (1) to open discussions of processes and practices of working with and through difficult texts and the roles that conversation and writing play in thinking and knowing, and (2) to widen our discussion of our topic, which was something like "academic knowing." We also read an essay by

Haunani-Kay Trask (1993) called, "From a Native Daughter" and Thomas Kuhn (1962) called "The Historical Structure of Scientific Discovery."

Courtenay's choices of text for her "lower" division English students were provocative yet interdisciplinary and complex. Reading Foucault gave them the opportunity to name and evaluate the role of power in society. The Trask (1993) essay helped students explore the impact of colonialism on native sovereignty as well as institutionalized racism and gender discrimination. Trask's work also illuminated the capacity of student activists to speak truth to power, while the Kuhn (1962) text problematized the concept of "discovery," asking readers to examine "great man" theories of historical events in favor of more contextualized, community-minded conceptualizations. Her students would sometimes "complain" that the reading was *so hard* and that they never even discussed all of it! They described spending entire class periods mulling over small sections of the full text that she had given them, discussing the meaning of even single sentences. However, this was all done with a particular purpose in mind, even amid some initial grumbling.

> I like making use of essays with some age because they take students away from being able to rely on a knowledge that they already have. I also like to use essays with more than one section, and often assign the second section first, so that students can examine relationships between parts of texts and how they create a single, cohesive argument. Particularly with Foucault, students make [the] most sense of [his work] where they begin reading "fresh." When we have started at the beginning, students rely on making sense of the argument through their understanding of isolation and surveillance during plague. Starting with Bentham/panopticon seems to help students see ways in which current systems of arrangement are designed with seeing at the center, quite literally . . . Because of the strong value I place in annotation on our meaning-making processes, I also insist that reading of longer, more complex text be done on paper copies. In the case of Foucault (and often whatever the first essay of the semester is), students are asked to reread after a month or so, and given a clean copy on which to take new notes as they read.

By engaging in annotation and rereading, Courtenay not only was exposing her students to critical theorists but was also helping her students stretch their scholarly muscles. Rather than drilling discrete skills or memorization, they were required to revisit ideas and refine their communication of their understanding.

Courtenay's purpose was twofold. Her students would not only have the opportunity to analyze discourses of power and race in the maintenance of the status quo, but they would also gain experience discussing ambitious texts in a manner that was not unlike what they could experience in a college English or philosophy class. Even if her students did not fully "get" Foucault or did not agree with his analysis, and even if Courtenay did not fully agree with everything in the text, giving her students another frame through which to view the world was important. In so doing, she was giving them the opportunity to consider other possibilities for their world and the tools to assert themselves.

Although discussions of Foucault likely did not yield the same easily reportable outcomes as the methods her administrators suggested, Courtenay knew critically engaging learning opportunities were more valuable to her students as literate young adults. She also knew this ambitious yet subversive teaching could meet the criteria for strong instructional design under the Danielson Framework (Danielson, 2014). It may not have aligned with her administrators' interpretations of efficient (i.e., convenient) evidence, but Courtenay's subversive creativity turned narrow interpretations broad. By leading students through rich discussions about socially constructed power, she was demonstrating a more sophisticated interpretation of Domain 1b ("Demonstrating Knowledge of Students"; [Danielson, 2014]) by integrating students' cultural, academic, social, and ethical development into her lessons. Courtenay had strong relationships with her students, knew who they were, and how essential it would be that they develop a critical consciousness. By spending each morning reworking her lesson plans to better suit where her students were positioned in relation to the texts at hand, she was enacting "Flexibility and Responsiveness" (Domain 3e; [Danielson, 2014]). Although the Danielson Framework (Danielson, 2014) is relatively silent on social justice except for the implications of Domain 4's emphasis on professional community and teachers as leaders in ethical and professional spheres (Clayton, 2017), Courtenay expanded the visions of this tool to the benefit of herself and her students.

Implications and Conclusion

Courtenay's efforts to subvert oversimplified evaluation interpretations are not uncommon. Others have noted the dangers of positioning teacher evaluation rubrics as the ends of efforts to improve teacher quality (e.g., Ball, 2003; Clayton, 2017; Meuwissen & Choppin, 2015), demonstrating that more work needs to be done to equip teachers to better critique and resist the subtractive experiences that can accompany metricized teacher practice. This is of particular importance for teachers in ELA and related disciplines that invite critical thought and action. Rather than simply surrendering her professional confidence and agency, Courtenay subverted policies that contradicted her values. Motivated by a critical perspective, she engaged in distinct strategies to push back against relatively static evaluation directives, using the Danielson Domains (Danielson, 2014) as a point from which to launch her students toward Foucauldian critical consciousness.

From an analytical perspective, Courtenay not only was exposing her students to texts about the influence of power on society and individual bodies but was challenging these authorities as well. Her very teaching and instructional design stood as subversive acts of resistance against some of the same rigid regulatory frames she was asking her students to call into question. By pushing back against her administrators' narrow interpretations of the Danielson Framework (Danielson, 2014), she was also challenging the oppressive tendencies of neoliberal reform. Such market-oriented policies have been found in most cases to marginalize students and teachers, narrow curriculum, and embed whiteness as the normative definition of quality (Au, 2007; Picower & Mayorga, 2015).

At the end of the school year, Courtenay felt that she could not be the teacher she wanted to be at Parsons. She left for a district more supportive of the kind of teaching she was committed to. Her new school district served a more diverse and historically marginalized population and was taking steps to integrate more opportunities for justice-oriented teaching and learning. Parsons is now certainly missing out with her absence, which brings into focus several questions.

Questions for Discussion

By examining Courtenay's perceptions and enactments at distinct moments in her career, we were afforded a more nuanced perspective on the ubiquitous impact of neoliberal education reform. The following questions are posed for teacher educators, preservice teachers, and in-service teachers exploring methods for subversion and resistance in high-stakes accountability contexts. We urge teachers and teacher educators to illuminate the presence of neoliberalism in school, state, and national policies in education.

First, reflect on where *you* see the reductive capacity of accountability policies at work. Where are they most prevalent and how else can social justice pedagogies in ELA counter these trends? Second, how can teachers be subversive in the interim while fighting for greater, more assertive voice in building/local/state school policies long term? What forces work in concert with these efforts? Third, what do you make of the fact that Courtenay left Parsons High School? What other options could have been present for her? What would you have done in her situation? Do you agree with the implications of her decision: that teachers working with students in historically marginalized communities may have more opportunities to integrate subversive social justice pedagogies? Finally, what do you make of the lack of emphasis on social context and critique across the Danielson Framework? How does this implicate teachers' capacity to act as agents of social change in their profession and on behalf of their students?

References

Au, W. (2007). High-stakes testing and curricular control: A qualitative metasynthesis. *Educational Researcher, 36*, 258–267. doi:10.3102/0013189X07306523

Ball, S. J. (2003). The teacher's soul and the terrors of performativity. *Journal of Education Policy, 18*, 215–228.

Ball, S. J., Maguire, M., & Braun, A. (2012). *How schools do policy: Policy enactments in secondary schools*. Routledge.

Clayton, C. (2017). Raising the stakes: Objectifying teaching in the edTPA and Danielson rubrics. In J. H. Carter & H. A. Lochte (Eds.), *Teacher performance assessment and accountability reforms* (pp. 79–105). Palgrave Macmillan.

Danielson, C. (2013). *Enhancing professional practice: A framework for teaching*. ASCD.

Danielson, C. (2014) *The Framework for Teaching Evaluation Instrument, 2013 edition*. Retrieved from https://danielsongroup.org/downloads/2013-framework-teaching-evaluation-instrument.

Delpit, L. (2006). *Other people's children: Cultural conflict in the classroom*. The New Press.

DeVault, M. L. (1999). *Liberating method: Feminism and social research*. Temple University Press.

Foucault, M. (1977). *Surveiller et punir: naissance de la prison* [Discipline and punish: The birth of the prison] (A. M. Sheridan-Smith, Trans.). Penguin.

Kuhn, T. S. (1962, June). The historical structure of scientific discovery. *Science, 136*(3518), 760–764.

Lipman, P. (2004). *High stakes education: Inequality, globalization, and urban school reform*. Routledge.

Lipman, P. (2011). *The new political economy of urban education: Neoliberalism, race, and the right to the city*. Routledge.

Meuwissen, K. W., & Choppin, J. M. (2015). Preservice teachers' adaptations to tensions associated with the edTPA during its early implementation in New York and Washington states. *Education Policy Analysis Archives, 23*(103). doi:10.14507/epaa.v23.2078

Mills, M. (1997). Towards a disruptive pedagogy: Creating spaces for student and teacher resistance to social injustice. *International Studies in Sociology of Education, 7*, 35–55.

Nichols, S., & Berliner, D. (2008). *Collateral damage: How high-stakes testing corrupts America's schools*. Harvard Education Press.

Peshkin, A. (1988). In search of subjectivity—one's own. *Educational Researcher, 17*(7), 17–21.

Picower, B., & Mayorga, E. (2015). *What's race got to do with it? How current school reform policy maintains racial and economic inequality*. Peter Lang.

Portelli, J. P., & Konecny, C. P. (2013). Neoliberalism, subversion and democracy in education. *Encounters in Theory and History of Education, 14*, 87–97.

Postman, P. N., & Weingartner, C. (1969). *Teaching as a subversive activity*. Dell Publishing.

Ravitch, D. (2010). *The death and life of the great American school system: How testing and choice are undermining education*. Basic Books.

Ravitch, D. (2013). *Reign of error: The hoax of the privatization movement and the danger to America's public schools*. Alfred A. Knopf.

Trask, H. K. (1993). *From a native daughter: Colonialism and sovereignty in Hawai'i?* University of Hawaii Press.

Zembylas, M. (2003). Interrogating "teacher identity": Emotion, resistance, and self-formation. *Educational Theory, 53*, 107–127.

ABOUT THE AUTHORS

About the Contributors

Dr. Carey Applegate is an associate professor of English Education at the University of Wisconsin–Eau Claire. Her areas of scholarship include urban youth and youth literacies, education narratives, issues of equity and social justice, and rhetorics of education reform/activism. Her work has appeared in the *International Journal of Critical Pedagogy, English Journal, Intercultural Education,* and several edited collections, including *Saviors, Scapegoats and Schoolmarms: Examining the Classroom Teacher in Fiction and Film for Teacher Education* (Routledge, 2016).

Janine Boiselle is a high school English educator in Cumberland, Rhode Island. She received her bachelor's degree in English and her teacher licensure in 2017 and 2018. Janine began her teaching career with four years at the middle-level and is also a teacher consultant for the Rhode Island Writing Project. She identifies as a cisgender lesbian, but chooses to let her appearance and attitude speak for herself. Rocking a mostly shaved head and male-signified attire, Janine is a vibrant radical in the classroom.

Tamara Brooks has been in the high school English classroom for over twenty-five years. She has taught in classrooms both nationally and internationally. She has worked for the Governor's Honor Program in Georgia for fifteen years, and currently works in the American School of Belo Horizonte, Brazil.

Ryan Burns, EdD, is a current high school English teacher in Rhode Island. As part of his recent doctoral research in Literacy, Culture, and Language Education, Ryan composed a multilayered autoethnography that explores and analyzes his experiences as a queer, White educator teaching for social justice during troubling times. Ryan is a founder and facilitator of Queer Educators as Storytellers (Q.U.E.S.T.), a community of LGBTQ+ educators who share and write about their experiences in and out of the classroom. Ryan's work also appears in *Educators Queering Academia: Critical Memoirs* (Peter Lang, 2016) and the second edition of *Queer Adolescent Literature as a Complement to the English Language Arts Curriculum* (Rowman & Littlefield, 2022).

Caroline T. Clark, PhD, is a professor in the Department of Teaching and Learning at The Ohio State University, where she serves as the faculty lead for the English Language Arts AYA 7–12 licensure program. Her research focuses on language and literacy practices in and outside of school and collaborative research with teachers, young people, and families for social action. From 2004 to 2018, she co-led a teacher inquiry group committed to supporting LGBTQQ and gender diverse students in schools and she recently received the American Educational Research Association's Queer Studies SIG Body of Work award for her scholarship in the area of literacy and social change.

Heather Coffey, PhD, is a professor in the Department of Middle, Secondary, and K12 Education at Cato College of Education. Heather serves as Co-Director of the Charlotte Writing Project and is the Program Director for the Masters of Education in Curriculum and Instruction in the Department of Middle, Secondary, and K12 Education at UNC Charlotte. Her areas of research interest include English teacher preparation and critical service-learning as pedagogy in teacher education. E-mail: hcoffey@uncc.edu.

E. Sybil Durand, PhD, is an associate professor of youth literature in the Department of Teaching, Learning & Sociocultural Studies in the College of Education at the University of Arizona. Dr. Durand's scholarship examines how students and teachers engage young adult literature written by authors from culturally diverse U.S. and international communities. Her work has been published in the *Journal of Adolescent & Adult Literacy*, *Research on Diversity in Youth Literature*, *Equity & Excellence in Education*, and *The ALAN Review*.

Steve Fulton, MEd, NBCT, is a former KMS Teacher of the Year and a North Carolina Outstanding English Teacher of the Year. He has been active in leading initiatives at the middle school and district levels focused around writing, making, and social change. Steve began as the Kannapolis City Schools AIG Coordinator in 2019, where he advocates for all students with potential for high ability. Steve is an active teacher consultant with the Charlotte Writing Project. His writing, speaking, and teaching often center on maker education, technology integration, critical literacy, and civic engagement. He can be reached at steve.fulton@kcs.k12.nc.us and on X (formerly twitter) @steve8071.

Lori Garcia is a high school English teacher in the Chicagoland area. Throughout her 13 years as an educator, she has taught a range of English language arts courses and levels, including electives such as Journalism and AP Seminar. She has presented on her experiences disrupting the canon at the International Literacy Conference and NCTE's Assembly for Research Conference. She is inspired by professional development that focuses on culturally responsive teaching and interrupting the dominant narratives evident in our educational institutions and has completed her Beyond Diversity training with the Pacific Education Group's Courageous Conversations protocol. She holds a master's degree in Curriculum and Instruction.

Dorothy E. Hines, PhD, holds a joint appointment as an associate professor in African and African American Studies and in the Department of Curriculum and Teaching in the School of Education at the University of Kansas. Dr. Hines is an award-winning writer and a former high school teacher. Her research examines the racialized and gendered schooling experiences of Black girls and how they thrive in educational spaces that have traditionally negated them. She can be reached at dhinesd@ku.edu.

Selena Hughes is the program administrator for the Engaged Pluralism program at Vassar College in Poughkeepsie, New York. As a former English teacher, instructional coach, and youth program manager, her experiences have cultivated a passion for creating culturally sustaining classrooms and spaces from Dutchess County, New York to Honduras to Kansas City, Missouri. She is also an avid fan of sci-fi, fantasy novels, and LARP.

Betina Hsieh (X [formerly Twitter]): @ProfHsieh) is the Boeing Endowed Professor of Teacher Education at the University of Washington. Her teacher education work is informed by 10 years of urban middle school classroom experience, K-12 literacy coaching and work as co-director of the Bay Area Writing Project. She is the co-chair of the NCTE Asian/Asian American Caucus with Dr. Jung Kim, and was the NCTE Research Foundation chair from 2021-2023.

Latrise P. Johnson is writer, scholar, mother, teacher, and intellectual. She works as an Associate Professor of Secondary English Language Arts and Literacy at the University of Alabama (UA). Before joining the faculty at UA, Dr. Johnson taught middle and high school Language and Literature in Atlanta Public Schools. She is an equity-oriented scholar whose research examines the literacy practices of historically marginalized youth in and outside of school. Her articles, "Writing the Self: Black Queer Youth Challenge Heteronormative ways of Being in an After-school Writing Club" and "The Human and the Writer: The Promise of a Humanizing Writing Pedagogy for Black Students," published in *Research in the Teaching of English,* both received the Alan C. Purves Award (2017/2020) for their impact on literacy education. She served as Professor in Residence at a local high school conducting research, teaching classes, sponsoring student groups, and working closely with students and teachers. Dr. Johnson serves the literacy field as Associate Editor of *Literacy Research: Theory, Methods, and Practice Journal* (LRTMP); as a member of *Language Arts, Research in the Teaching of English* (RTE), and *Equity & Excellence in Education* (EEE) editorial boards; and as past Chair of English Language Arts Teacher Education (ELATE). Dr. Johnson was a CNV (Cultivating New Voices) Fellow (2010-2012) and teaches yoga to her friends and family.

Meghan A. Kessler, PhD, is an assistant professor of Teacher Education at the University of Illinois Springfield. Her research and teaching interests include early career professional learning, preservice teacher evaluation, and social studies teaching and learning. She can be reached at makessl2@uis.edu.

Jung Kim is Professor of Literacy and department chair at Lewis University. She is a former high school English teacher and literacy coach, mom of two, a school board member, and an ultra runner. Her research interests include adolescent literacy, teaching with graphic novels, the racialization of Asian American teachers, and children's and young adult literature. You can find her on X (formerly Twitter) @ jungkimphd, where she will always rep #AsianAmAF and #MidwestIsBest.

Angela M. Kohnen is an associate professor of English Education in the School of Teaching and Learning at the University of Florida. Her research explores multiliteracies pedagogy, digital literacy, and critical literacy in authentic classroom contexts. Prior to earning her doctorate, she taught high school English in the St. Louis, Missouri area.

Amanda Lacy has been teaching high school English and reading for 14 years. Her professional interests include young adult literacy, social justice, creating culturally relevant curricula, and, of course, sharing literature and poetry with her students. She hopes to see the nullification of high-stakes standardized testing by the end of her teaching career.

Rossina Zamora Liu, PhD, is an assistant clinical professor in the College of Education at the University of Maryland. She earned her MFA from the Iowa Nonfiction Writing Program and her PhD from the Language, Literacy, and Culture Program, both at the University of Iowa. Her work interrogates the onto-epistemologies of White supremacy and fosters cross-racial collaborations. She received the J. Michael Parker Award from the Literacy Research Association (December 2016) for her ethnographic study exploring the labors of vulnerabilities in crafting trauma counternarratives. She is coauthoring a book on the psychology of White supremacy and White privilege for Oxford University Press.

Michael Manderino, PhD (@mmanderino), is the director of Curriculum and Instruction at Leyden High Schools outside of Chicago, Illinois. He is also a graduate faculty scholar and codirector of the Social Justice Summer Camp for Educators at

Northern Illinois University, where he was a professor of literacy education for 6 years. Michael taught high school for 14 years and was a literacy coach. He is the coauthor of three books and has published in multiple peer-reviewed journals in the areas of disciplinary and digital literacies.

Angela L. Masters is a veteran social studies teacher at a high school in central Illinois, where she teaches courses on U.S. history as well as Civics & American Government and Advanced Placement Economics. She earned her PhD in Curriculum and Instruction from the University of Illinois in 2018. Angie's scholarly interests center on questions related to teachers' lives and experiences, especially related to reform, and teachers' professional development and learning. She can be reached at masters854@gmail.com.

Leah Panther is an assistant professor of literacy education at Mercer University in Atlanta, Georgia. Her experiences with teaching, teacher education, and research center on identifying and sustaining youth and communities' language and literacy practices. Her most recent work includes the edited volume *Critical Memetic Literacies for English Education: How Do You Meme?* for Routledge and articles for the *Journal of Language and Literacy*, *Multicultural Perspectives*, and *English Journal*.

Katie Roquemore is an assistant professor of education at Landmark College, a college exclusively for neurodivergent students. She earned her PhD in Cultural Foundations of Education and Disability Studies in 2020. She previously taught high school English at a small urban high school in North Carolina where she was a Service Learning Teacher Leader for the district. Her research interests include experiences of disabled teachers and students in elementary and secondary schools, including how policy has an impact on those experiences.

Sandra Saco is currently a teacher-researcher and doctoral student studying English Education. She formerly worked as a high school English teacher for seven (7) years and currently teaches pre-service teachers in methods of teaching language courses. Her research interests are on the effects of culturally sustaining pedagogical practices and culturally diverse young adult literature (YAL) in the secondary classroom. Her work can be found in *The ALAN Review*. Sandra's current research focuses on how Latinx students unpack the Latinx diaspora through critical discussion, storytelling and reading YAL.

Stephanie Anne Shelton, PhD (@stepshel78), is the Director of Diversity and an Associate Professor of Qualitative Research in the College of Education at The University of Alabama. Previously a high school English teacher and teacher educator, her research regularly focuses on LGBTQIA+ issues and social justice topics in secondary education, especially in sociopolitically conservative contexts. Her work includes multiple edited books, book chapters, and articles published in journals including *English Education, English Journal, Journal of Language and Literacy Education, Qualitative Inquiry,* and *Teaching and Teacher Education.*

Melanie Shoffner is a professor of English education at James Madison University (Harrisonburg, VA). Her research and writing focus on the dispositional, relational, and reflective development of preservice English language arts teachers. Her most recent work includes the co-edited book *Reconstructing Care in Teacher Education after COVID-19: Caring Enough to Change* (Routledge, 2022) and chapters in *International Perspectives on English Teacher Development: From Initial Teacher Education to Highly Accomplished Professional* (IFTE, 2022) and *Textiles and Tapestries: Self-Study for Envisioning New Ways of Knowing* (Creative Commons, 2020). A former high school English teacher, she is also a former Fulbright Scholar, a researcher for *Henry Ford's Innovation Nation with Mo Rocca* and the current editor of *English Education.*

Crystal Sogar is in her third year of teaching AP English Language at Summit Preparatory Charter High School in Redwood City, California. She graduated from Purdue University's teacher education program in 2017.

Jill Stedronsky is a teacher of language arts for eighth graders in Bernard's Township, New Jersey. Her research focuses on intrinsically motivating students and cultivating an authentic inquiry-project-based, gradeless classroom. She works with the staff in her district in all these areas. She is an adjunct instructor at Drew University and a teacher leader for the Drew University Writing Project.

Scott Storm, PhD (@ScottWStorm), earned his PhD in English Education from New York University and is a Visiting Assistant Professor of Education at Bowdoin College. His work is informed by 15 years of experience as a high school English teacher in urban public schools. Scott studies literacy, learning ecologies, and social justice teaching and is particularly interested in the ways that students critically engage with literature and aesthetic forms. Scott's writing has appeared in *Journal of Literacy Research, English Teaching Practice & Critique, English Journal,* and the *Journal of Adolescent & Adult Literacy* among others.

Anna Mae Tempus (@AnnaTempus) is an early-career English language arts instructor in Wisconsin. In 2016, she received the Wisconsin Council Teachers of English award for Outstanding First Year Teacher for her dedication to a justice-based curriculum and passion for multicultural literacies. She is a master's candidate at the Bread Loaf School of English and contributing writer at edutopia.org. Anna Mae's research interests include critical Whiteness and Critical Race Theory in the classroom.

Kristen Hawley Turner, PhD (@teachkht), is a professor and director of teacher education at Drew University in New Jersey. Her research focuses on the intersections between technology and literacy, and she works with teachers across content areas to implement effective literacy instruction and to incorporate technology in meaningful ways. She is the coauthor of *Connected Reading: Teaching Adolescent Readers in a Digital World* (2015, NCTE) and *Argument in the Real World: Teaching Students to Read and Write Digital Texts* (2017, Heinemann) and the editor of *The Ethics of Digital Literacy: Developing Knowledge and Skills across Grade Levels*. She is also the founder and director of the Drew Writing Project and Digital Literacies Collaborative.

Diana Wandix-White, PhD, has been an educator for more than 20 years. She has taught various levels and aspects of English/language arts at the middle and high school, junior college, and university levels and has served in administration. She earned a BA in Communication Studies from Washburn University, an MEd in Reading Education at Prairie View A&M, and she recently completed her PhD in Curriculum and Instruction at Texas A&M University, where she researched urban education and the culture of care in K–12 public schools. Dr. Wandix-White is currently furthering her research as a postdoctoral fellow at Texas A&M University.

Jill M. Williams, PhD, is a Curriculum Specialist for Westerville City Schools and an adjunct lecturer at The Ohio State University (OSU) in the School of Teaching and Learning. She has also worked as a program manager for the Middle Childhood MEd program at OSU and a full-time English teacher in Westerville, Ohio. She is a coauthor and editor of *Acting Out!: Combating Homophobia and Heterosexism in Schools* (Teachers College Press, 2010), recognized in 2010 as an "Outstanding Academic Title" by the American Library Association and winner of the National Association of Multicultural Education Philip C. Chinn book award. Jill was awarded "Teacher of the Year" by Westerville City Schools in May 2011 and was awarded the Holloways Human and Civil Rights Award by the Ohio Department of Education, also in the spring of 2011. In 2019, she was the recipient of the National Council of Teachers of English CEL Innovative Leadership Award.

Jemimah L. Young, PhD, is an assistant professor at the University of Iowa. Her areas of expertise include multicultural education, urban education, and the sociology of education. Her research interests center on (1) the academic achievement and assessment of Black women and girls, (2) educational outcomes for students of color, (3) educational experiences of marginalized and minoritized populations, and (4) culturally responsive pedagogy. She can be reached at jemimah-young@uiowa.edu.

About the Editors

Jeanne Dyches, PhD, is an associate professor and the associate director of the School of Education at Iowa State University. A former high school English teacher and literacy coach, Jeanne researches intersections between racial literacies and curricula, subversive literacies, and critical disciplinary literacy. Her research has been published in numerous journals, including *Journal of Literacy Research, Journal of Adolescent and Adult Literacy, Teachers College Record, Journal of Teacher Education, Urban Review,* and *Harvard Educational Review.* The Iowa Academy of Education, American Reading Forum, and American Educational Research Association have all recognized Jeanne's scholarly contributions.

Brandon Sams, PhD, is an associate professor of English at Iowa State University, where he teaches undergraduate and graduate courses on young adult literature and English methods. A former high school English teacher, Brandon focuses his research and scholarship on the potential of critical, aesthetic, and contemplative reading practices to interrupt and renew "schooled" reading practices shaped by the epistemologies of audit culture. His work has recently been published in *English Teaching: Practice and Critique, The ALAN Review, Changing English,* and *The Journal of Language and Literacy Education.*

Ashley S. Boyd, PhD, is an associate professor of English education at Washington State University, where she teaches graduate courses on critical and cultural theory and undergraduate courses on English methods and young adult literature. A former secondary English language arts teacher, Ashley's scholarship examines practicing teachers' social justice pedagogies and their critical content knowledge; explores how young adult literature is an avenue for cultivating students' critical literacies; and investigates the implementation of state-mandated tribal curriculum in secondary schools in Washington. She is the author of *Social Justice Literacies in the English Classroom: Teaching Practice in Action* (2017, Teachers College Press) and coauthor of *Reading for Action: Engaging Youth in Social Justice through Young Adult Literature* (2019, Rowman & Littlefield). She has published in the *Journal of Teacher Education,* the *Journal of Adolescent & Adult Literacy, English Journal,* and the *International Journal of Critical Pedagogy.*

INDEX